I0820914

VOLGA BLUES

ALSO BY MARZIO G. MIAN

Karadzic

Artico—
La battaglia per il Grande Nord

Tevere Controcorrente

Maledetta Sarajevo

Guerra Bianca—
Sul fronte artico del conflitto mondiale

VOLGA BLUES

A Journey into the Heart of Russia

MARZIO G. MIAN

■ ■ ■

Translated from the Italian by Elettra Pauletto
Photographs by Alessandro Cosmelli

W. W. NORTON & COMPANY
Independent Publishers Since 1923

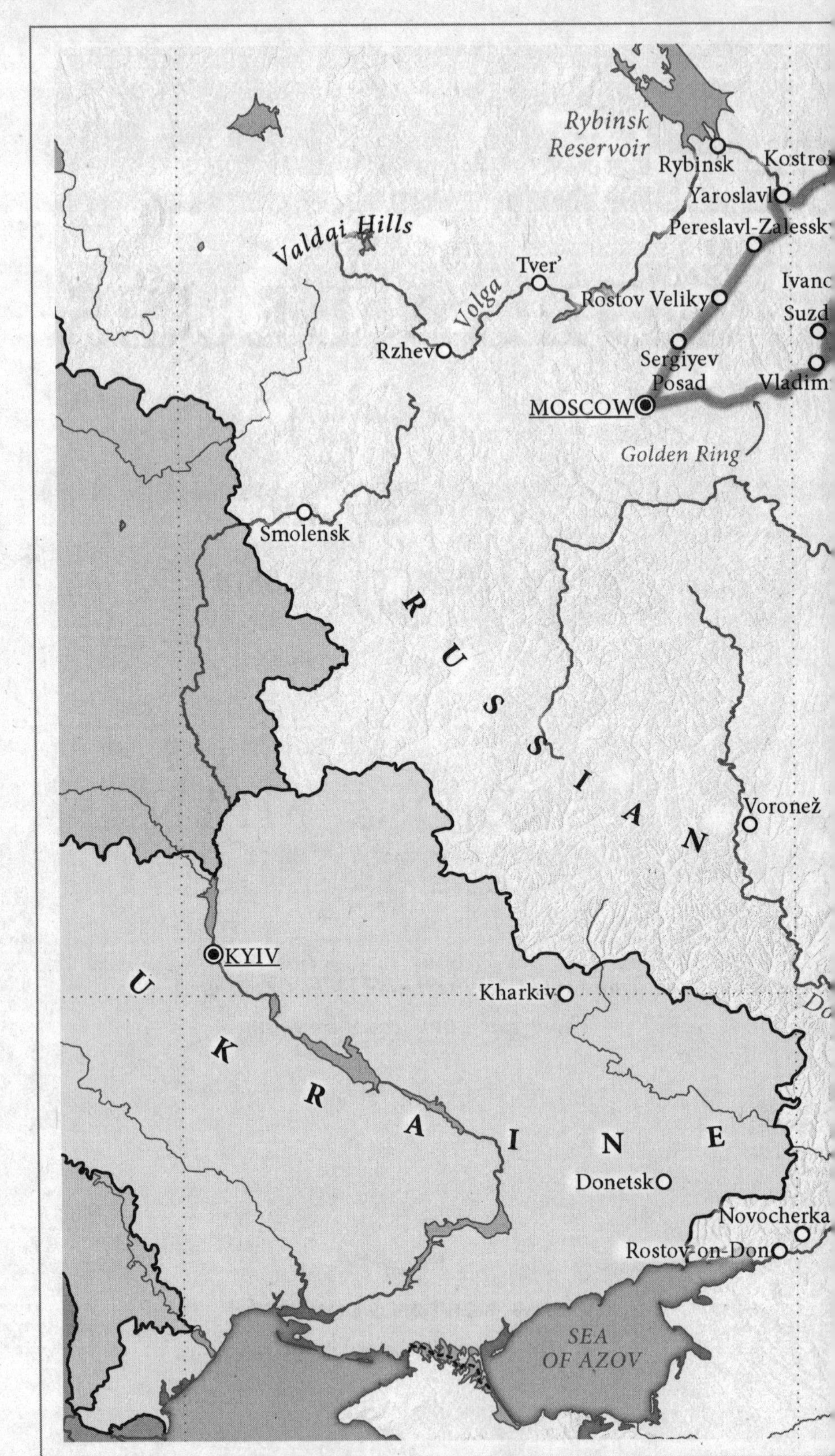

Rybinsk
Reservoir
Rybinsk
Yaroslavl
Pereslavl-Zalessk
Valdai Hills
Tver'
Volga
Rostov Veliky
Rzhev
Sergiyev
Posad
MOSCOW
Golden Ring
Smolensk
R U S S I A N
Voronež
KYIV
Kharkiv
U K R A I N E
Donetsk
Rostov-on-Don
SEA
OF AZOV

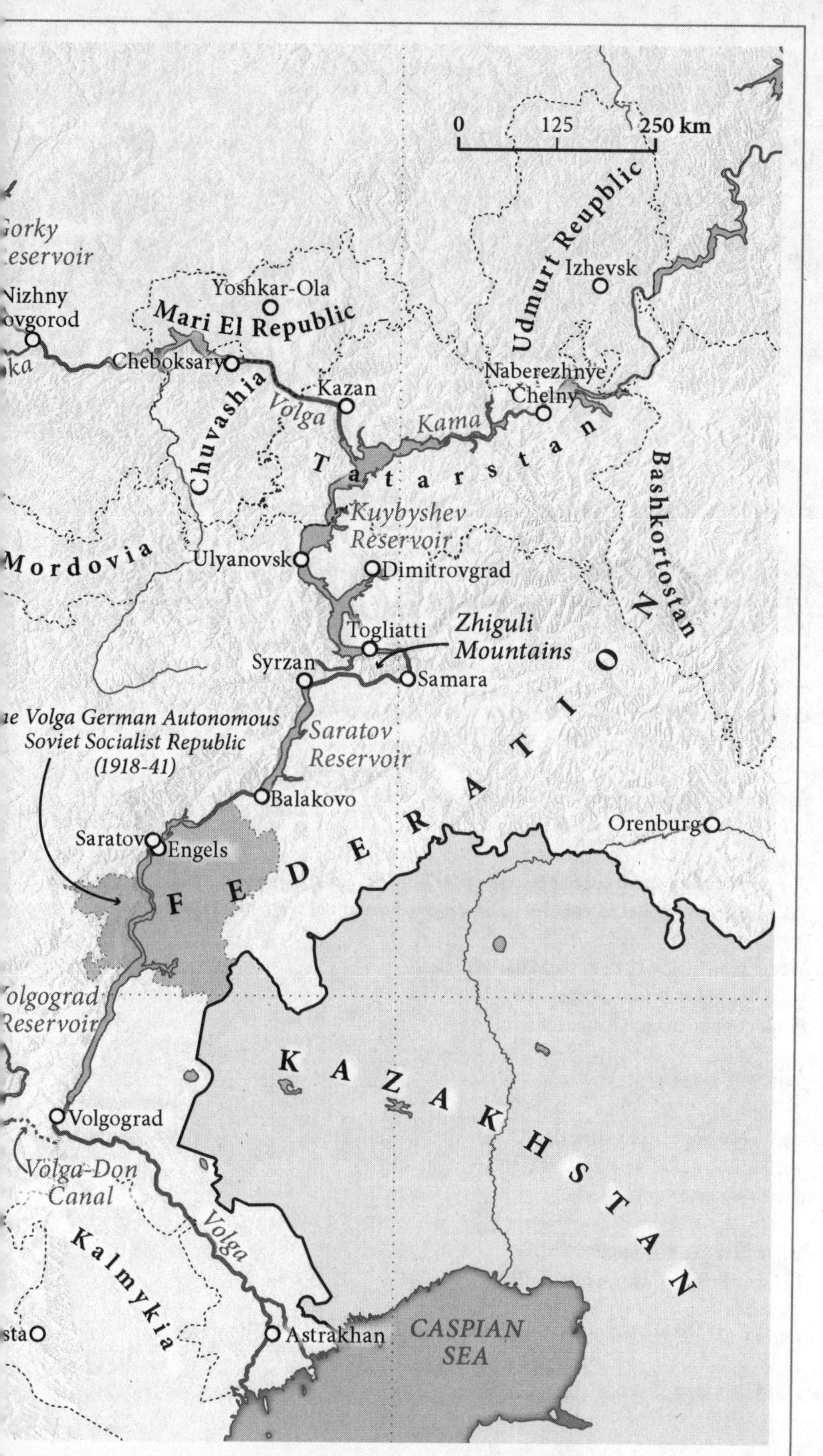

0
125
250 km
Gorky
Reservoir
Nizhny
Novgorod
Yoshkar-Ola
Mari El Republic
Cheboksary
Chuvashia
Kazan
Volga
Udmurt Reupblic
Izhevsk
Naberezhnye
Chelny
Kama
Tatarstan
Bashkortostan
Kuybyshev
Reservoir
Mordovia
Ulyanovsk
Dimitrovgrad
Togliatti
Zhiguli
Mountains
Syrzan
Samara
The Volga German Autonomous
Soviet Socialist Republic
(1918-41)
Saratov
Reservoir
Balakovo
Saratov
Engels
Orenburg
RUSSIAN FEDERATION
Volgograd
Reservoir
KAZAKHSTAN
Volgograd
Volga-Don
Canal
Volga
Kalmykia
Elista
Astrakhan
CASPIAN
SEA

First published in Italy in 2024 by Gramma Feltrinelli

Printed in the United States of America
First American Edition 2026

For information about special discounts for bulk purchases, please contact W. W. Norton Special Sales at specialsales@wwnorton.com or 800-233-4830

Manufacturing by Lake Book Manufacturing
Book design by Lewelin Polanco
Production manager: Anna Oler

ISBN 978-1-324-11103-0

W. W. Norton & Company, Inc.
500 Fifth Avenue, New York, NY 10110
www.wwnorton.com

W. W. Norton & Company Ltd.
15 Carlisle Street, London W1D 3BS

Authorized EU representative: EAS, Mustamäe tee 50, 10621 Tallinn, Estonia

1 2 3 4 5 6 7 8 9 0

To the house in Fanna,
land of enchantment and calycanthus.
To Gastone and Eleanor—my source.
The start of the adventure, to bathe in
light and then flow away into the steppes
loved and reckless, with your eyes in mine.

I could care less that Homer and Ovid
omitted people like us from their tales
covered in soot and scars
I know
that the sun would fade at the sight
of the golden sands of our souls.

—**VLADIMIR MAYAKOVSKY,**
"A CLOUD IN TROUSERS"

Contents

Preface 1

PART ONE—*PASSIONARNOST*

1 The abbess at the source: "God does not suffer cowards" 9

2 The evil stepmother: "Death explains it all" 25

3 The philologist of the dead city: "The past is unpredictable" 47

PART TWO—*SMUTA*: TIME OF TROUBLES

4 Dinner with the Chechen: "Fuck the '90s!" 65

5 The widow's *izba*: "Damn you, Pavel" 89

6 Among mercenaries: "Now let's take care of the Poles" 114

PART THREE—*NA GRANI*

7 The sausage oligarch: "Thanks for the sanctions!" 149

8 The Tatar merchant: "Allah roots for Putin" 165

9 In Lenin and Oblomov's neighborhood: "Today we ask ourselves again: What do we do?" 184

10 The island of pacifists: "Boys don't cry" 204

11 The *batyushka* of the steppe: "Let's burn it all down" 228

Closing Credits 259

Acknowledgments 261
Bibliography 263
List of Illustrations 265
Index 267

VOLGA BLUES

Preface

It takes one month, they say, for a drop of water to flow from the source of the Volga in the Valdai Hills, between Moscow and Saint Petersburg, to the delta in Astrakhan, on the Caspian Sea. One month was also the duration of our voyage.

The Volga is the longest river in Europe. Its source, on the same latitude as the North Sea, is in a different time zone than its mouth, which is on the same parallel as Lake Michigan. When we left the source in June, snowdrops, blueberries, and wild strawberries dotted the taiga underbrush beneath the larches and pines. By the end, in Astrakhan, the steppe was toasted by the sun, lotus flowers bloomed on the delta, watermelons were ripe and sweet.

As grand as the Volga's physical and geographic footprint is, its metaphysical reach is what makes it the River Jordan of Orthodox Russia. Officially, its sanctity dates to 2017, when Vladimir Putin and Patriarch Kirill I, the leader of the Moscow-based Russian Orthodox Church, consecrated the source in grand style, equating it to a baptismal font. A plaque proclaims that the waters of the Volga have been "blessed by God to save the soul of the Russian people." It calls to mind Mussolini's inscription at the source of the Tiber River, among the beech trees of the northern Apennines, which says, "Here is born the river sacred to the fate of Rome"; or the statue of Tiberinus, the god of the Tiber River, placed at the point where the Thames emerges among the hills of the Cotswolds to link the Roman and British Empires.

Great rivers have always been great turbines of rhetoric.

In the land of great rivers, the Volga is *the* river. Not due to the vast space it traverses or to its more than 2,000 miles of flow (the Lena River, in Siberia, boasts 2,600 miles). Not due to the breadth of its waters or to the nature of the lands it runs through. As the eminent director of the Hermitage, Mikhail Piotrovsky, told me in Saint Petersburg before the start of my journey, "Russia would not exist without the Volga. It was everything, and it remains everything. It's the life force of a nation. Symbol and destiny. It's the autobiography of a people."

I wanted to know what he thought of my idea of descending along the river to understand a Russia that, as seen from the West, has become distant, mysterious, and hostile—a world unto itself, plunged into deeper obscurity than in the darkest days of the Soviet Union. My photographer, a longtime colleague, Alessandro (Ale) Cosmelli, set out with me to witness the unspeakable, intimate truths the Volga had to tell.

Piotrovsky received Ale and me in his modest office on the museum ground floor, where he has carved out a corner among piles of books, papers, tea pots, sculptures, and wrapped paintings. "The Volga has produced great minds. Unrivaled writers like Maksim Gorky, Ivan Goncharov, the poet Velimir Khlebnikov. It makes you aspire to greatness. It is an intimate space, sheltering, with bright skies, not like the wide-open lands of the steppe or Siberian rivers, which make you feel like a speck in the cosmos. Astonishing ideas, on the Volga. Lenin, who was born and raised in Simbirsk, now Ulyanovsk, set everything on fire and changed the history of the world."

Piotrovsky, who is originally from Armenia, is an illustrious scholar of Islamic and Arabic studies. I've known him for years, but we normally talk about the Italian painter Canaletto, Byzantium, the great Islamic explorers, or his beloved Sicilian white wine. Now here he was, in full war fervor. And not just to defend his prestigious position, or to show dedication to his dear friend Putin, whom he's known since the early 1990s, when Putin became vice-mayor of Saint Petersburg after returning from his KGB post in Dresden with a Western-manufactured washing machine tied to the roof of his Trabant. At seventy-nine years old, Piotrovsky could simply keep his head down and say nothing, as most Russians do. He spoke in his usual calm tone but looked feverish, as if something were devouring him from the inside. The photographs hanging on the wall, which showed him with Putin and the illustrious Western visitors he would bring to the Hermitage—a smiling Tony Blair, a dour Angela Merkel—are now relics of another era, not unlike the tapestry hanging on the wall, gifted by an Egyptian sheikh to Catherine the Great in the eighteenth century. The mild-mannered Piotrovsky that I used to know, jacket draped loosely over his hunched shoulders, had become a warrior.

"Russia is many peoples, but one nation," Piotrovsky declared. "Along the Volga, it was able to incorporate everyone. Twenty different nationalities live along the river, including Finno-Ugric people and southern nomads. Islam, like in Tatarstan, is just as much a part of Russian tradition and identity as is Christian Orthodoxy. In Europe, in America, you speak of multiculturalism, but your cities are bursting with hate. Here, it wasn't hard to include everyone, because we're an imperial civilization." He did not mention the words of Stalin—"I'm a Russian of Georgian nationality"—who wreaked havoc on Volga cities with horrific massacres and deportations of Tatars, Cossacks, nonaligned Christians, and kulaks, who were considered "enemies of the people."

"Just look at the Hermitage!" Piotrovsky said, spreading his slim arms with renewed vigor. "It's the encyclopedia of world culture, but it's written in Russian because it's our interpretation of world history. It may be arrogant, but that's who we are."

He took a deep breath and began to talk of Stalingrad, his Jerusalem. "I don't call it Volgograd, but Stalingrad. It is our reference point now more than ever, an unparalleled symbol of resistance, our enemies' worst nightmare. During the Great Patriotic War, we used it to defend the Volga as a vital supplies corridor. And it's been the same in the past few months. The Volga and the Caspian allow us to trade with Iran to oppose the sanctions, export oil to India, and import what we need." He removed his glasses and cleaned them with his jacket. "If the Nazis had taken Stalingrad, they would have cut off the Volga and conquered all of Russia. A very material thing that became spiritual. A warning that remains current. Whosoever tries it will meet the end of all the others—the Swedes, the French, the Germans, and their allies. Russians are like the Scythians of the steppes: They wait, they suffer, they die, and then they kill." Piotrovsky's words were fearsome, but they pointed me in the right direction.

If the Mississippi is the Father of Waters, the Volga is the *matuška*, the Little Mother—Russia's epicenter of culture, faith, and identity. Where the czarist and Soviet empires first put down roots. Where the Mari, Chuvash, Tatars, Cossacks, and Kalmyks still live, between the Baltic and the shores of the Caspian Sea. When Catherine the Great, called the "Prussian," was crowned czarina in 1767, she wanted to make herself known to the various ethnic and religious groups in the empire, so she gathered a small fleet and sailed down the river from Kazan, on the eastern shore. She wrote to Voltaire saying, "My friend, I'm in Asia!"

Officially, the geographic border between Europe and Asia is farther east, on the Ural River, but the Volga is where the two continents meet and separate, historically and culturally: The river is a bridge or a wall, depending on whether the compass of Russian history points west or east. Based on the conversations I had during the trip, one truth emerged: For Russia, the West is now the enemy.

We arrived in Russia by land, from Helsinki, in very uncertain times. The showdown—real or staged—between Vladimir Putin and oligarch/mercenary leader Yevgeny Prigozhin had just culminated in the latter's threat to march the Wagner Group's troops on Moscow. Ale and I crossed into the country without journalism visas, going in blind with two inscrutable Russians, Vlad and Katya, our travel buddies and fixers. Their names have been changed for security reasons, as have those of other characters we met along the way.

We traveled from Saint Petersburg to Astrakhan by way of Tver', Dubna, Rybinsk, Yaroslavl, Nizhny Novgorod, Kazan, Ulyanovsk, Samara, Saratov, and Volgograd: almost four thousand miles to the Caspian Sea without ever seeing a single Westerner, without hearing any language but Russian, something I'd never experienced before. In Putin's paranoid Russia, stifled by the FSB (the security services, remnants of the KGB), there is a constant state of disquiet that can sometimes turn into panic.

Especially if one goes around asking questions and taking photographs.

While the following pages can't account for the evolution of events since they've been written, they do offer a glimpse into the deep heart of a country whose future is fundamental to the fate of humanity.

PART ONE

Passionarnost

■ ■ ■

You are millions. And we are legions
Legions legions.
Just try to fight us!
Yes, we are Scythians! Yes, we are Asians,
With greedy and slanted eyes!

—**ALEKSANDR BLOK,**
"THE SCYTHIANS"

1

The abbess at the source

"God does not suffer cowards"

OLGA, THE TERRIBLE

On the edge of a little wood with very tall birch trees there is a spring, the source of the Volga, and a small spruce chapel resembling a Finnish sauna: the same smell, the same damp air, and even the slatted benches outside the hut, which was built on the water and can be reached by an elegant white walkway. Inside, lit candles, icons, and austere devotionals watch over all those who enter. A plump babushka kneels on the wooden planks beside a bucket full of water drawn from the Volga. She dampens her face and head, then dips a small cross into the bucket, along with the framed picture of a little girl. She cups her hands and takes a few sips of the water. She is very calm, at least until she stands up and furiously makes the sign of the cross, bowing toward the icons, then toward the stream glinting in the candlelight and setting sun. Vlad, one of our travel companions, pays his respects too, eyes shining, by wetting his head and sending selfies to his mother.

About six hundred feet from here, the Volga wends into the black-green taiga before flowing into a series of lakes: The brochures say that on a clear day, you can see the river current run across them, as if miraculously separate from the surrounding lake waters.

The temple of Saint Nicholas the Thaumaturgist stands guard from a bluff to the left of the chapel, and in the valley to the right is the Church of Transfiguration, built with Valdai red stones in a similar style to Saint Basil's Cathedral in the Red Square. Guardianship over this sacred clearing is entrusted to the order of the sisters of Saint Olga, the mythical Varangian princess of Kyiv and the Rurik dynasty—Vikings who followed the Volga and planted the roots of Kyivan Rus, the first East Slavic state, in present-day Ukraine. Six centuries after Olga's death in 969, the Orthodox Church proclaimed her a saint of apostolic stature, not because of any special miracle but for having been the first of the dynasty to be baptized in Constantinople. Her grandson, Prince Vladimir, later adopted Christian Orthodoxy as the state religion, which sealed Russia's fate more than any other event in the thousand years that followed, even though Vlad's choice had reportedly been inspired by trivial considerations: He excluded Islam because it prohibited alcohol, and Judaism because he thought God had abandoned the Jews for spinelessly delivering Jerusalem to the Romans.

Before finding her faith, Saint Olga, who is always represented in paintings with a blissfully kind face, introduced a "Russian style" of power that was later adopted in various iterations by Ivan the Terrible, Lenin, Stalin, and Putin.

After being widowed at a young age, she found herself up against the Drevlians, an East Slavic tribe whose leaders wanted her to marry their prince, Mal, and place him on the throne of Kyiv. They sent twenty warriors to persuade her, but she buried them alive. Then she announced a change of heart: She would take Mal as her husband, but to confer dignity to the event she asked to be escorted to her betrothed by the most eminent men of his tribe. When they arrived to retrieve her, Olga suggested they refresh themselves with a warm bath, but after they entered the *hammam*, she locked the doors and set fire to the building, burning alive all those who wished to rule Kyiv. Once she had truncated the elite (as Stalin did with the Katyn Massacre on the high Volga, or Putin in Chechnya), the Drevlians disappeared from the face of the earth and the reign of the Rus began under the sign of Christian Orthodoxy, with aspirations to become a Holy Empire.

THE APPARITION

Saint Olga, the czarina, assassin, and patron saint of widows, is buried in Kyiv in the Church of the Tithes. In Russia, she watches over the sacred source of the Volga by way of Abbess Sophia, who heads the monastery of cenobitic nuns in what is little more than an *izba*, a little log house easily mistaken for a tool shed or for the home of the cathedral's custodians.

In the early twentieth century, the Tver' consistory decided to erect a temple-sanctuary at the source of the Volga and entrust it to the order of the sisters of Saint Olga, "to connect this place to the dawn of our country's Christian history," the abbess explains when we meet her. They called it the Olginski Monastery. Its library contained liturgical, literary, and scientific works and textbooks to educate the children of local farmers. Its school, named after Cyril and Methodius, served the area's orphan girls. The sisters provided the Red Cross with linens for Russian soldiers wounded in World War I and organized pilgrimages for widows to the Church of the Holy Sepulcher in Jerusalem. In 1917, the monastery was shut down and the land was confiscated by Soviet decree. But the sisters didn't go far: They felt that the atheist rampage would soon expire, "because without God, Russia will die of thirst," the abbess says. They set up a secret monastic commune in the forest, as partisans of the faith, and in 1924 they founded a women's agricultural cooperative, where they raised pigs and spun flax. They prayed and sang odes at night. "When you go to Nizhny Novgorod, you'll have to visit the Serafimo-Diveevsky Monastery, dedicated to Saint Seraphim of Sarov, a nineteenth-century starets," the abbess suggests. "It's on the Volga. A thousand nuns were arrested there in the days of Nikita Khrushchev—he was the worst of all. They were accused of vagrancy, deemed idle and homeless, since their monastery had become a school for radio telegraphists. They were sent to a gulag in Uzbekistan and few survived. Those who returned formed a secret society that lasted until the 1980s: Only the confessor priests knew the nuns' real names. They used code words to gather and pray."

During the Great Patriotic War, a term used in Russia to describe the battles fought on the eastern front of World War II, the Germans occupied the Olginski Monastery and then burned it down, as they did with everything else during their retreat from Moscow. Until the fall of the USSR, schoolchildren and tourists would stay at the Saint Nicholas Cathedral and temple while visiting the source. Then the crosses reappeared and with them came the priests, archimandrites, and archbishops to celebrate the *moliebny*, liturgical processions. More and more pilgrims started to arrive every year on May 29—a date dedicated, since the early 1990s, to celebrating the source's sacredness—to sing anthems to Saint Olga and to bathe and drink from the source.

As we approach the monastery, the forest around us sways in the wind and the first drops of a storm pierce the dusty road like bullets. We're expected for dinner. The dining table is laden with chickpea soup, breaded carp, and buckwheat dressed in honey. To drink, there is elm tea or *kvas*, a type of beer made with stale bread and hops.

Before dining, the nuns invite us to pray under the portrait of Kirill, the patriarch of all the Russias. When we turn to sit down, we see the abbess, dressed in black, face as white as a candle, standing motionless in the doorway by a braid of hanging onions. More an apparition than a presence. She looks straight at us without speaking. Her expression is one of indifference, or disappointment, perhaps because we're late. Her oval face is framed by a monastic *koukoulion*, but her hair is not shaven, unlike that of many of the nuns, because a thin blond lock pokes out above her forehead. Her hands, crossed over her stomach, emerge from her sleeves to reveal large knuckles, strong and reddened by work. A large silver cross adorned with an emerald on each end hangs from her neck, along with a Saint Olga medallion. Her rimless glasses accentuate the cerulean translucency of her eyes. She smiles when we tell her about how moved we felt at the source. "No one has ever left the source with an empty soul," she says.

LOVE IN RUINS

The abbess arrived at the source in 2005 after traveling up the Volga—she did not want to say from where. She found nothing but the burnt foundation of the monastery destroyed by the Nazis. She and nine other nuns restored it: They oversaw the carpentry and masonry work, cared for the chickens, cows, goats, and honeybees, and tended the gardens, where they now grow aromatic herbs. She keeps her eyes down as she tells us this, looking up only when making a point. This is our entertainment on this stormy night: an entirely alcohol-free conversation, perhaps the only one of the trip.

Before coming to the monastery, the abbess was a young math and physics teacher, an atheist daughter of atheist Communists: Her father called religious people fanatics, parasites, and failures. When she decided to take the trip, she was in unspeakable pain, abandoned by the only man she'd ever loved. "I told myself that absolute love cannot exist. It's just a fairy tale like the ones priests tell."

She followed the river she'd grown up on to reach its source—a worthy distraction from her suffering. When she arrived among the birch trees and alders, she found the sisters of the Serafimo-Diveevsky Monastery of Nizhny Novgorod "singing and praying like angels from heaven, with sacred icons clutched to their chests, barefoot in the muddy earth." Watching them, she thought these nuns must be the happiest women in the world: They had nothing superfluous, only the essential—only God.

"It was a Russia I'd never seen or imagined before. I wondered where it had been hiding. I felt like I had walked into a new dimension made of earth, people, and truth. I knelt before the source, searching for the words to pray but unable to find them, I didn't know them. Then God embraced me, loved me, and never left me."

Theology studies, vows, and meetings followed; her spiritual father is the archimandrite Tikhon Shevkunov, superior of the Sretensky Monastery in Moscow. By 2007, she had become abbess, and that year, the sisters received permission to rebuild the Olginski Monastery, in below-zero temperatures. "We were a formidable team," the abbess remembers. "Six of us slept in a single hut, on hay, with seven chickens, three goats, and a guard dog who was more afraid than we were. There was no water or electricity. We melted snow to bathe, cook, and mix cement. It was our mission, and we were happy. Everything you see here we built with our own hands." I ask her what Russia's mission is today. "To save itself from the devil!" she exclaims, as if she were stating the obvious. "The rest of the world may do as it pleases, but Russia must fight the devil to the death."

THE INVENTION OF GOD

After the fall of the USSR, Christian Orthodoxy filled the void left by Communism. It began to shape a new identity drawn from centuries-old traditions. The mystique of the Russian homeland was modeled on the birth of Russia itself, which occurred when Constantinople fell and Russia declared itself the only heir to Christianity, forever turning its back on Catholic Europe. This mystique has now become a creed leaders use to cloak the rhetoric of a Great Orthodox Russia in spirituality as they endeavor to reclaim what they believe belongs to Russia by right. In 2020, the armed forces got their own cathedral outside Moscow: The floor is made of molten German tanks, and a mosaic commemorates the 2008 invasion of Georgia, the 2014 annexation of Crimea, and the role of the Russian forces in the Syrian civil war. The space also includes recent quotes from bishops like Elizbar Orlov, of Rostov, who says the Russian army "is cleansing the world of a diabolic infection." Crusading prelates spray soldiers and missiles headed to Ukraine with holy water as if to say that while soldiers fight on the ground, angels bless them from above. Yet none of Russia's four hundred bishops have made public statements on the invasion. Three-quarters of Russians identify as Christian Orthodox even though they descend from the first atheist state in history and only 5 percent of them are practicing.

A friend in Moscow told me what a Russian priest, Innokenti Pavlov, said about state clericalism: "They learned their lesson from the scientific atheism of the USSR, which taught that if God didn't exist, he would have to be invented. What a great idea, they thought, let's invent this God!" Pavlov was found dead in 2020 in unusual circumstances.

According to the abbess, Russian literature "kept the mystery of faith alive in our hearts in the days of state atheism. There were no Bibles, but we had Gogol, Pushkin, Tolstoy, and Dostoyevsky to remind us of our true Russian souls." Meanwhile, women safeguarded the roots of the culture. "The bravest of the family. Thanks to them, God never abandoned Russia."

Vladimir Putin's grandmother baptized him in secret in 1952, when Stalin was still alive. As president, Putin attends important occasions alongside Patriarch Kirill, the Russian priest who elevated the "special operation" in Ukraine to the rank of holy war. Putin also has the same *duchovnik*, or confessor, as Abbess Sophia: Father Tikhon Shevkunov fully supports him in his crusade against the Western Antichrist.

OPERATION BYZANTIUM

The Sretensky Monastery in Moscow is next to the Lubyanka building, which was the headquarters of the KGB, Putin's former employer, and now serves as FSB headquarters. In its various incarnations throughout the twentieth century, officials working out of this building had killed or imprisoned about three hundred thousand members of the church. In Soviet times, the monastery now led by Father Tikhon hosted the KGB barracks. In commemoration, there is a cross in the interior courtyard with a bronze plaque that reads, "In memory of the Orthodox Christians who were tortured or killed here in the years of the atheist terror."

In 2008, Tikhon, who studied film before converting to Christianity, shot a documentary for state TV called *The Fall of an Empire: Lessons from Byzantium*. It covers the Crusaders' pillage of Byzantium, the capital of Christian Orthodoxy. Tikhon's theory was that without the material and intellectual riches Europe plundered from ancient Byzantium, it never would have known culture. "The vindictive hate of the West toward Byzantium and its heirs continues to this day," he declares in the documentary. "If Russians don't understand this, we risk forgetting where we came from, who we are, and what our task is. Being Christian Orthodox is a matter not just of faith but of defending the sacred world of Russian Slavism."

The Fourth Crusade, which took place in the thirteenth century, remains an open wound for many Russians. At the time, the West saw Byzantium as deviant, effeminate, and corrupt. But for Russian nationalists, Byzantium was a beacon of civility and political stability—a Christian empire that protected an ungrateful Europe from Arabs, Turks, and Persians for more than a thousand years. The documentary even concludes that the Italian Renaissance couldn't have happened without Byzantium's cultural blossoming in the eleventh century. In the West, no one recalls the events of April 1204, when Crusaders, led by the Venetians, massacred the people of Constantinople, razed churches to the ground, burned libraries, and stole ancient treasures. Who even remembers the blood Venice spilled to obtain the four bronze horses in Saint Mark's Square? Father Tikhon remembers.

The theologians of Great Russia (a term czars applied to the lands occupied by ethnic Russians) believe that April 1204 has the same foundational value as that assigned by Greater Serbia to the 1389 Battle of Kosovo, when the Serbs were defeated by the Turks. An occasion for martyrdom, memory, revenge.

Today, Russian Orthodox believers see the fall of Constantinople in 1453 as an excuse to take on the mantle of the Byzantine Empire, thus justifying Russia's fight against Western-dominated liberal globalism. In their minds, this narrative solidifies the idea of a powerful Slavic state that thinks and speaks in Russian and embraces Eurasia.

THE LAND IN BETWEEN

The abbess doesn't want to talk about it, but her ties to Father Tikhon—known as the "Richelieu of the Kremlin"—indirectly grant her a high status within Russia's ultraconservative, nationalist, warmongering crowd. This group wants to restore Russian imperial (and Christian) greatness through force and through a system of Eurasian alliances able to challenge Western hegemony.

These are the same tactics espoused by Aleksandr Dugin, the regime's philosopher and political analyst, whose relevance to Putin's vision of a neo-imperial Russia was confirmed when Ukraine's secret service tried to assassinate him. But on the night of August 20, 2022, he wasn't with his daughter, Darya Dugina, when her car was blown up, killing her. According to the Israeli paper *Haaretz*, whoever wants to understand Putin's idea of geopolitics and his vision of the world, including his campaign in Ukraine, would do well to hear what Aleksandr Dugin has to say.

This modern-day Rasputin cut his teeth in the depths of Moscow's 1990s alcohol-fueled Nazi-punk counterculture and apparently likes to refer to himself in the third person. In 2007 he declared that "Putin is becoming more and more like Dugin. Actually, he's achieving something I've been working on my whole life. The closer Putin gets to us, the more he finds himself. When he becomes 100 percent Dugin, he'll have become 100 percent Putin."

Dugin's Eurasian orientation ascribes to the idea of *passionarnost*, an irrational school of thought developed by Russian historian Lev Gumilev. It seems ironic that such an important linguistic contribution to Russia's glorification should come from someone who experienced harsh and lengthy torture in a Siberian gulag. It refers to a rare ability to overcome inertia and give oneself to a cause bigger than oneself.

The idea is popular among anti-Communist dissidents, Fascist sympathizers, and staunch supporters of the USSR. Passionarnost espouses a special Russian super-ethnos, a term Gumilev used to refer to a merging of peoples, in this case to form a Slavic civilization that is opposite and superior to the Western one and that can bring many nations under Moscow's umbrella—an appealing thought for the new reactionaries that have emerged in full force since the end of the Cold War. To them, passionarnost sounds like an affirmation of Christian Orthodox values and Russian cultural supremacy.

According to Putin, passionarnost is "the inner energy of the nation, the ability to sacrifice oneself for the greater good," a sort of manifest destiny. Russian literature has shown how ideas can become concrete acts that generate monsters and cause millions of deaths. Stavrogin, from Dostoyevsky's *Demons*, is a fanatic devoured by an idea. Raskolnikov, in *Crime and Punishment*, kills just to prove a theory, prompting his friend Razumikhin to say that if he'd come up with a different theory, he probably would have done something a thousand times worse. This black humor tragically foreshadowed the fate of twentieth-century Russia.

In an interview, Tikhon responded to a question on Western perceptions of Russia by citing Emperor Alexander III, according to whom "the West fears our vastness." He then noted the opinion of Christoph von Münnich, who moved to Russia in the eighteenth century: "The Russian state's advantage is that it is governed directly by Our Lord and Savior. There is no other way to explain its ability to survive." According to Tikhon, "Many Western analysts don't understand that Russians will always oppose any form of external imposition. Therein lies the main conflict between Russia and the West. For a combination of geographic, historical, spiritual, and cultural reasons, Russia lives its own autonomous life between Europe and Asia. Generations have experienced this incredible Russian life, sometimes tragic but always full of deep spiritual wonder."

Putin has long used the term "Atlantic" to refer to anything relating to the West, and "Eurasia" to encompass the Russian world: the *Russkiy mir* of space, language, and common cultural, communal, and spiritual values. *Russkiy mir* is a relatively new concept—not a philosophy, but a creed encompassing everything pertaining to Great Russia, where Orthodox Christianity, Fascist impulses, traditionalism, and a certain "Asiatic" Soviet despotism coexist. Just as Putin's support for the Russian Orthodox Church coexists with the rebirth of the Stalinist myth: It seems like blasphemy, but in Russia, it works without too much cognitive dissonance. State crimes end up in the mass grave of collective memory. As the war in Ukraine rages on, Stalin no longer appears as an exterminator. As a young man, he'd been a seminary student, and his first ambition had been to become patriarch. Now he is being depicted as a pragmatic leader who in 1945 championed, not Communism, but the Russian people. A leader who united Russians against the Nazi invasion and revived love of country and spirit of sacrifice by seeking help from the priests—the few who remained. And the priests have not forgotten.

KHRUSHCHEV, THE ULTIMATE EVIL

Father Tikhon, the poster child for post-Soviet monastic fundamentalism, Putin's confessor and spiritual father of the abbess, in 2012 published *Everyday Saints*, a book of mystical testaments that sold many more copies in Russia than *Fifty Shades of Gray*. His book aims to bridge the distance between the church and Russia's Communist past, normalizing an era that was not at all normal and placating the secret discomfort many Russians feel about the crimes (or sins) of their fathers or grandfathers. The book attacks godless people like Marx, Lenin, and Trotsky without mentioning Stalin or Putin. It tells of miracles, revelations, prophecies, visions bordering on the paranormal and the occult, close encounters with the devil, and exorcisms. Russia appears as an otherworldly place, where manifestations of the divine and holiness itself are everyday occurrences.

Tikhon, born in 1958 and baptized at twenty-four years old, writes of his experiences as a novice and as an archimandrite in the Pskov-Caves Monastery in the Baltics. It was one of the few the Soviets were never able to close down, perhaps because of the hassle of dealing with fourteen thousand bodies buried in the recesses of the convent that, inexplicably, didn't reek of corpses but smelled of violets, Tikhon claims. This small fort became the site of heroic deeds, resistance, and martyrdom—a gallery of saints offered to the pantheon of a Russia returning to its God, all thanks to the KGB, apparently. The freedom to do good assumes the freedom to do bad. Those monks, many of whom were former soldiers in the Great Patriotic War, were tortured and sent to the gulags but never tamed. Now, they are deemed patriots of a Russian Christian faith that stands in contrast to the Western Antichrist. "God does not suffer cowards," according to the abbess.

Tikhon does not speak of dark days but of a time when Russian faith was put to the test. In short, Soviet repression was God's will to strengthen the heirs of Byzantium.

But Tikhon's real target, and that of the reactionary intelligentsia intent on absolving seventy years of Soviet rule, is General Secretary Nikita Khrushchev, guilty of denouncing Stalin's thirty years of crimes. In 1957, *Time* lauded the first Soviet attempt at glasnost by naming Khrushchev person of the year. But for Putin and Tikhon, the fact that he aired Russia's dirty laundry, and exposed the blood on the hands of a man who led the USSR to dominate half the world, makes him enemy number one. Not to mention that he also ceded Crimea to Ukraine (where he had formerly been political commissar) and ordered purges against the church. *Everyday Saints* also devotes several pages to Father Alipius, the Pskov-Caves Monastery financial officer who fought valiantly in the Battle of Moscow and the Battle of Berlin, where he was severely wounded. But when peace was restored, he had to fight against the very state he'd shed blood for—both wars, against Hitler and Khrushchev, were matters of life and death.

Tikhon's theory is that Khrushchev needed a big victory to rival Stalin's win against the "Nazi Antichrist," so he set out to annihilate the Orthodox Church and erase a thousand years of Russian history. As he did with Stalin's crimes, he openly declared that the world had seen the last of the Russian priests and their foul beards. Tikhon details how Khrushchev blew up thousands of churches, cathedrals, and monasteries or transformed them into warehouses, taxi garages, and factories; exiled thousands of religious figures; and closed 90 percent of seminaries and religious training schools, leaving only two authorized monasteries: Trinity Lavra of Saint Sergius, in greater Moscow, and the one in Pskov, which Tikhon refers to as Indian reservations for tourists.

KIRILL THE MODERATE

But Tikhon's book makes no mention of devils in cassocks, that is, Orthodox dignitaries who worked for the KGB and oversaw selections and promotions.

Nobody knows this criminal page of the Soviet era's Orthodox Christian Church better than Father Gleb Yakunin, who was excommunicated in 1993 for having snooped into KGB archives. There, he found an agent "Mikhailov" who seemed to travel a lot: He went to Australia, Thailand, and New Zealand on the same days—according to patriarchate records—as an archimandrite named Kirill, who worked for the department of foreign relations. In 2009, that same Kirill, now sporting a long white beard, was appointed patriarch of the Russian church. According to Yakunin, the entire episcopate was being bankrolled by the KGB. Now it responds to Putin, who seems to be fashioning himself into a modern-day czar as he gains increasing control over Russian institutions. "The church is being used to help people forget the past, not to dredge it up," Yakunin said.

But Tikhon, also known as the bishop of Lubyanka, remains Putin's most trusted general. While Kirill initially opposed the invasion of Ukraine—before offering to bless it for political reasons—and refused to celebrate the annexation of Crimea in 2014, Tikhon sees Russian power and Moscow's mission to become the Third Rome as inextricably linked. The Kremlin's fight against Western values and LGBTQ+ culture is Tikhon's brainchild, and he has supposedly proved that a return to pure, hard orthodoxy wouldn't require historical purification or a denial of the Soviet past.

In 1990 Tikhon began publishing articles in which he warned that an emergent democracy in Russia would be a threat to the Orthodox Church. In those days, Putin was head of the FSB, and Tikhon would join him on foreign trips. As Kremlin envoy for religious affairs in Crimea, he supported annexation. Now he spearheads opposition to Kirill from the right, accusing him of ecumenism, or of being too communicative with the Catholic pope—whom he considers a heretic, as per a Russian Orthodox belief that Catholics aren't a church and are therefore not Christian.

Indeed, a large number of Russian Orthodox believers consider Kirill a traitor who was colluding with Pope Francis to sell out the Russians to the Catholics. Their meeting in Havana in 2016 elicited rumors of a secret joint liturgy and a mutual communion with Rome. Kirill was also crucified for talking to the heads of other Christian churches—all heretics, according to Orthodox fundamentalists. Then, when Western journalists reported on the prodigious fortune of "Putin's altar boy," as Pope Francis once called Kirill, early in the war—villas on the Black Sea, yachts, Swiss bank accounts, and watches costing tens of thousands of euros—antisemitic voices close to Tikhon inundated Kirill with accusations of being bankrolled by Jewish oligarchs. This aligned with Tikhon's belief in an antisemitic conspiracy theory according to which Nicholas II was murdered in a Jewish ritual killing. The *Novaya Gazeta* wrote that "our president's personal priest is an antisemite."

VLAD'S STRAWBERRIES

Back in the van, Vlad and Katya belt out American pop songs (which seem to air on the radio more than their Russian counterparts) and point out a giant plant they see along the road. Its green flowers seem to be invading pits and untended fields everywhere: It's called "Stalin's revenge" because it was introduced as animal feed after the war and now it punishes any unsuspecting saps who might urgently have to defecate in the field and who "rightly burn their butts off," Vlad says. "Those big leaves look like a lifesaver but they're worse than caustic soda. You can hear people screaming from miles away—it's great."

During these first few days of the trip, Vlad's not touching alcohol and remains vague when the subject comes up. We know he's been sober for months but that Katya insisted on coming with us to keep watch on him. Or so she told us after downing four beers back in Saint Petersburg. Katya is generally talkative like that, but her silence in certain moments—like when we read news about Ukrainian drone incursions into Russia on Telegram—suggests she sees us as willing victims of Western fake news.

As we cross the immense forest, we start to talk about America. I don't know if it starts from Vlad's curiosity, since he often asks us about our experiences in America, or from a joke we make about the songs he and Katya listen to—only American ones. Ale and I hoped to enjoy some Russian music on this trip—maybe not the great Russian classics, which the radio seems to ignore, but at least some contemporary pop (especially since Katya claims to have been a pop singer in Saint Petersburg), and maybe even some folk music. We're in Russia, for crying out loud! But wherever we go, all we hear is the music of the enemy: Radio 7 and Radio Retro, the most widespread stations on the upper Volga, seem to play only American rock, songs that evoke the classic American road trip. We want the *dusha*, the mysterious Russian soul, but we get only the usual American soul, rock, and blues. "Russians are obsessed with America," I say, in an effort to provoke Vlad and Katya. "Everything you think is cool is always American. You confiscated all the McDonald's but left the label and renamed the Big Mac 'Bolshoi Mac.'" Vlad laughs and calls the Russian-American relationship sadomasochistic. He says Russians have a lot in common with Americans, their ideas of grandeur, for example, maybe due to the vastness of their spaces. "You feel small, but you find strength in belonging to a great land. Our land certainly is. From Florida to Alaska, from Vladivostok to Saint Petersburg, it's still America, it's still Russia, isn't it? I think this is what gives us and them a sense of power over the rest of the world. It brings us together while pitting us against each other, like two alpha males trying to dominate the pack."

"And add to that all the cultural, social, ethnic, and geographic diversities that exist in America and in Russia," Ale adds. "This is disorienting for us Europeans: We're ensconced in our own little communities, and aside from a certain national pride inherited from history, we no longer have a greatness to be proud of."

As Ale and I watch Katya and Vlad, we feel observed in return. They seem to be holding back on expressing themselves fully, but only out of a lack of familiarity with us, likely because we are Westerners. They remain guarded with regard to sensitive topics, out of politeness and because they know how to be friendly, even with each other, without having to talk about the invasion, the police state, murdered journalists, and so on. Although they do wax poetic about any aspect of being Russian, as long as it doesn't stray into the realm of right and wrong, truth and lies.

We get back on the M11 and turn onto a road that snakes through the forest. Above us, the moon fights to emerge from a cage of clouds. Vlad slams on the brakes. He says he feels the call of the wild. "I have to breathe, shit . . . There's something really immense in there that bites you here, in the heart, especially early in the morning and at night. Not like those shitty convents." The abbess, the nuns, and all those saints had visibly depressed him, deflating the emotion he'd felt at the source.

Vlad has just returned to Russia after spending a year in northern Europe, and to feel truly home he must get drunk "on nature, at least," he says. "The smells of the Russian underbrush get you high, man. Better than the glue we used to sniff as kids in Saint Petersburg." After wending through pines and birch trees for about twenty minutes, he emerges covered in mud and scratches, pockets full of wild strawberries.

He looks ecstatic, almost exhausted with happiness, wearing the dazed grin of a teenager who's just lost his virginity. Vlad, who was born in Siberia but has lived in Saint Petersburg for many years, is thirty-five years old but has the face of a kid and the almost ephebic features of Tadzio from *Death in Venice*. Yet he has already lived a full life, in a Dionysian escape from boredom and from the present, conforming to Chekhov's idea that Russians prefer the memory of having lived to life itself. But more than anything, Vlad has a penchant for excess and is driven to self-destruction.

When we first met Vlad—especially upon visiting the source of the Volga—Ale and I got the impression that he is a very complex person. Extraordinarily Russian. But we also felt an immediate connection to him, and we became fast friends. Conversely, there is something opaque about Katya, who makes us feel uneasy, even alarmed.

2

The evil stepmother

"Death explains it all"

BAGS FULL OF BONES

Eighty-five thousand tons of human flesh—Natalia Dranova, a local historian who agreed to show us the "forest of bones" just south of Rzhev, reaches this figure when she adds up the carnage from the "Rzhev Meat Grinder," the fifteen-month battle that took place northwest of Moscow between January 1942 and March 1943. She estimates that the average Russian man weighed 145 pounds and that the battle killed 1,300,000 soldiers. "Piled up, they'd be as high as that five-story building," she tells us, pointing at a crumbling Khrushchevka prefab apartment block from the 1960s, which looks out over the Volga. "Who else would give their lives for their country like that? More than our weapons, what the

West fears is our willingness to sacrifice our lives. It alters the calculus and forces our enemies to face a destabilizing human element. You can be as technologically advanced as you want, but heart always wins out. Heart is our real atomic bomb."

In a town of about fifty thousand inhabitants, only 297 houses remain standing. "Everyone talks about Stalingrad, but without resistance in Rzhev, it wouldn't have been so significant," Natalia says. "Hitler would have crossed the Volga and reached Vladivostok, where Japan would have invaded. The USSR would have crumbled fifty years sooner." Rzhev is known as the forgotten war because Stalingrad overwhelmed the history books: In his memoirs, Georgy Zhukov, the Soviet general who led Operation Mars (the offensive against the Germans) before transferring to Stalingrad, doesn't even mention the outsize sacrifice suffered in Rzhev.

Natalia leads us to the fresh skeletons of the day: Yellow military tape cordons off an area bordering an old cemetery, which was initially located far from the urban center, as is customary in Slavic Orthodox tradition. But the neighborhood has since been swallowed up by suburban projects, a sports complex, and an abandoned chicken farm. The graveyard is more than a century old, so it would have been part of the battlefield during those terrifying months.

The old tombs are laid out haphazardly: They sprout like mushrooms among the roots and trunks of ash and birch trees—the souls of the dead are said to find peace among the trees. Pagan beliefs seem to dominate this gothic wilderness.

The fresh mounds are hard to make out among the thick vegetation, but I can clearly see the colorful plastic flowers and wrought iron fences that surround them, poking out from brambles planted on the border between life and death. Among the ivy, crosses covered by little wooden roofs resemble birdhouses but are designed to make the soul of the dearly departed feel like it is still in its *izba*, a cozy Russian cottage. The neglect has its own aesthetic, like an English garden, where wilderness artfully blends with form. The pathways are clear, large cats doze under the tombstones. The silhouettes of several visitors stand out in the dazzling light that filters through the trees—they are sitting on benches by a grave, smoking and conversing in low voices. An old woman is on her knees arranging fresh flowers and candles in a little glass greenhouse, a sort of freeze-proof shrine. Almost every grave has one. Little glasses and vodka bottles to drink to the health of the thirsty souls are laid out on wooden tables along with candy for souls with a sweet tooth. I see signs of five recent funerals, a massacre of empty bottles and cigarette butts on the ground, photos of the boys who died in Donbas during the Russian invasion over the past month, stamped in black and white on gray marble—Sergey, twenty-one years old, on his motorcycle; Daniil, twenty-four, his bare torso covered in tattoos. A car drives by, blasting music. A few dozen feet from the corner where the newly dead are buried, four men in unzipped white chemical suits gather around the loose earth. Suddenly, they all start laughing, maybe from a joke; one of them laughs so hard he erupts into a raspy cough. In the distance, beyond the yellow tape, we see three open black bags containing piles of bones and a chest of old objects and fabric scraps. The remains of the Rzhev Meat Grinder victims.

Natalia recites Aleksandr Tvardovsky, the last words of an unknown soldier: "He was killed near Rzhev / in a garden with no name." The steppes are those of Stalingrad, where the Red Army turned the tables of World War II, "but without the Meat Grinder things would have been different," Natalia says. Every year, Rzhev unearths the remains of two to three thousand soldiers from that era. Bands of stray dogs and wolves dig up and munch on human bones—at least according to urban legend. Either way, in the competition for who is most Russian and anti-Nazi, locals remain proud of how much blood they spilled along the Volga front. "Stalingrad recorded two hundred thousand fewer deaths," Natalia claims. "Operation Mars stopped seventy divisions of the Wehrmacht. With a clever disinformation trick over the radio, General Zhukov made the krauts believe that the biggest counteroffensive would take place here, between Rzhev and Tver', which was still called Kalinin back then. This left the Germans undefended so he could surround them in Stalingrad as part of Operation Uranus." I think I hear a cannon roar, but it's just thunder in the distance.

THE DEAL WITH THE DEVIL

"All my efforts are directed at Russia: If the West is too dumb and blind to see that, I'll have no choice but to join the Russians, attack the West, and after its defeat, turn all my might against the Soviet Union. I need Ukrainian grain so as to not go hungry, as we did during the last war." This is what Hitler told his generals in August 1939, a few days before Germany signed a pact of nonaggression with Moscow. Hitler's obsession with anti-Bolshevism since the days of *Mein Kampf*, along with his antisemitism, could easily accommodate a deal with the devil, so long as he could later stab him in the back. On the other hand, after Germany attacked Poland, Stalin—then the most hated man in the Soviet Union, which had been bled dry from his purges—decided Soviet Russia would stay out of a wider conflict. Moreover, the pact called for the partition of Poland: Its Ukrainian and Belarusian lands would be returned to Russia, as in the days of the czar. Stalin also claimed parts of Estonia, Lithuania, and Finland.

This unnatural alliance upset the West and disoriented Communists, Fascists, and liberals. When Hitler's armies crossed beyond Germany's eastern border on September 1, 1939, Stalin was amazed by the speed with which they overwhelmed Polish defenses, whose strength lay in their cavalry, not in tanks. On September 3, France and England declared war on Germany, marking the beginning of World War II. It wasn't until September 17, when the Polish resistance was practically in tatters, that Soviet soldiers entered Poland—the "bastard of the Treaty of Versailles," as the Soviet minister for foreign affairs, Vyacheslav Molotov, called it. It was the first time since the Russo-Polish War ended in 1921 that Russian troops crossed into a foreign country. Stalin handed Hitler the German Communists who'd escaped to the USSR, just as Churchill delivered to Stalin, like sacrificial lambs, the Cossacks who had joined the war on the side of the Axis and were later captured by the British. In a telegram to Hitler, Stalin said, "The friendship forged in blood between the Germans and the people of the Soviet Union has every reason to be solid and long-lasting." As per the agreement, Stalin set up Soviet bases in the Baltic states and ordered Helsinki to adjust the borders, counting on the Finns to yield before a daunting force. But they did no such thing. The Red Army, guided by hastily assembled generals, penetrated the forests of the Karelia, between Russia and Finland, leaving 160,000 wounded and 50,000 dead in the snow: an enormous price in terms of human life, with significant political consequences. Finland forced an interim peace, and Stalin revealed his weakness to the world, confirming Hitler's suspicions: Bloody purges had weakened the foundations of the presumed military giant.

In 1939 the Soviet Union was the third-largest industrial power in the world after the United States and Germany. Stalin's forced industrialization had succeeded, at the expense of the lives or deportations of about ten million farmers. The USSR had only ten years to catch up with the century of innovation afforded to more advanced countries, "or we'll be swept away," Stalin said. Ninety percent of land had been collectivized. Experienced, high-ranking Red Army officers who had trained in French and Prussian academies counted among the eight hundred thousand people executed in the purges of the 1930s for suspected Trotskyism or collusion with reactionary forces. So when the war came, the USSR produced more ammunition and weapons than Nazi Germany, but it had no officers to lead history's biggest military mobilization.

THE MOST TRAGIC HOUR

Operation Barbarossa began at four in the morning on June 22, 1941, on the Russian front. The Germans had amassed a force that was six times more numerous than Napoleon's Grande Armée: three million men, two thousand planes, more than three thousand tanks. Only the number of horses was the same. Stalin had ignored warnings from his secret service and from Churchill, and had banned the commanders at the front from engagement, only to execute them for not resisting Hitler's attack. Shocked by the failure of his calculations and faced with an enemy who was advancing without resistance along a two-thousand-mile front, Stalin retreated to his dacha resigned to his fate and dazed as a boxer who's just received a terrible blow. For the first time in his life, he had no one to blame or enemies to eliminate. He seemed to have given up. A politburo delegation arrived to find him three sheets to the wind and terrified. Maybe he expected to be shot, which is what he would have done in their shoes. But no one was willing to take his place in that moment: They needed his legendary calm and cunning, qualities with which he'd secured his czar-like cult of personality. He was the *vozhd'*, the leader of the people, ruthless and uncaring of the lives of others. He was the only one who possessed enough inhumanity to lead in times of war, after honing it so keenly in times of peace. They convinced him to mobilize the people, even if the generals themselves doubted the loyalty of their troops, sons of farmland devastated by collectivization.

Yet the people sacrificed themselves beyond all expectations: By the end of the war, 27 million people had died, more than half of whom were civilians, 800,000 having fallen in the nine hundred days of the siege of Leningrad. The Americans lost 407,000 men and the British 450,000. Within a few weeks, Hitler's generals started to suspect they'd underestimated the Russians. They saw that they were not going to their deaths for the sake of the regime, Communism, or Stalin, but for Russia's very survival. They had seen the atrocities committed by the advancing Germans and wanted to defend their homes. As for Stalin, he did not invoke the spirit of Lenin or the proletarian revolution, but Orthodox saints and czarist heroes: Alexander Nevsky, Dmitry Donskoy, Aleksandr Suvorov, and Mikhail Kutuzov—leaders who'd fought the Swedes, Mongols, Turks, and Poles and leveled the French. The war against Hitler thus became the mother of all wars: the Great Patriotic War.

Germany began its march on Moscow in October 1941, but men and equipment soon sank into the mud and snow: the same fate met by the Napoleonic troops, or worse, because it took the Nazis three additional months to come within forty miles of the Kremlin. "The word 'Moscow' will disappear forever," Hitler had declared. Lenin's corpse was secretly placed in a refrigerated van and taken to Tyumen, in eastern Siberia. A bunker was built in Samara, then known as Kuybyshev, on the lower Volga—which ironically had been the capital of the Whites in the civil war—under the Palace of Culture to evacuate Stalin and the entire government in case Moscow fell. The city is about 510 miles from Moscow, and if the Germans had wanted to attack it, they would have had to advance much farther east than planned and cross the river, which is extremely wide there. Foreign embassies, international correspondents, and a few ministries also moved to Kuybyshev.

But Stalin didn't budge: He didn't want to cut and run like Alexander I before Napoleon. One of his first moves was to save the industries, which were concentrated in European Russia. He had to snatch them out from under the enemy, who was looking not to acquire new lands but to access raw materials from Ukraine and the Caucasus and take over heavy industry. Aside from trying to erase Communism from the face of the earth, Hitler wanted to use the USSR as a reservoir, silo, or blast furnace. The plan took shape in one night: The entire politburo was involved in the operation, one of the most impressive demonstrations of efficiency, tenacity, and energy of Soviet power throughout the entire conflict. Some 1,523 factories were disassembled and transferred to the Urals. Workers and common folk suffered superhuman losses. And even though the secret police watched over the operation with its usual brutality, the resistance, counteroffensive, and eventual victory worked because of the active and enthusiastic participation of the people.

Moscow's most tragic hour came on October 19. The city was under siege, and trenches were dug outside the Kremlin. But it was also the day Stalin conceived one of his most brilliant political acts. He decided to celebrate the anniversary of the 1917 revolution anyway, with a full military parade and fireworks, challenging Hitler's generals, who watched in disbelief through their binoculars. Then he ordered that the Virgin of Vladimir, one of the most ancient and significant icons in Russian history, be flown over Moscow and Leningrad in a military twin-engine plane to bless the cities and save them, just as the Madonna had saved Constantinople from the Turks and Moscow from the Tamerlane hordes. Stalin then addressed crowds at the Mayakovskaya metro station, which served as an air-raid shelter. He called not on Communism, Lenin, or the Soviet people, but on the "great Russian nation of Georgi Plekhanov, Vissarion Belinsky, Nikolay Chernyshevsky, Aleksandr Pushkin, Leo Tolstoy, Anton Chekhov, Maksim Gorky, Aleksandr Suvorov, and Mikhail Kutuzov."

Before the war, nationalism would get you shot or sent to Siberia; now it was the only path to salvation. Stalin leaned on the national spirit: Though Georgian, he took on the mantle of the heir to Russia's past, tradition, and culture. He knew that what Vladimir Putin now calls *passionarnost*—the interior energy of the nation, the ability to sacrifice oneself for the common good—was not about the ideological conflict between Communism and nationalism but about Russian wounded pride and rage toward the German invaders. In his speech, he listed the reasons why Hitler's blitz failed, even though German troops extended from the White Sea to the Black Sea. Western allies hadn't given in to anti-Soviet sentiment and had fought alongside the USSR. The Soviet regime had withstood; German hopes—for conflicts between workers and farmers, popular uprisings, interethnic clashes—had been dashed. Despite its losses, the Red Army's morale remained high because "the Russian nation is defending the country from the foreign invader."

"Russia cannot lose," Stalin concluded.

"Russia cannot be beaten," Putin declared recently—even though he started the war in Ukraine. In the battle for Moscow in late November 1941, the Red Army lost almost three million soldiers: twenty for every German killed, more than the British suffered in all of World War II. The counteroffensive began in early December, at –4 degrees Fahrenheit and in almost two feet of snow. The Russians pushed back the Nazis—their first blow since the start of the war—who headed west, for Rzhev. In the fifteen-month battle that followed, the Red Army used 400 tanks and 1,300 cannons to block seventy German divisions and stop them from descending on Stalingrad. On February 6, Hitler ordered the retreat from the northern front and on March 1 he listened, live via radio, as upper Volga bridges were blown up to be sure the Red Army couldn't follow.

"Rzhev was the red line," Natalia tells us. "We didn't let them through. The earth beneath our feet was literally soaked in blood. They had to set up fishing nets outside Tver' to block the thousands of bodies that were flowing downstream." Until the end of the 1990s, the Battle of Rzhev didn't even appear in schoolbooks, perhaps because it had been considered part of the battle for Moscow or, more likely, according to Natalia, because the human sacrifice had been so horrific it would be "hard to make it pass for heroism. It undermined the myth of victory, which probably could have been achieved without the soldiers acting as mere cannon fodder."

Natalia believes the Russian people have not changed since then: Soldiers gladly fight the "new Nazis" in Ukraine and "would give their lives by the millions if Russia's survival were on the line. All the cowards have gone abroad, damn pussies." She's referring to the eight hundred thousand Russians, mostly young people, many of them intellectuals, who left the country in the first months of the war out of dissent or to avoid enlisting.

We're strolling through thick, dark pine trees that blanket the plains like a shroud. Natalia says she lost ten family members in the battle of Rzhev. "Some of them don't even have graves. I wonder if some of those bones they pulled out today belong to them." She doesn't deny her resentment, maybe even hate, toward the "degenerate" West—even though she studied in Switzerland and is the daughter of a businessman, wife of an engineer, and paragon of the Russian provincial middle class that wears Versace and renounces "the depths of despair that was daily life in the Soviet Union." She also realizes that the past alone cannot give post-Soviet Russia its own identity. But she believes "the time for self-flagellation is over" and that Russia "has given its best to the world and gotten little in return. The West wants to see us on our knees again. We must establish a new order: The bones in those black bags demand it."

As Vladimir Mayakovsky wrote, "I've seen richer, more beautiful, more civilized nations, but a land with more pain—that I've never seen."

AND THE CRANES TOOK FLIGHT

When Putin decided to erect a monument to the Soviet soldier on the Rzhev rise, plans for a conflict in Ukraine were revving up, the war machine was going full throttle—$80 billion, that year—and the central bank was setting aside reserves for a winter of austerity, expecting tougher sanctions than the lukewarm ones levied in 2014, when Russia annexed Crimea. It was February 2020, exactly two years before the invasion. Putin wanted to build the first monument to the Soviet soldier on the banks of the upper Volga, in the land of the Meat Grinder, a stone's throw from the European Union—and he did it in five months. The monument—eighty feet of molten bronze—is larger than the one on the Mamayev Kurgan hill in Volgograd dedicated to the heroes of Stalingrad, the one in Murmansk to the defenders of the Soviet Arctic Circle, the one in Sevastopol to the Sailor and the Soldier, the one on Poklonnaya Hill in Moscow to victory over Germany, and the Piskaryovskoye Memorial Cemetery in Saint Petersburg. Putin wanted this new monument to communicate that he has not forgotten the Battle of Rzhev and to signal the end of mourning for the Soviet Union. This is all part of his Great Game: Starting with hostilities in Ukraine, he wants to demonstrate that the space that had belonged to the Soviet Union is neo-imperial Russia's backyard and that countries of the former USSR can no longer ignore their history or geography.

Although Putin had asked that the statue face west, toward NATO, sculptor Andrei Korobstov designed it to face east, toward Moscow, a detail the press in Poland and the Baltic states did not fail to notice.

The statue stands on a thirty-two-foot-high and three-hundred-foot-wide artificial mound that is visible from six miles away. He's not in a combat stance: He's holding his assault rifle at his side and seems weary. The battle is done and won, but the soldier doesn't seem to have the strength to rejoice—perhaps he is thinking of his massacred comrades or of what's to come: He will need to fight more battles to win the war and push back the German invader.

From up there, with his head skimming the clouds, his hair soaked in sweat, his jaw clenched, his face slightly bowed and his brow furrowed, the soldier looks you straight in the eyes, serious, proud, saddened, or threatening—depending on whether you're Russian or foreign. If the latter, the iconography of the figure may be lost on you: The body is held up not by legs but by a bronze fade-out of leaves and birds in flight. These are cranes, which became symbols of the Rzhev Meat Grinder after a poem by Rasul Gamzatov, who wrote in Avar, a language of the northeast Caucasus. It became a famous song after it was translated into Russian and put to music by Jan Frankel, a Soviet composer born and raised in Ukraine:

> Sometimes I think those fallen soldiers
> who never left the battlefield
> were not buried to decompose and rot
> but became white cranes that coo gently as they migrate.*

The soldier's assault rifle is thirty feet long and weighs almost three tons. Its visual impact is so impressive it almost overwhelms the monument. It is a PPSh-41, nicknamed "the Godfather," a weapon that was just as iconic in the war as the German Stahlhelm helmet that many Russian farmers still use today, hooked to a pole, to scoop out the contents of their outhouses. Once the Godfather became widely deployed in 1942, it transformed the combat tactics of the war. Along with harsh Russian winters, it was the Red Army's most trusted ally: It could deliver a thousand hits per minute—twice as fast as the German MP40—with a range of more than six hundred feet. A single patrol armed with PPSh-41s could unleash as much firepower as an entire

* Videos of white cranes in flight were projected at Alexei Navalny's funeral to give new wings and new life to the dissident's memory.

company using traditional firearms. It was practically immune to frost and dust, ideal for urban or forest guerrillas, and it later enjoyed a fruitful career in Korea and Vietnam.

At the monument's inauguration, Putin admitted Russian amnesia: "It was too difficult to dwell on what happened here, there was too much pain. The number of victims was horrific, unthinkable, and inexplicable." But, he added, "I am here to say that the significance of that long and bloody battle for victory over Nazism was enormous. The lesson is still very compelling today. Each time a soldier fell, another would stand up. That is who we are. Step by step, day by day, the battles of Rzhev brought us closer to triumph at Stalingrad, to the end of the siege of Leningrad, and to the liberation of Belarus, Ukraine, and the Baltic states. . . . This memorial pays tribute to the great and selfless actions of our heroic soldier, our liberator soldier, our triumphant soldier. Our fathers', grandfathers', and great-grandfathers' valor and resistance, and their undying love and loyalty to the motherland, constitute our moral compass. They are the ties that bind generations of Russians."

SOBORNOST LESSONS

At the memorial, we meet Marina Ganicheva, a writer and the vice president of the Union of Russian Writers. We are standing in the complex's great semicircle, surrounded by walls of reinforced concrete where the names of more than a million victims of the Meat Grinder are engraved; black-and-white images of the battle scroll past us as a funereal soundtrack inspires silent contemplation. Suddenly, Ganicheva—a curvy woman with a slight limp and thick glasses—walks into the clearing followed by a group of decorated elderly people and about twenty kids, some in navy jackets, some holding up banners with the image of Admiral Fyodor Ushakov, who in the second half of the eighteenth century won all forty-three of his naval battles—a sort of Russian Horatio Nelson. The medal of the military order is dedicated to him, as are the Kaliningrad naval institute and a small planet discovered by a Russian cosmonaut. He was also made a saint, charged with protecting the Russian navy and strategic nuclear bombers.

Ganicheva translates Putin's 2020 speech for us. "Saying those things here, a year and a half before the start of the conflict in Ukraine, was an intentional political act. His words are still relevant today, because the motherland is calling us all to duty."

She explains that her group is on a pilgrimage along the Admiral Fyodor Ushakov trail, which also includes Stalingrad. "We've been traveling for a month, praying to our admiral to protect our soldiers." We walk out of the monument and reach the museum, where stalls sell Stalin and Putin T-shirts, fridge magnets with victory signs, and flags with the letter *Z* in the black-and-orange colors of the Order of Saint George, a symbol of Russia's war in Ukraine that first gained prominence around the time of the annexation of Crimea. Here you can buy antique revolvers, and one of the hawkers picks one up, showing off her long flat nails painted in the colors of the Russian flag.

There is an unpleasant feeling in the air. The flags with the *Z*'s whip us in the face as they flap in the wind. Some of the kids from the group start playing the accordion, the balalaika, and the ancient, heart-wrenching gusla, then the whole group joins in, singing patriotic

songs as a small crowd gathers around them. Two particularly powerful singers stand out: Ganicheva and Katya, our travel companion. This is worrisome. Even Vlad seems uncomfortable: Maybe he's wondering what we're thinking, maybe he feels the toxicity in the air.

Suddenly, Katya can no longer contain herself and goes to sit among the choir, her eyes tearing up with emotion. She suggests some songs and motions for one of the younger kids to come sit on her lap: The child, scrawny, silent, fearful, and lost in his oversize navy shirt and red, white, and blue sash (the flag of the Luhansk People's Republic in Ukraine), is grasping an icon of Ushakov. It turns out that these kids are from occupied Donbas and are being given a crash course in Russification: a full immersion in "the values of their homeland," as Ganicheva explains. Were they deported? Are they among the twenty thousand children Kyiv has declared stolen? There is no way to verify this and it's risky to ask—the limitations of being a clandestine journalist. But their gloomy faces are immediately impressed on my memory: These children look like they've seen something, they know the chaos of war and the smell of death, and now they have been torn from their real homeland—their mother, their schoolyard, their street, the smell of their wet dog—and made prisoners of mad foreigners.

One of them, about thirteen years old, seems extroverted and can speak some English. In a moment of adult distraction, he approaches us and asks if we're with NATO or if we're "peace men." But Ganicheva quickly jumps in and asks him what he's talking about. She gives him a smug pat, like a mother teaching an important lesson. "We're sheltering them in the Writer's Home, outside Moscow," she says. "They're getting to know their homeland and the value of memory. They feel the heartbeat of the real Russia, they see how our land has suffered, and we help them understand how to defend what our ancestors defended. They write letters to soldiers at the front every day, moving letters. Our job is to keep the flow of memory coursing between the generations, as our president says. It's called *sobornost*, staying united in faith and country. Russia won't survive just on the prayers of the elderly and the saints. We need the courage of the young."

Marina Ganicheva knows all about saints and children—she is an established fairy tale writer who toes the propaganda line of God-Country-Family and the values of *Russkiy mir.* Her stories are based on current events, like the one where she praises the beauty of a Ukraine gone by, when Soviet children would visit their grandmothers in the summer and see that "Ukraine was a paradise, the homeland, the land of the prosperous sun, of light and cherries, of grain and white bread." Once upon a time there was the good Ukraine, but then came the zilkop, a giant, black, two-legged insect that eats little girls. It turned Ukraine into a hellscape, killing whoever calls on God or Russia.

ONCE UPON A TIME

In Russia, power and *skazki*, or fairy tales, share a long history. Some of the stories Aleksandr Afanasev gathered in *Russian Popular Legends* in the nineteenth century were censored for being too erotic or anticlerical. The Soviets also banned some for ideological reasons, while using others as educational tools. Compared to the fairy tales of the past, those written in the time of the USSR were modern and served the political objectives of state atheism. Instead of magic, they told of technological innovations and scientific inventions. During Moscow's space race with Washington, stories featuring cosmonauts abounded. In Putin's Russia, nationalist fairy tale writers like Marina Ganicheva are also very useful to the cause—their stories bridge high and low culture, popular traditions and nationalist lore, fields and cities, parents and children. Fairy tales allow people to talk about a world that resembles reality but isn't exactly real; to create propaganda and to circumvent it.

These aren't the fairy tales where pumpkins turn into carriages. *Skazki* are taken very seriously—the word means "what was said," or "history," and for centuries they were the only form of culture accessible to the masses. They bring fierce characters to life, like the *bogatyri*, great knights who defend Russia from wizards, witches, and foreigners.

Yet Russian literature developed rather late. In the Middle Ages, Orthodox monasteries did not spread culture, as Catholics did in the West.

Poland and Lithuania started their first universities in the fourteenth century, while Russia first did so only in the eighteenth century. Russia's first literary works were published in the seventeenth century: popular ballads about Tatar wars, adventures, saints, and intimate thoughts, like *The Life of the Archpriest Avvakum*—a messy autobiography published in 1861 that many scholars consider the first example of Russian fiction.

Catherine the Great led the first push to develop the arts in the eighteenth century, setting European parameters. A century later, Russian authors struck gold: Russia itself. Through novels, they explored nature, the human soul, and the fate of the Russian people. They drew on their ancestral roots, the tradition of the fable, to unlock the mysteries of the landscape and unmask the spirits of fields and forests, including archetypes of the popular imagination: Koshchei, the immortal; Baba Yaga, the dark lady of the woods—a mythical character with magical powers, sometimes a witch, if required by the story; and the legendary Firebird. Stories that bring out Russian fascination for superhuman audacity and the supernatural world. Russians still tell their children these stories, which were a training ground for authors like Pushkin, inspired by tales he heard from his nanny as a child. The world of poetic folklore and imaginary peasants allowed him to shape a new language. Modern Russia was heavily shaped by Pushkin's *Fairy Tales*. Alyosha in Dostoyevsky's *Brothers Karamazov*, Prince Myshkin in *The Idiot*, Chekhov's *Uncle Vanya*, Pierre Bezukhov and Platon Karataev in Tolstoy's *War and Peace* were modeled on the typical benevolent simpleton of fairy tales. Fairy tales were diamond mines for Russian creativity. They also inspired composers like Mussorgsky, Rimsky-Korsakov, and Stravinsky.

THE PLAGUED

The Russian Bear, the symbol of Russia, is also a type of fairy tale, one that gets updated by whoever's in charge—usually before a new expansionist push. Putin used it in 2014, on the eve of the annexation of Crimea. "They want to reduce us to vassals, but they won't chain the Russian Bear. The Bear should live peacefully off berries and honey, but they want to chain him and tear out his teeth and nails and stuff him. But we know that when cornered, the Russian Bear will always claw his way out."

Marina Ganicheva, therefore, shouldn't be underestimated because she writes fairy tales. Indeed, it gives her the status of a genuine Russian writer, one who takes part in the most authentic, secular tradition of national literature. The fact that Ganicheva is also vice president of the Union of Russian Writers shows that she holds a privileged position among the champions of Putin's orthodoxy. She's a witch hunter.

The control and persecution of dissident or bourgeois intellectuals was an original sin of Soviet Communism. In 1917, Lenin created the All-Russian Extraordinary Commission to fight counterrevolution and sabotage—the Cheka—which sent enemies of Soviet power to the gulag (84 in the prerevolutionary period and 315 in the three years of Lenin's leadership), including writers who did not lend their services to the revolution. Lenin's wife, Nadezhda Krupskaya, determined which books to censor or ban.

In 1934, the Union of Soviet Writers, founded in 1932 by the Central Committee by order of Stalin, took control over authors' works. "Literature aims to teach Marxism," said the statute, therefore "there is no such thing as literature that is not class literature, there is no apolitical literature." The union required "professional" writers to sign up and barred unregistered writers from publishing. Unsurprisingly, the union's offices were adjacent to political police headquarters.

The union's first president was Maksim Gorky, whom Stalin enticed back from the Italian island of Capri. It was an indecent page in his biography, because he lent his talents to justifying phony trials and smearing writers whom Stalin disliked. Subsequent presidents were generally mediocre, little-known writers who zealously applied directives, encouraged members to inform on colleagues, and rewarded the "good" with publications, spacious lodgings, and health care while punishing the "bad" with censorship, marginalization, or denunciation to the police.

It was so easy to end up in jail that, as the story went, if a prisoner asked a guard for a book, the answer would be no, they didn't have that book, but they did have its author.

Stalin made only one exception among the elite of the Silver Age, the postrevolutionary period that ran between the 1890s and 1920s: Mikhail Bulgakov.

Although Bulgakov's *The White Guard* and *Heart of a Dog* had placed him at the top of the watch list, Stalin admired his talent and kept him in a gilded cage: After poet Vladimir Mayakovsky died by suicide, he offered Bulgakov a job as a director's assistant at the Moscow Art Theater, effectively ending his career as a writer.

But while Bulgakov died peacefully in his bed, Isaac Babel, a revolutionary like Mayakovsky, was arrested and executed in 1940, while poet Anna Akhmatova, a giant of twentieth-century literature, was expelled from the Union of Soviet Writers for alleged aestheticism and political disengagement. She endured severe poverty and was banished from publishing houses and universities. Osip Mandelstam was deported and died on the way to the gulag: He was arrested for having recited epigrams against Stalin and his "cockroach mustache," verses that had never been written on paper but had been memorized by his wife. Joseph Brodsky, having refused to sign up to the Union of Soviet Writers, was arrested in 1964 as a "social parasite." A worse fate befell Boris Pasternak, who was driven to poverty and isolation even though he was registered in the Union of Soviet Writers and had written odes to Lenin and Stalin. All because the union judged his *Doctor Zhivago* too apolitical.

Almost all the persecuted Silver Age intellectuals passed through Lubyanka, and if they came out alive, it was only to be sent to forced labor.

Writer and journalist Vasily Grossman wrote that the Lubyanka building was the tallest in the USSR because from there, you could see Siberia from the basement.

A HISTORY OF CENSORSHIP

Russia's tragic love story with literature includes a long history of censoring and repressing writers. The written word is powerful and dangerous: A creative act is also an act of liberty.

Since the 1990s, when the chaos of the collapse of the Soviet Union meant no one—including the state—paid much attention to writers, the dawn of Putin's twenty-year reign has gradually returned Russia to its old traditions.

"In Russia, everything changes every ten years, yet nothing changes in two hundred years," wrote Pyotr Stolypin, a minister in the Russian Empire.

At least initially, Putin seemed to have learned from Soviet horrors and granted ample freedom to writers—this gave a human face to the regime, which was still crypto-authoritarian. Literature was no longer the main source of cultural consumption, as it had been in the USSR. Stalin had been an avid reader since childhood—at the seminary he devoured Victor Hugo, whose books were banned by the Orthodox hierarchy, and he published some decent poems. All we know of Putin is that he has read all of Hemingway's works.

But journalism was different. During the democratic opening of the 1990s, reporters became increasingly inquisitive and influential. Many started disappearing even before the end of the decade, but in the West, we only realized that being a journalist in Russia was a suicide mission after the assassination of Anna Politkovskaya on October 7, 2006. She was known for writing scathing articles about Putin. By 1999, there were more than fifty—two hundred, according to some sources—unsolved murders of journalists. In Putin's Russia, novels, poems, and essays are no longer that influential (the book market shrinks by 7 percent every year): Ideas and news come from print media, TV, and the internet, and that is where the state comes down hardest.

Everything changed with the invasion of Ukraine. It gave rise to the Federal Service for Supervision of Communications, Information Technology, and Mass Media: a sinister organization that monitors internet traffic and publishing for "foreign agents." Its existence is one reason why some of Russia's most brilliant writers, like crime writer Boris Akunin or Ludmila Ulitskaya, have escaped abroad. The government has declared Akunin a terrorist and extremist, while no decree or official incrimination was levied against Ulitskaya—who for years has been slated to win a Nobel Prize—but her books have been removed from bookshelves in Moscow and reportedly sent to the pulping mill. Ulitskaya's crime is apparently unforgivable: She opposes the invasion of Ukraine and donates some of the proceeds from her books to Ukraine.

Many of the writers who stayed behind work in the Presidential Council for Culture and Art, effectively expressing support for the regime and the war. The Union of Russian Writers has returned with a vengeance, with Marina Ganicheva as its vice president. The statute does not state that literature must spread Marxism, as it did in Pasternak's day, but it does have to promote patriotism. In February 2022, the union released a statement of support for Putin, the FSB, and the army, and denounced any intellectuals who stood against the invasion. At a conference with the union, Putin announced that 2025 would be the "year of Russian literature," launching a campaign to persuade young people to read more books and promising state support for writers, just like in the days of Stalin and Gorky.

UNCLE YURI

As we walk away from the memorial museum, I ask Ganicheva if writers are required to register with the union. "They do it voluntarily!" she says, her eyes sparkling with excitement behind her thick lenses. "It guarantees their rights so they can travel, write, and create in peace while earning decent pay. It's a matter of managing the publishing market, which is worth more than $2 billion," money she says must be managed in a politically and morally correct way. She seems to suggest that whosoever refuses to toe the patriotic line—by not joining the union—should change jobs (even if they don't currently risk torture in some basement, or a penalty of breaking rocks until death) regardless of whether they are writing transgressive verses.

Her dedication to Russian institutions was likely passed down to her by her father, a president of the union until his death in 2018. "Good parents have only good children," she confirms. While I don't quite get an idea of what type of writer her father was, I do learn that he'd been an important member of the literary *nomenklatura*, a great friend of cosmonaut Yuri Gagarin, with whom he'd spend vacations on the Don. "Uncle Yuri was an incredible swimmer," Ganicheva tells me. "He'd cross the Don as if it were nothing. He used to take me crab fishing." Her father, she tells me unapologetically, promoted nationalist, antimodernist, and antiliberal positions at the union through the 1990s, in opposition to Yeltsin's pro-Western conversion. He and another union president, Alexander Prokhanov, used to throw memorable galas to celebrate subversive intellectuals like Eduard Limonov, Aleksandr Dugin, and Valentin Rasputin. Prokhanov was the brains behind the operation. He was an uncompromising ex-Communist, a leading star among so-called "patriotic front" writers, a radical-reactionary movement that brought together factions that missed the USSR and longed for neo-imperial autocracy. Prokhanov was a prime-time regular on Russia 1, a state-owned television channel, and guest of presenter Vladimir Solovyov, who was sanctioned in 2022 and deprived of his villa on Lake Como.

These people, Putin's literary inner circle, make up the cultural soup that has fed Russian ideals over the past decade. Even if he has read only Hemingway, he knows he can't move troops or keep alive the dream of an imperial Russia without intellectuals (even mediocre ones), monks, or priests.

MEMENTO MORI

Ganicheva's group is about to file back onto the bus and leave the memorial, one of the last stops on the "patriotic way." The Soviet soldier watches over the Meat Grinder plain, frowning. I ask Ganicheva about the rules that govern the modern Russian nation—what makes people feel like they belong to this land. She thinks about it briefly, scanning the ground, and blows her nose with a lace handkerchief. "Unlike you, individual success doesn't matter to us. It's not enough. Death may be the key to understanding the Russians." Her voice trembles and she spreads her arms to take in our surroundings. "Think about our saying, 'Meeting death is not scary when you're among Russians.' Death can be horrible, but not if it's useful to the Russian people. This is the root of our patriotism. We're not as practical as you, but we have bigger hearts."

3

The philologist of the dead city

"The past is unpredictable"

BLOODRED BRICKS

The Proletarka was once an elegant housing complex in bloodred bricks built by the Morozov merchant family outside Tver' for workers of their city-factory—an industrial powerhouse of the last czarist Russia. In its heyday, the complex boasted a spinning mill, cotton mill, dorms for some twenty thousand workers who had been torn from their farmlands in the countryside, swimming pools, a Bolshoi popular theater, daycares, schools for children and illiterate adults, libraries, a hospital, an observatory, and a resort on the Volga.

Now, all that remains of Proletarka and its two hundred industrial buildings is a reputation that causes a lump in the throat of anyone old enough to remember the 1980s and '90s, when the whole world came crashing down on the area and production lines, mixers, spinners, wrappers, and printers closed up shop one by one as the cotton mill shut and the majestic apartment blocks—in Bauhaus-worthy design—sank into squalor. The last salaries were paid in rolls of fabric, and the mecca of the Soviet proletariat became a terrifying mob hub for drug trafficking with Chechnya, Berlin, and Vienna.

Today, no taxi driver from Tver' would dare cross Kalinin Boulevard, beyond which lies a landscape of ruin, a graveyard of bloodred bricks, the necropolis of a forgotten civilization. A magnificent dilapidation colonized by weeds, crows, cockroaches, people of the abyss, spectral presences, failed gangsters, ex-cons, alcoholics at the end of the line, toothless prostitutes, tuberculosis-ridden squatters, traffickers in homemade opioids, criminals hiding out to avoid being sent to fight in Donbas.

THE STROLL

I first learn about Proletarka from philologist Mikhail S. His story is so vivid that even before we get there, I feel an irresistible attraction to that mound of ruins that is the still-warm corpse of the Soviet Union. The site has passed directly from contemporary history to archaeology, joining the ranks of Cartagena, Babylon, Pompeii, and Angkor, the capital of the Khmer empire swallowed by the Cambodian jungle.

Mikhail and I meet on the elegant, eighteenth-century promenade in Tver', where the Volga, still in its infancy, flows peacefully but steadily, half a mile wide, ready to take in the powerful thrust of the Tvertsa River and face Russia with the brash confidence of the preordained.

Sailboats float by in the pale sunset, and a tour boat is anchored on the opposite shore, by Saint Catherine, a whitewashed convent with green onion tops. I watch couples cuddle on benches and elderly people walk their dogs under the linden trees while the smell of grilled meat fills the July air, breaking the oppressive sensation of tedium common in provincial settings the world over. A tall, blonde woman in a long yellow dress rushes past me clutching a bouquet of daffodils to her chest. A man in camouflage and with a red hammer and sickle tattooed on his bicep ambles along after her, bottle of liquor in hand, a little monkey crouched in silent contemplation on his shoulder.

CAPITALIST CIGARETTES

As we walk along the river, Mikhail and I stop in front of a memorial to read verses by Soviet poet Andrey Dementyev: "Here I became son of the Volga, here begins my story, here I saw glorious events and followed the path to dawn." Dementyev was born in Proletarka, like Mikhail, and rose to fame for writing saccharine, rhetorical, and patriotic songs popular in the upper echelons of the Communist Party in the 1970s and '80s, and for penning a fictional biography of Mikhail Ivanovich Kalinin, a significant figure in the upper Volga—Tver' was known as Kalinin until 1990. Kalinin had been a foundry worker and unionist in Saint Petersburg, then Petrograd, before becoming the city's mayor in the October Revolution. He was among Stalin's most trusted allies and chairman of the Presidium of the Supreme Soviet.

"Dementyev used Kalinin's story to glorify his own social redemption, but in fact, Kalinin was Stalin's minion," Mikhail tells me. "A sort of puppet-notary who signed hundreds of thousands of execution orders in the 1930s." He said nothing when Stalin accused his wife of Trotskyism and declared her an enemy of the people. Despite being the second-most-powerful man in the USSR, at least on paper, he stood by as his wife was tortured for months, and imprisoned in Siberia for fifteen years.

One episode is particularly representative of Stalin and Kalinin's perverse relationship. When Yugoslav President Josip Tito attended a banquet at the Kremlin in 1946, Kalinin—who showed signs of blindness, possibly senility—was the butt of most of Stalin's jokes. When Kalinin told Tito he'd like to smoke a Yugoslav cigarette, Stalin hissed, "Comrade Mikhail Ivanovich! How dare you? Those are capitalist cigarettes!" To which Kalinin started to stammer, hands shaking. His cigarette fell onto the tablecloth and Stalin burst into a booming laugh. According to witnesses, Tito was the only one to remain perfectly serious, confident enough to resist Stalin's diabolical parlor games.

According to Mikhail, Kalinin also contributed to the Katyn Massacre, where twenty-five thousand Polish prisoners of war—police officers, civilian officials, journalists, professors, and industrialists—were killed between April and May 1940 in various locations, including present-day Tver'. Kalinin knew the terrain and was able to establish prison camps in locations that would ensure that even a large-scale massacre could remain shrouded in secrecy. One was in Ostashkov, an isolated town near the source of the Volga, in the Valdai Hills. Some seven thousand Polish prisoners were massacred there within a two-week period.

BAREFACED LIARS

At this point, Mikhail sees that I am lost. "Are you disappointed?" he asks. He knows that the point of our trip is to understand what it means to be Russian in this moment in history, when the Russian Bear has emerged from hibernation with a hunger for revenge, expansion, and glory. A time when Putin, with the war in Ukraine, upset America's world order and rehashed a clash of civilizations with the West. "I get it," he continues. "The Russian enigma can drive you mad. Here, absolute love for humanity and bloody atrocities have always lived side by side." He seems to feel physical pain as he says this. "Any idea you make of us could be immediately replaced by another, antithetical one, even while talking to the same person. Deep down, we know the fundamental truths of life and history, yet we live, or survive, in the denial of those truths. After all, aren't many of Dostoyevsky's characters driven by a hatred of lies? That was even before the court of the people and state atheism. We're still the same liars we've always been."

Mikhail is referring to a type of lie called *vranyo*, which regulates social and political life. "You know I'm lying, and I know you know, and you know that I know you know, but I persist in my barefaced lie, and you nod along. Now, as in the days of the Soviets or the czar, power doesn't care that everyone knows it's lying. But it does not tolerate, and therefore it punishes or eliminates, anyone who questions its honesty."

We've reached an area formerly known as Lenin Square: The statue is still standing, despite having been temporarily replaced with a giant swastika during the Nazi occupation. Now the square is called Saltykov-Shchedrin, after the nineteenth-century writer who brought prominence to his home region of Tver' by flagellating the Russian character. Mikhail recites a famous line: "Wake me up in a hundred years, ask me what is happening in Russia, and I'll tell you with my usual frankness: We steal, we drink, we make war." He sighs. "I have to agree. They say people have been drinking much more since the war started, especially young people. Imagine what it means to drink more, in Russia . . . Well, what happened recently here in Tver', where rates of alcoholism are through the roof, should give you an idea of the atmosphere in the era of artificial intelligence and the metaverse. On sobriety day, Savva, a famous bishop, flew over the city in an old twin-engine and dropped seventy liters of holy water to bless the people and save them from drink, drugs, and fornication. He held an icon of John the Baptist out the window as the plane flew at low altitude, because it apparently has miraculous powers against alcohol. In what Western city could such a thing happen?" Mikhail asks.

"But let's not forget how much Russia influenced modern European culture in the nineteenth century. We were a cultural superpower. Russian metaphysical thought is at the basis of modern Western philosophy. Anti-Western Dostoyevsky 'turned the heart of man into a battlefield,' as Mitya Karamazov says, to test the mettle of your knowledge, to discover the spiritual nature of evil."

Giant Ilyushin military transport aircraft have been flying slowly over us for a while, among the masses of black clouds, headed south. "Yet here at the gates of Europe," Mikhail continues, "where we should have absorbed some modicum of Western logic, everything gets jumbled: faith, tradition, ideology, empire, Stalinism, nationalism. It's not like Putin has injected us with some concoction to rile up ordinary Russians. This rough and incoherent soup of identity has been flowing through our veins for generations. We'd do anything to overcome the trauma of the end of the Soviet Union and the humiliation of the '90s. We want to believe in something extraordinary, for which we're willing to die. I feel this too, I must confess. I've always considered myself a rational man, an enlightened atheist of Marxist extraction, but I sometimes find myself swallowed up by this irrational, reactionary idea that is rising from the deep: the Russian ability to suffer and sacrifice ourselves to change the world, to reclaim our Eastern souls begotten of Mongol domination, to reject contamination by a corrupt and declining West. I'm not that horrified by Russia's mission because the Bolsheviks also believed in the redeeming mission of Communism, where the proletariat embodied the Messiah. Now everything is dangerously mixed up: passion, feeling, indifference, state violence. We've turned our backs on the West."

He looks out at the Volga. The lights from a restaurant boat are reflecting on the water. "And the call of the steppe is taking root again."

He gives me a scornful smile. "Where will our unpredictable past lead us now?"

TOO LATE

Mikhail's own past unfolded just around the corner: an enormous graveyard of memories, colored bloodred by the bricks of Proletarka. The city-factory's story is his story, the world where he was born and raised, where he sang and loved. That was before he left for the big cities and libraries; but his memories are anchored in that Soviet homeland, in those dusty or muddy courtyards, halls that smell of cabbage and cancerous cigarettes. Now, looking back, everything seems wonderful to him. "It was the Soviet Union, and I was young," he says. When talking about the USSR, Mikhail doesn't think about the fifteen socialist republics, the world superpower that divvied up the planet with the United States, or of cosmonaut Yuri Gagarin, or of literary writers like Maksim Gorky, Andrei Platonov, or Vladimir Tendryakov. He sees the faces of the workers in his block, his summers on the Volga, and he tears up. Not once has he crossed Kalinin Avenue to Proletarka since the city died, sometime at the end of the twentieth century, along with the empire.

In the prerevolutionary period, the Romanovs had envisioned Proletarka as a model worker city, in a desperate attempt to keep up with Europe. They entrusted it to the Morozov industrial dynasty, an old merchant family that had risen from serfdom after its patriarch, Savva Vasilyevich Morozov, bought his own freedom. Mikhail tells me that Morozov became a broker of cheap labor in the textile and paper industries. "He was one of the most unscrupulous loan sharks in the region. He fleeced hungry farmers by forcing them to abandon the fields around Tver'. He bought the first steam-powered textile machine from Germany and built plants and homes for workers."

Savva's grandchildren expanded the city-factory, turning it into one of the most innovative industrial centers on the continent in terms of technology, productivity, and social commitment, providing cutting-edge housing, hygiene, and education, and paving the way for women's emancipation—a veritable Marxist haven. "Too bad," Mikhail says, "that Marxist architects and urban planners in the second half of the twentieth century became known all over the world for having brutalized popular housing."

The Romanovs' race against time had been desperate and gasping. Czar Alexander II authorized the end of serfdom in 1861, four years before the abolition of slavery in the United States. Then came a series of concessions to local governments, greater access to education, an overhaul of the judicial system, reforms that incentivized social mobility, and the creation of something resembling a bourgeois class. In 1881, a few hours before his assassination, Alexander II even approved a reform proposal that could have led to a British-style constitutional monarchy. "A story that has not been told enough," Mikhail says. "The truth is that the czar, in his decline, was catching up on many fronts. Even in science, with Dmitri Mendeleev and his periodic table, and Ivan Pavlov and Élie Metchnikoff, two of our first Nobel Prize winners. Finance Minister

Sergei Witte reformed the banking system, introduced the stock market, facilitated the flow of capital from the West to build infrastructure like the Trans-Siberian Railway, the longest railroad in the world, which helped launch a quest for modernization in the Far East and define the idea of a Eurasian empire, also geographically. And we had Sofya Kovalevskaya, the first woman in the world to teach math at a university. In 1895, women were already being admitted to the university of Saint Petersburg, long before they could get into Cambridge. In the early twentieth century, Russia boasted more women PhDs, lawyers, and teachers than any other European country." Even though Russia had missed the memo on the Renaissance, it seemed to be proceeding full throttle into the Enlightenment.

In 1913, on the eve of the revolution, Russia was the world's fourth-largest producer of steel and iron. While most of the population still comprised illiterate farmers surviving on subsistence-based agriculture, the last czar was processing enough grain to support a budding export industry. But wealth stagnated among landowner classes and the aristocracy. "Any attempt to install a liberal elite or ideology was stymied by the pro-Slavic orthodoxy, which feared Western and Catholic contamination like the plague, and which was preparing the ground for the bloodiest revolution in history by rousing the industrial working class—which was then a small minority concentrated in the northwest, between Moscow and Saint Petersburg."

At the dawn of the twentieth century, Russia was feeling the winds of a reformist change: The economy was taking off and Russian culture was injecting European progressive movements with new energy. But the Romanovs had precious little sand left in their hourglasses. As Russia crossed into the new century, it witnessed the fall of two empires, two revolutions, the installation of an extraordinarily brutal regime, two world wars won at the expense of millions of lives, and various famines, purges, and repressions. "Twice in one century the state risked disappearing. Only Genghis Khan's Mongol horde had ever presented such a serious existential threat," according to Mikhail.

THE DIVA AND THE TYCOON

In Mikhail's telling, Proletarka's story was a mirror of the times, the particular contained in the universal. After Communists took the Winter Palace at the start of the century, the oligarchic Morozov family was bound to cross paths with them. The Morozovs had unwittingly nourished their enemies by allowing union strikes, authorizing union activity, and creating a factory council and a collective of women workers—all of which eventually emboldened a Communist ideology that was antithetical to the Morozovs' capitalist methods. The wives (and lovers) of the Morozovs had flirted with radical socialists in the first years of the twentieth century. Varvara Morozova, a former worker who repeatedly suppressed factory protests, was in the crosshairs of the czarist secret police, suspected of being a double agent and of bankrolling the Soviets. But the Bolsheviks didn't care for Morozova's labor or emancipatory spirit either, because it was ruining their plans. "They feared it would dilute their working-class conscience," according to Mikhail.

When the revolution broke out in 1905, Savva Morozov was the richest man in the empire and an early supporter of the revolution—not out of ideological fervor but to curry favor with Maria Andreeva, a diva of Moscow's Art Theater and "the Russian Eleonora Duse," as Mikhail calls her. Andreeva was a radical Marxist with ties to clandestine revolutionary movements, and she used Morozov's love—and anti-czarist sympathies—to force him to raise workers' pay and to financially support the cause, posting bail for detained comrades, sending money to exiles in Siberia, and paying for indoctrination trips to Germany, Switzerland, and England. According to Gorky, who later married Andreeva, Morozov was doling out 24,000 rubles a year to the *Iskra*, a social-democratic paper.

Meanwhile, the Bolsheviks called him "father" and accepted thousands of rubles a year from him, but this didn't stop them from organizing a violent strike against his cotton mill. Morozov sank into a depression and left Russia. On May 13, 1905, in a hotel in Cannes, he ended his life with a shot to the head.

But no one believed it was suicide. A year before, Morozov had taken out a 100,000-ruble life insurance policy, listing Maria Andreeva as the beneficiary. After his death, she took the money and distributed it to her comrades. "At Morozov's funeral," Mikhail concludes with a wry smile, "she and Gorky were conspicuously absent."

Back in the 1960s, when Mikhail was a child, Proletarka brimmed with crockery, fine carpets, paintings, and golden mirrors from the 1917 expropriations. "On holidays we'd decorate a long table in the hallway and take out these chipped Gzhel ceramic plates in cobalt. The old folks told us they came from Morozov's estate. My daycare was housed in the same building where the servants of the pre-Soviet directors lived. We made good use of everything that had been left behind."

LIFE IN THE BARRACKS

As we sit down to a beautiful plate of grilled meat, Mikhail struggles to talk about his old home. His difficulty is an affliction the Russians call *toska*—you can't articulate it while sober, but maybe you can drown it in alcohol. It's a complex feeling made of nostalgia, melancholic apathy, dissatisfaction, and grief. It can be a sense of loss or oppression, or a feeling of perpetual uncertainty. It's a form of Russian meditation, or existential steeping: It can become a vision of the world, generating passivity, dark humor, art, or the urge to destroy everything. For Mikhail, *toska* means Proletarka: nostalgia for life in the Soviet worker paradise and regret and anger over lost opportunities.

He tells me about his paternal grandmother, who lived in block 119, and his maternal grandmother, who grew up in block 47. They'd been laborers in the Rzhev countryside and fled during the Great Patriotic War. "Grandma told me that after the war, widows helped one another raise the children. When my parents got married, they were given a 270-square-foot room in block 50, a standard space for a *kommunalka*, shared accommodations. Since my father was a supervisor, he was offered an apartment on Lenin Avenue, but he turned it down: It was cold there, while the barracks were always nice and warm. And our yard was close to everything: school, swimming pools, the theater, the bakery. Our room was divided in two by a large chest: my grandmother and auntie on one side, the rest of us on the other. The men would gather in the shared kitchen and drink and play dominos around the Cube, a large cast-iron pot we also used to make tea and hard-boiled eggs. A screen allowed the women to bathe the children behind the Cube in the evenings. Food scraps would end up in a bucket and were sold to farmers as chicken feed. We used the money to buy sweets on New Year's for the whole floor. My mom told me about how in 1953, all the female workers got together to listen to Stalin's funeral over the radio—I never knew whether she was crying because of Stalin's death or because of the friends she'd lost. In the basement of our block, there was a mess hall where you could buy soup if you didn't have time to cook. I liked it even better than my mom's soup. Every block had its own library, but each room also had a lot of books. The floor leader kept order and gave weekly reports to the party. A bell rang every night at nine to signal that everyone had to go back to their rooms and that children couldn't go into the hall anymore. In the morning, the bell would ring twice: at six for wake-up, and at seven to start work or school. During elections, the first block that voted was praised. I remember old Gosa walking through the hallways with his accordion, trying to motivate people. A line of people would form behind him and walk down the stairs, singing. My aunt Irina would follow, arm in arm with a boxer popular in Proletarka who suddenly disappeared one day: We heard he'd been arrested, and my aunt was inconsolable. The important holidays, like International Workers' Day and New Year's Eve, were held in block 70, on the fifth floor. The building was in art nouveau style, and we called it 'Paris.' It was so majestic, children could ride their bikes inside. Anastasia lived there, she liked to dance, she wrote poetry and rock songs. We got engaged there one evening, while listening to Viktor Tsoi—he was like our Jim Morrison, and the front man for Kino. We kissed on the stairs, in a spot with no light. It was 1987, and we haven't been back since," Mikhail says, nodding at the world beyond the railroad tracks. "We rarely spoke of it. It hurt to hear about what happened to our city. Now that Anastasia is gone too, Proletarka really is just a pile of bricks and rust."

VILLE LUMIÈRE

Before he was arrested for hiding Lenin's arm under his bed, Oleg, an ex-con who agrees to show us around Proletarka, lived in "Paris." He, his former partner Alesya, and their seven children lived crammed into two rooms in block 70, the only one with separate apartments—until the last days of the USSR, it housed the leaders and engineers of the party. But at least they had gas, glass on the windows, toilets, a shared kitchen at the end of the hall, and a working sewer, one of the first ones built by the Bolsheviks when they nationalized the city-factory.

When we first meet him, we find him sitting on a sidewalk under the linden trees on the avenue leading to Paris. He tells us his story going back to the 1990s, when he was trafficking meat in Tver' for the Tambovskaya Bratva, a Saint Petersburg–based gang led by Vladimir Kumarin, known as the night governor. "We lived the high life in Paris. It had everything we needed. Electricity, running water in the bathrooms down the hall, and we could take turns bathing on Sundays. We never wanted for food. Alesya, the mother of my children, worked in foreign currency. We lived well."

The three entrances to Paris are guarded by goons with guns at their hips. About five hundred people live here now, some of them the children and grandchildren of former workers, but most are immigrants who arrived in the 1990s from the former Soviet republics of the Caucasus. They served the crime bosses in those years of gang wars, fake democracy, and hunger.

Oleg did his fair share of work for the *organizatzia* too. He is fifty-five and flies by the seat of his pants. He takes a nip from his flask at the end of each sentence to regain the strength to speak. He seems exhausted, but he's alert and somewhat fit: Just a few weeks ago, he says, he beat up someone much bigger than he—he gestures to give us an idea of the man's heft. "One of the guys that go out with my ex," he says. Indeed, Oleg has the face of a boxer, or more accurately, of someone who's been beaten up a lot: a shattered nose, a spiderweb of scars with traces of fresh wounds. His hair and beard are reddish, kept with care.

We're waiting for Alesya so that she and Oleg can be our guides through the meandering halls of this legendary block. We even picked up a gift for her, at Oleg's request (he was hoping to make off with a bottle of something). But when she arrives, she immediately starts throwing rocks and bottles at Oleg—whatever she can find on the ground. She grabs a pipe and aims it at him, and we decide to retreat quickly toward Oleg's den of iniquity in block 72, which was once inhabited by the administrators of the cotton mill and is now a common area on the fourth floor.

Ale sits him down in a sinking, half-burnt armchair in the middle of a spacious room. It looks like the walls may have once been a charming pink, and we can still see the old stucco peeling off the ceiling. The space is empty and bright, but the ground is littered with human and animal feces, the bay window has no glass, and a blue curtain frayed by the wind snaps like a whip with every gust. As Ale moves in for a photo, Oleg looks straight at the lens, the green and yellow of his eyes glinting in the sun.

Oleg tells us that last night, someone stole the door to his room for the third time. But he knows exactly who it was—he's just waiting for the right moment to handle the matter.

He introduces us to his new roommate, a disabled elderly man from downstairs who lost his lifelong partner ten days ago. He has a smashed nose too, and he looks terrified. He says he had to sleep next to his lady for five days because no one would come pick up the body.

According to Oleg, Putin himself, as head of the security services under Boris Yeltsin, cleared out Proletarka in the 1990s with a series of stings and truckloads of arrests. Only the outcasts remained—even the worst prisons didn't want them.

For a while, Oleg worked as an assistant driver on a freight train in

Togliatti, on the lower Volga. But he was already an alcoholic, so one night, they threw him off the train in the middle of the steppe.

Back in Paris, things changed. He had to make ends meet with petty theft, so he was always in and out of prison. He did two years for stealing a cell phone from the kid of some big shot. He claims he'd found the bag with the phone in the woods and had every intention of returning it.

After prison, he got into the scrap-metal trade, a popular activity in Proletarka at the time, around 2010. People would take apart cast-iron railings and staircases, while the Finns were buying up the legendary, colossal "Stalin stoves" popular during the Great Patriotic War and designed to burn peat instead of wood. They had been the nerve center of social life in each block. And then there was the Lenin statue—incredible that it was still there at the park, amid the poplars, just two blocks from Paris, in front of the old People's Theater. Russian authorities had torn down thousands of Lenin statues in the 1990s as they sought to purge the symbols of its Soviet past to make way for a neoliberal rebirth. But in Proletarka, all that beautiful bronze had remained in place.

So without much ado, in just a few nights, Oleg took Lenin apart with an angle grinder. On the third night, the police descended on Paris: They made a beeline for Oleg's room and under his bed found Lenin's arm, the one that pointed the proletariat toward a radiant future.

Oleg hadn't known of the tacit agreement to leave that particular Lenin in place, nor was he aware of the statue's great value. It was the last keeper of this "paradise of Communist workers," and for the survivors of block 70, it represented a world where they had been young and alive once. Oleg also had no idea that Proletarka's Lenin was one of the first monuments built in his image. It was erected in 1925, a year after his death, and designed by the great sculptor Georgi Alekseev, one of the fathers of socialist realism. Oleg had already sold most of Lenin to a blast furnace in Tver'. He had kept the arm for a rainy day.

After spending two years in prison for this offense, Oleg showed up outside the Paris block, where he was violently beaten by a dozen residents as Alesya and their children looked on. It was not so much about avenging Lenin—the beating would help Alesya get rid of her husband without having to go through the system. And to think, Oleg tells us, that as a token of love, and to offer a tangible sign of change (and maybe also to clear his criminal record), he had stopped by the registry in Tver' to adopt Alesya's last name: Abramovic.

He still calls her "my sun," even though he's not allowed to go near her and feels condemned to await his dying day alone in the abyss of block 72.

He spends his afternoons on the avenue, sitting on his heels, watching the high life of Paris from afar.

PART TWO

Smuta: Time of Troubles

■ ■ ■

Confusion, madness, darkness
the blood of Asiatic revenge . . .
The crows caw, "Craw!"
No, gentlemen! Cleanliness!

—PAVEL BAULIN

4

Dinner with the Chechen

"Fuck the '90s!"

DRINKING TO REMEMBER

It's early morning in Dubna, the city of the atom—during the Cold War it was the Soviet answer to the Manhattan Project site at Los Alamos. Ale and I are alone on the beach contemplating the Volga, asking ourselves, as Lenin did, "What shall we do next?" We've survived a tense night, after a dinner where we realized how dangerous Katya might be for our mission. "I hear my brain going tick-tick," Ale says. "She's like a time bomb." Even Vlad seemed tired last night, but said everything would be fine in the morning, probably. He told us to meet him on the beach right about now, for a quick swim. But there's still no sign of him or Katya.

Although the Volga starts to turn east here, it still gives off a Baltic aura, a metallic luminosity. A cruise ship sails down the river slowly, seemingly unmoving, as the gurgle of the propellers on the surface of the water cuts through the quiet morning air. Passengers in bathrobes wave from the deck at the swimmers below, who float there, waiting for the wave to pass so they can resume their slow and steady laps. Everything is white: the beach; the monument to Mendeleev, inventor of the periodic table; the elegant gazebos hosting chess tournaments; the skin of the scientific elite on vacation. Families quietly descend to the river, crossing the pine forests below the rows of pastel buildings and villas belonging to nuclear researchers and directors. Some of the homes have large verandas, others are in neo-rationalist style, with gray concrete and light wood. They look like they were built in the 1950s, when Dubna was Russia's atomic laboratory. We could be anywhere in the world, on some other shore, or in another time, when people knew how to wait patiently for history to unfold. Again, we wonder what to do. Who is Katya, really? An enigma or something worse?

We first became worried when we noticed her agitation at the monument to the Soviet soldier. But on the road to Dubna, we started seriously to fear her. She is not the ideal companion for foreigners driving through Russia without a journalism visa. She constitutes yet another unknown variable and could derail an already risky trip.

In the van she talks incessantly without saying anything interesting. Aside from being unnerving, she's keeping us from getting to know Vlad, who, day by day, is winning us over with his childlike crassness and the wonder and euphoria he expresses as we delve deeper into Russia, as if he finds the place new and exotic. He entertains us with jokes in different languages, imitating various accents, but he also surprises us with brilliant observations and profound confessions. He continues not to touch alcohol and seems satisfied with that. When driving for long stretches, he fills the void by gorging on cigarettes, brightly colored drinks, gooseberries, currants, chocolate, liters of coffee, and especially ice cream, which he can down in two bites—he consumes a daily dozen of Eskimo ice-cream sandwiches, sublime relics of the Soviet era. "Elton

John had to cancel a concert after eating too many Eskimos!" Vlad told us one day before intoning a verse from "Rocket Man." But at night he's restless, he paces up and down, he hears the call of his demons.

Katya, on the other hand, orders beers as soon as she can and holds forth on what constitutes a "civilized" consumption of vodka, which one isn't supposed to sip, as we European troglodytes do: We have to get it all down at once, never drink alone, and never consume water between shots—inhale, exhale, and swallow, maybe sniff a slice of black bread after the shot, without letting too much time pass before the next one, because "the later you drink the second one, the more you waste the first." Apparently, good vodka has no aftertaste, otherwise it's Polish shit, in which case you can down a whole bottle without falling over, as long as you bite into a slice of lemon or cucumber.

One night, she told us she had to forget to drink, not the other way around. "I want to remember what life was like when it was life." We haven't forgotten that she's supposed to be here to keep an eye on Vlad's drinking. She brought a huge red suitcase full of little dresses and sandals and we assume she's Vlad's girlfriend—she's obviously madly in love with him. They sleep in the same bed, but Vlad seems embarrassed to show affection toward her, which upsets her. Another mystery.

Katya has important contacts. She says she knows Maria Zakharova, the spokesperson for Foreign Minister Sergey Lavrov, and if needed, she could email her or call her. Is she bragging? Is it true? Would it be an advantage for us or a hindrance? Will Katya's contacts enrich our trip or land us in a black FSB van, accused of being "foreign agents"? This trip already feels like a tightrope walk, and managing unforeseen events tied to her presence makes it even more stressful.

We were just a few miles outside Dubna when she told us about her friend, the son of a big cheese from Moscow, who was consulting for the Kadyrov government in Chechnya. Ramzan Kadyrov has been accused of assassinations and torture and is known as "the butcher of Grozny." Putin promoted him to colonel general for supporting the war in Ukraine and advocating a "final solution."

Katya called her friend "an expert in brand identity." They'd studied communications together in college. Since her friend was passing through Dubna, did we maybe want to meet him, since we were so obsessed with "Russian identity"?

THE OVERFLOWING GLASS

So last night, we had dinner with Andrey K., thirty-five years old and bald, with a Chechen beard. Outside the restaurant, which was between the business quarter and a pine forest, we noticed a parked car with two men inside. The engine was running and the lights were off, but Andrey told us not to mind them. "Russians can sit for hours talking in the car, and the running engine is a habit from winter that persists throughout the year. Access to gas spoils you. Actually, Russia's really lucky: We have long, cold winters, but also a ton of oil and gas."

The restaurant was spacious, decorated with dark wood and black iron, with a bar in the center of the room. A spotlight highlighted twinkling bottles stacked in an otherwise dark corner. The cocktail menu was full of improbable names, like Hiroshima, Drunken German, and Russo-Japanese War. But they also served an excellent Sambuca Akademic Pontekorvo, in honor of Italian physicist Bruno Pontecorvo, who grew up in Rome with "Via Panisperna boys" like Enrico Fermi. He was expelled from the Manhattan Project for being a Communist and became a Soviet citizen in 1952. A member of the Russian Academy of Sciences, Pontecorvo died in Dubna in 1993, an orphan of two nations: Italy and the Soviet Union. Aside from the drink, Dubna dedicated an important street to him and erected a bust on the Volga, where he seems very melancholic.

Andrey doesn't drink, so we started our meal with *svekolnik* and *okroska*, traditional cold summer soups. The menu noted that radishes, kefir, and others were local products, and that the vegetables were grown without chemical fertilizer. "That's the good part about the sanctions," Andrey said. "We used to import fertilizer and pesticides, but now we eat only healthy Russian food; the sanctions have prompted a sort of patriotic slow food movement."

I asked him how he would define the Russian brand. "Everything revolves around the Russian soul, which is very difficult to describe," he said, stroking his beard, which resembled that of a mujahideen, or a Puritan pastor from New England. He quoted from memory the romantic poet Fyodor Tyutchev:

Russia cannot be understood by the mind
or measured with a common yardstick:
Russia is unique
it can only be believed in.

"The Russian soul is pure feeling," Andrey explained. "Each brand is made of logic and emotion. The logical part is represented by our great past, the emotional part by our great soul."

Andrey has worked a lot on the soul "from a moral and political standpoint," he explained. "When Western commercials arrived in the 1990s, they changed the Russian mind, brought new ideas that didn't exist in Soviet times. Publicity shakes up your thoughts using irony and humor: People think it can't hurt because it's fun, but it can destroy an entire culture. That's what happened in Russia. I remember Sprite's big posters. They were changing our cultural codes. Young people on trams no longer gave up their seats to the elderly. A new social ideal took root based on egocentrism, hedonism, and narcissism. But we've always been a communal society, collectivist, anti-individualist. In this sense, Lenin found fertile ground, a collective consciousness ready for his historic experiment.

"During Soviet times, Russians had very strict ideas about good and evil. In the 1990s, these ideas changed, and everyone started to decide for themselves, à la carte, like on this menu. The minds and nature of Russians were changing. We were told we could get things done without effort or sacrifice, that it's best to do what's easy, fun, quick, and superficial, and that depth and spirituality were for dinosaurs. These ideas came from the West and were like water filling a glass, like this"—he slowly poured water into his glass to illustrate how ideas were disorienting Russians without quenching their thirst. "The glass is full, and the water has started to overflow." Finally, we asked him to stop, to avoid soaking the tablecloth. "Russians couldn't take it anymore."

I asked for a specific example. "Let's take the LGBTs," he said. "They came to Russia from the West. They told us that if we wanted to be modern, in lockstep with the evolved world, we had to share this type of culture, according to which everyone can decide their sexual identity and how to experience it and that it's not rude to flaunt it in public, without regard for anything or anyone. Well, this idea for Russia is . . . let's say . . . too strong."

At this, Katya laughed hysterically, turning red in the face. In the background, a song by Sekret came on, a pop group from the 1990s. It reminded me of a band that was big in Milošević's Serbia, under NATO bombings, but it also resembled some Neapolitan songs. "Today it's raining and it's shitty and we haven't seen each other in a hundred years . . . / But in general, you know, things are going fine." Katya sang along with Sekret, in a lovely scratchy voice. She came alive with nostalgia upon hearing those notes, like an old lady remembering her youth.

"Those were crazy years, though, Andrey," she said.

"Fuck the '90s," he said. "The more I look back, the more I realize what we risked. It was one of the most dramatic times in our history. Russia has only ever been that close to dissolution under Ivan the Terrible and after the revolution, during the *smuta*." This term, meaning time of troubles, was also used by Putin during Prigozhin's mutiny. "Not a single Russian misunderstood Putin's call when he said 'smuta,' which evokes an existential threat to the nation," Andrey explained.

Failed revolts and coups in Russia bring disorder and collapse, but also greater repression of dissidents and a tightening of the autocratic reins. By referring to a smuta, Putin reminded Russians of the profound dangers of dissent while also declaring his historic, if not divine, mandate to suppress it. Chaos reinforces the brutality of the central power but also the call to unity, which in Russia is synonymous with passivity, submissiveness, and acquiescence. A centuries-old dynamic, as predictable as the cycle of snow and thaw.

Andrey is a regime intellectual, but he was lucid and not too reticent. He cited the 1825 Decembrist revolt, Lavr Kornilov's march on Saint Petersburg in 1917, and the 1991 attempted coup—though I wasn't clear on whether he thought Mikhail Gorbachev was the victim or the instigator. Each challenge revealed the fragility of the man in charge, while giving him the chance to sink his iron talons into the nation and launch his "Siberian season" of sprucing up the old gulags and building new ones. "Russians know to never wish for the death of a bad czar, because the next one could be even worse," Andrey said.

The recent smuta took root in the '90s, as did the Putin syndrome and the expansionist push. Andrey insisted it was all about identity, calling it the holy grail of our time. "When the USSR collapsed, the West tried to destroy us by poisoning the source of our identity. We have a traditional culture. We demand the right to safeguard the values our parents and grandparents passed down to us. More than democracy, what counted was the freedom not to have to submit to Western cultural impositions. At a certain point, when the glass was full to the brim, we said that's enough."

When I expressed the opinion that traditional culture has become a utopian dream in a society with a world record for divorce (the end point of 75 percent of marriages in Russia), Andrey moved on to Chechnya, a topic he'd said he wanted to avoid. "I'm very familiar with the Caucasus and Russian Islamic communities: I have no problem admitting that their idea of good and evil is very similar to that of our elders. Paradoxically, Russian Muslims today are the ones defending traditional Russian culture. When you go to Kazan, in Tatarstan, you'll see—no other region is more conformist. The governor is one of Putin's closest allies and the mosques are unified in their support of central power. There is a general conviction that we're living in dramatic times, and that Russia must defend itself and fight back, reinforcing its self-awareness first and foremost. The sanctions have helped us rebuild the idea of unity. Apple considers us animals that don't deserve to buy its products even if we spend our entire paycheck on them? Then we'll survive just fine without Apple. I can't take my son to Florence? We went to Stalingrad and it was wonderful. It's a clash of civilizations, harsher and fiercer every day, on both sides. It will last many years. Luckily, as often happens in Russia in times of necessity, our people know how to transform the threat into rebirth. It's a matter of circumstance: Had there been no Peter the Great, Stalin, or Putin, someone else would have taken their places. Leaders are born of necessity—they arrive when they are most needed, because important things have to happen and we must be ready. These men are expressions of the energy of the people. We decide when the time has come for them to act."

Andrey's frightening psychopolitical interpretation of the aggressive Russian reawakening showed me that our trip along the Volga, a driving force of history in this part of the world, is a voyage into the collective mind of a nation. Not only has Russia broken the taboo of invading a sovereign nation, but it has amassed so many resentments, excuses, and bullets that the expansion of the conflict beyond Ukraine has become more than just a theory.

THE GREAT ROBBERY

"Do you remember Alexander Rozenbaum?" Vlad asked Katya and Andrey. "I think he's very representative of those years. He sang about love through stories of criminals. His music was romantic, poetic, but also full of pain because everything was going to hell." Katya intoned a heart-wrenching Rozenbaum song from the late '90s about autumn and a carpet of yellow leaves, a thin dress, and a saxophone, a wonderful dream, of a Boston waltz, and folly.

Her voice was morbidly languid, like a saxophone. Illusions, corruption, deception, hunger, and killings: Those were the true follies of the Russian '90s, the cursed decade. It started with the post–Cold War euphoria that infected the world, Russia included, despite an uncertain future. The prospect of ending nuclear brinkmanship—the game of deterrence that had given rise to laboratory-cities like Dubna—seemed realistic. Not all Westerners circled the wounded Bear like vultures: Some felt true compassion for a people brought to its knees, forced to survive on international charity. Just as many Russians sincerely hoped for a new system where their country could ascribe to the Western liberal-democratic model and maybe even join NATO. But the sinister precedent of Weimar—when a humiliated Germany, defeated in World War I and hungry for redress, laid the groundwork for national socialism—loomed large. A similar fate soon befell Russia. In the mismanagement of a crucial juncture in contemporary history, the West bears enormous and undeniable responsibility.

Yeltsin liberalized the movement of capital, privatized much of the state economy, and left Russia with a reform hangover worthy of his reputation as a drunkard. It was called shock therapy, and those in charge of it, from inside and outside the country, were highly paid Western "experts," especially Americans: consultant-manipulators who infiltrated universities, banks, heavy industry, the oil industry, ministries, and towns. These people didn't know anything about Russia and wanted only to bleed it dry, thereby putting an end to America's greatest challenger. Doctors, office workers, army officers, and pensioners weren't paid for weeks; workers were given whatever remained in the warehouses as severance payments, while the elderly sold their old watches and coats. The health system crumbled, hospitals lacked needles, and sailors in the Pacific fleet were literally dying of hunger: The Northern Fleet had to beg the Norwegians for soup. Inflation went wild. The defense budget in 1998 was a quarter of the Soviet one; the country was bankrupt and couldn't finance even a peacetime defense. The national GDP fell by 34 percent between 1991 and 1995—a larger decline than in the American Great Depression. The percentage of the population living under the poverty line went from 1.5 percent at the end of the Soviet era to 45 percent in the mid-1990s. The death rate caused by cardiovascular disease, alcoholism, and violence—including suicide—rose by 60 percent in four years.

The historical solidarity of Russians in times of war or famine mitigated the impact of the neoliberal economic shock, but a class of unscrupulous and criminal former party officials, former Soviet bankers, economists, and scientists saw unfettered opportunity to exploit the chaos, setting up private banks to finance their pillage and collecting capital from abroad with the help of their new Western banker friends. Great wealth fell into the hands of a few criminals, while everyone else became a vast proletariat of beggars: The Great Mother Russia was flung into the free-market square.

"My aunt had saved up for twenty years," Vlad told us. "She wanted to buy a car. As the ruble plummeted, she decided to take her money out of Sberbank: All she could afford with it was a pair of shoes. A neighbor with long red hair cut it and sold it to a wig company to buy milk for her children."

The biggest country in the world, after seventy years of Communism, was forced at gunpoint to adopt unfettered capitalism: drink or drown. Millions of people lost their savings in a Russian roulette of Ponzi schemes. The state stopped managing housing, and only those with enough cash to bribe public officials could participate in the real estate market—families would cram into a few hundred square feet, like in the 1930s. "Profit" and "bankruptcy" were key words in the new vocabulary.

The country became a lawless place run by criminal gangs, a parallel state of Mafia bosses who'd risen through the ranks in Soviet gulags and prisons. These were gangsters in uniforms of fuchsia jackets, black shirts, black ties, flashy jewelry, and tattoos that marked their place in the hierarchy. They drove Vaz-2109s, 940 Volvos, and Chevrolet Tahoe company cars to mark their status. These bandits could make their own rules and offer *krysa*, or protection. If you had *krysha* from a good gang, you'd be fine; if you didn't, you might as well invest in a tombstone. Armed confrontations were the order of the day, as were lines outside grocery stores, as in the days of the old USSR whenever bananas came back in stock. Being an assassin was a job like any other: Of the thirty-two thousand murder investigations conducted in 1996, two thousand were found to be cases of murder for hire. Businesses that provided armored doors to keep out thieves and murderers did very well in those days.

The honeymoon with the West was short-lived. It ended as soon as people caught wind of what was happening with the privatizations: In closed-door auctions, the Kremlin was signing contracts allowing oligarchs to share the spoils of Soviet industry and Communist Party funds in exchange for political neutrality. Democracy and reform became synonymous with hardship, crime, and the end of welfare. Wealth, trendy restaurants, and foreign cars were concentrated in Moscow, where provincial steel kings, Siberian oil barons, and traveling canned-food salesmen were evicting the uppity intelligentsia from their elegant urban neighborhoods. Rusty Zhiguli and Volga cars circulated on country roads. State shops were replaced with improvised local stalls selling stolen goods from closed factories, homemade sweaters and preserves, or used clothing from China and Turkey. A third of imports came by way of *chelnoki*, an informal economy participated in by millions of Russians, mostly unemployed professionals, going back and forth between Turkey or eastern Europe to pack merchandise into big plastic checkered bags. People used their meager savings to buy foreign currency—everyone was obsessed with the dollar-ruble exchange rate. Proletarians were forced to become speculators to protect what little they had left.

Then there were illegal brokers. Katya remembered the bags of rubles, dollars, deutsche marks, and British pounds piled up in her living room. Her mother had managed an important black-market currency exchange in Saint Petersburg. Katya's '90s were roaring. She had everything she wanted: a Japanese stereo, VHS tapes with Hollywood movies, fancy clothes, trips, horse-riding lessons. She went to an international high school for the future class of post-Communist leaders, where the dregs of the old *nomenklatura* and the children of ex–KGB officers mixed with the nouveau riche, traffickers, and loan sharks. Flash robberies were in vogue. Katya told us about getting kidnapped and nearly killed when she was fourteen.

She had swapped her red designer jacket with her best friend's white one. The friend was the daughter of a big shot who imported Scandinavian furniture and Italian tiles. They were walking down the street when three gunmen, no doubt following the instructions of their handlers, loaded the girl with the white jacket into their Mercedes. Katya was rendered unconscious and woke up a few days later in a basement, covered in cockroaches and tied to a pipe. She managed to free herself, climb out a window, and slither into the 5-degree Fahrenheit night, in the snow, and without the white designer jacket. After roaming for many hours in the woods, she came across the Saint Petersburg–Moscow train rails and had to decide which way to go—a choice that could lead to survival or death by exposure. She went left and followed the tracks for a few miles, she said, before she found a ride. When she got to Saint Petersburg, it was the dead of night. Rather than run home, or to the police, she went dancing at a club in the Nevsky district, whose opening night she'd missed because of her kidnapping. The bouncer was her ex-boyfriend, who let her in to take a shower. "A Finnish symphonic metal band was playing," Katya told us, pouring herself another glass of bad white wine. "My friend was there too, wearing my red jacket. She told me the bandits had called her house for the ransom and she had answered the phone herself, sending them to hell. Shit, we laughed so hard thinking about those guys tracking me through the woods to kill me."

POST-ATOMIC HUMANITY

Those mad and desperate years caused irreparable damage. Hitler was big in the Russian underground. A hodgepodge of misfits and stoners used drugs and alcohol to contact the occult, practice esoteric rituals, and cultivate the myth of the SS. They adopted extreme thoughts and behavior to fill the void left by Communism, in defiance of NATO and American consultants. In other words, they were fertile ground for the rise of Nazi mystic thought gurus like Aleksandr Dugin, the philosopher who has most influenced Putin's belief in a Russian civilization that can stand up to the West.

Those were the years when Dugin gathered the ingredients for the ideological pastiche he now uses to support propaganda posts on social media, which bind right- and left-wing reactionaries in the name of anti-

Western sentiment. Russian writer and poet Eduard Limonov described him as "a vodka Nietzschean," as he isn't known for sobriety or for intellectual coherence—he's more of a "centaur," as nationalist Communists are sometimes called. Followers recall Dugin yelling "Sieg heil!" on the metro with a bottle of port in hand. In squatter houses or circles that opposed Yeltsin, Dugin stood out with his shaved head, messiah beard, and the mannerisms of a nineteenth-century Slavophile. Guitar always around his neck, he would use it to improvise ballads decrying liberal democracy, the genocide of Native Americans, and the bombing of his Serbian brothers. Limonov wrote about the mayhem Dugin supporters created at opposition rallies: "Orthodox monks holding up pictures of Stalin, retired Red Army commissioners next to the new Cossack officers, calls for proletarian internationalism, and vehement antisemitic lectures . . . It was a post-atomic humanity."

Dugin's crowd was a variegated world of orphans, survivors, and nonaligned who, in the chaos of the '90s, stumbled and fumbled in search of rebirth: They wondered how to reclaim their pride in Russia, what role their country could play after the fall of the USSR, how to avoid ending up as historical rejects, pariahs. Former Soviet republics and eastern European countries were quickly regaining their national identities, eager to appear victims of Moscow's colonial and ideological yoke. Only the Russians seemed destined to pay for their Soviet past, with interest, even though many non-Russian entities had willingly acted as executioners for the Kremlin—including Ukraine, East Germany, Prague, Bucharest, Budapest, and Sofia.

Throughout the '90s, those who defended Communism as an inevitable chapter in Russian history joined forces with Dugin's far-right chauvinists, broke up, fought, came together again, spied on each other, betrayed each other, and even carried out assassinations of political enemies with the backing of the nouveau riche and old KGB hands. This galaxy of misfits was united in its search for an organic nationalist ideology. Xenophobes, anti-neoliberals, skinheads, libertarians, and neo-Bolsheviks were all looking for the holy grail of Russian resurrection. When Putin arrived, these same forces supported his call to national pride and his muscular approach to regional and international politics. Even some of Putin's political opponents, who have paid for their dissent with jail, the gulag, and death, have long supported, in their own ways, bloody antiterrorism and antiseparatist campaigns, repression of ethnic conflict in post-Soviet lands, the war in Georgia, the annexation of Crimea, and Putin's answer to the "Ukrainian question."

OPPOSITION WANTED

Alexei Navalny, the opposition leader who represented hope for a democratic Russia before dying in a Siberian prison in early 2024, was the most evolved representation of nationalism: He fashioned himself as a European-style right-wing conservative activist, but never missed a radical nationalist gathering, where his liberal flags mixed with swastikas and Celtic crosses. Despite being a charismatic figure of the Yabloko liberal party, he was expelled from it for calling immigrants from the Caucasus "chachi"—a racist slur that comes from the name for a typical Azeri dish. In one of his popular online broadcasts, Navalny called southern Caucasus Muslims "cockroaches," then picked up a gun and explained how to eliminate them. He quietly opposed multiculturalism and spoke of "ethnic substitution" and "ethnic criminality." In 2006, he participated in an ultranationalist march in Kondopoga, a city in Karelia, near the Finnish border, where clashes between Russian and Caucasian kids had led to a pogrom in immigrant neighborhoods. After these events, he founded the *narod* movement, meaning "Russian people," a concept that is now more supremacist than populist.

It is thus misleading to say that Navalny cultivated a Western worldview, in the sense of an open society, though it may help attack Putin: Navalny was a nationalist, but with no specific agenda—certainly not a neo-Fascist or European liberal. Navalny told his biographer, Konstantin Voronkov, that participating in "patriotic coalition" demonstrations meant "responding to the concerns of the majority. I wouldn't worry too much about their 'Sieg heil' bullshit."

Navalny's mainstream Russian views were not what made him the Kremlin's strongest and most feared critic. It was his direct attack on the corrupt autocracy, on the "Putin System," which he did by deploying two disparate traits: a talent for using the internet to reach "Generation P"—young people in big cities who never knew any leader other than Putin and who don't follow traditional news sources—and a suicidal drive to unmask the corrupt, amoral, and criminal network propping up Putin's power.

His 2021 inquest into Putin's million-dollar assets on the Black Sea garnered ten million views in one week. Navalny was a relentless activist who became increasingly iconic, more for his aspirations to martyrdom than as the leader of the opposition—such a person can hardly exist in Russia, since there is no real opposition.

The situation further degenerated after the Ukraine offensive. Enemies of the Kremlin are a patchwork of bloggers, activists, and pundits, who don't form a critical mass. Those who escaped abroad are free but ineffective; those who remained in Russia are dead or in prison. It's not enough to be well organized, like Navalny. An opposition needs a political structure, which antiregime activists outside parliament cannot access. There is an opposition within parliament, which is tolerated as long as it doesn't disagree too much with United Russia, the regime's only real party. Official opposition parties are mere crutches and alibis for the ruling class.

"We're not talking about a saint," Andrey said. For him, Navalny was also a product of the smuta. "It all makes sense. Putin and Navalny were both born of chaos, but one saved Russia and the other pandered to Russia's enemies." Katya let out another attack of the giggles and added, glass of wine in hand, that Navalny must be a product of Western disinformation, probably of the CIA. She said she knew what that looked like after debunking so much fake news. She was familiar with its mechanisms because of her longtime interest in the mudslinging machine run by some European media outfits with regard to the war in Ukraine. Ale, sitting opposite me, reacted immediately: His eyes flung wide open, like a deer caught in headlights. He was already on edge because when he went out for a smoke, he'd seen the car with the two men still there, parked with its headlights off, engine running.

SON OF THE COLD WAR

By the end of the accursed 1990s, the masses were calling for order and bread. Putin delivered both. He also sensed the anger and humiliation suffered by the loss of superpower status and what it represented for the Russian soul. People were tired of the glasnost and its painful revelations. Putin saw that the time had come for the third edition of czarism, after absolute monarchy and Communist dictatorship. He crushed Chechen rebels in the south, called on his old KGB buddies to blackmail and kill his rivals in Russia or abroad, abolished gubernatorial elections and installed Kremlin-backed politicians, and expropriated national TV channels and used them as the Comintern would have. This suited Russians just fine. When a fire breaks out, as the Russian proverb goes, you don't ask questions about the guy putting it out. Putin, son of the Cold War, had heaven on his side: First came a boom in oil, gas, and raw materials, which paid salaries and pensions and reduced the enormous national debt. Social services improved and people could access credit and take out loans. Stability took hold along with a prosperity Russia hadn't seen in thousands of years. The economy took off, consumption rose, and a middle class started to take shape. Stores were filling up thanks to a powerful new logistical network. Defense funds were flowing in, old rusty military bases in the Arctic were reopening, and Russian atomic arsenals were, once again, forces to be reckoned with at international summits. Dubna, the beating heart of Soviet nuclear research, training ground for Chernobyl engineers, became significant again: Having been reduced to a ghost town in the 1990s, when its population halved, it returned to its former splendor and then some, welcoming a new university and one hundred new missile-innovation companies. Nationally, unemployment and poverty in 2012 was half that of the Yeltsin years.

But the obsession with Western products continued unabated. The relative well-being and economic power attained in the vast Russian provinces by "Putin's henchmen"—entrepreneurs given free rein to enrich themselves by taking over public factories, lands, and collective farms, so long as it suited the power center—had set off a consumerist race known as "biznes fever." Cyrillic absorbed globalist words like *cool, shopping, dealer, biznes launche, kottedge, kreizy*. Only foreign items like designer labels, IKEA, or trips to the Mediterranean, Thailand, Dubai, or Miami counted as trendy.

But there was a schizophrenic aspect to all this: On the one hand, the irresistible attraction to a materialist world; on the other, the strong push to fight Western contamination. The identity and revanchist thinking that had developed within the counterculture of political and intellectual activism was now taking root in society, encouraged by Putin's macho narrative and by the priests, who were taking back the stage, the riches, the power, the mission. The initial indignant reaction to declassified KGB files was gradually dissipating, and the offices of the Memorial Society—cofounded by nuclear physicist Andrei Sakharov to document and report Soviet crimes—closed down. Russians were now told to forget about the execution of their relatives, to doubt that millions had been killed in the first place, and to focus instead on the

irrefutable: the heroic victory in World War II, the great conquests that had made Stalin's USSR, Russia, a superpower.

"Democracy was never a dogma here," Andrey told us. "No one really believed in it: Russians know that in such a vast country, excessive freedom leads to anarchy. We saw the devastation wrought by the diktats of the democratic West. We developed new priorities. What mattered most, when Putin came, was to regain our dignity. It was time to reclaim our position in the world and in history. After taking the blame for the events of the twentieth century, were we really supposed to stand by as they called us corrupt, mobsters, killers, and thieves? How could we tolerate a soulless Westerner trying to teach us morality, and then take American and NATO hatred in stride?"

THE CLINTON CURE

Despite the manipulations and falsehoods accepted by Putinists like Andrey, the growing Russian disillusion with the West, which has escalated into geopolitical confrontation, is not without foundation.

Before the invasion of Ukraine, I had spoken about it at length with Andrei Kozyrev, Yeltsin's ultra-reformist foreign minister, the former prodigy of the New Russian diplomacy who now lives in Florida. He'd been with the White Crow, as Yeltsin was nicknamed, when he boarded a tank during the August 1991 attempted coup. Just as he'd been at Brezhnev's old hunting lodge, in the Belovezha forest, when Russia, Belarus, and Ukraine held a secret meeting to secede from the USSR and claim recognition of their national sovereignties. Kozyrev's job was to negotiate Russia's future with the United States and resupply Yeltsin with bourbon after every trip to America. Today, he is among Putin's enemies, since he considers the 1991 borders inviolable and therefore the offensive in Ukraine a criminal endeavor. He hasn't been back to his homeland in many years and lives peacefully in the United States, even though he believes the country played a crucial role in the escalation of Russian nationalism and Moscow's anti-Western drift. He's especially angry with Democratic administrations, especially Clinton, whom he accuses of treating Russia, the Balkans, and NATO's eastward expansion as his personal collection of trophies. Even though it was a Republican who fueled the fire: In a State of the Union address in 1992, Bush Sr. declared that "by the grace of God, America won the Cold War. . . . A world once divided into two armed camps now recognizes one sole and preeminent power, the United States of America." But had it really been a victory? According to Kozyrev, and the then–American ambassador to Russia, Jack Matlock, the end of the Cold War had been the result of delicate negotiations where each side had something to gain and wanted to guarantee future cooperation. Matlock even went so far as to say that America was treating Russia as a defeated enemy, and in so doing "was fomenting feelings of humiliation and revenge," when there had actually been "a pledge not to take advantage of Russia's weakness."

Clinton stepped on the accelerator. As did his aide, Strobe Talbott—who, Kozyrev told me, had said "the United States must take responsibility for Russia, like when you make kids eat spinach. It's for their own good."

In that context, Kozyrev had become a lightning rod. "Nationalists and those nostalgic for the Soviet era opposed me, but also moderate Russians and, at one point, all of public opinion. They accused me of having conceded too much to the West, of betraying Russia. I protested, I wrote directly to Clinton and said we were done putting up with being told what they'd do to us, whether we liked it or not. 'Don't add insult to injury,' I said, 'by saying it's in our own interest to obey your orders.'" Talbott's reply came swiftly, according to Kozyrev: "Either Russia adapts to the new reality, or it sinks, like the Soviet Union."

NATO's expansion took place in this climate. Three months after the fall of the wall, American Secretary of State James Baker proposed an agreement with Gorbachev: NATO wouldn't budge an inch eastward once Germany was unified. Soon after, in March 1991, Western allies decided that European countries in the former Soviet bloc wouldn't be allowed to seek NATO membership. But these assurances were never formalized, pen on paper, in a language agreed on with Russia, since Gorbachev was too weak to demand formal legal acts. Nor were the

Americans willing to tie their own hands by adopting signed and countersigned agreements. Eastern countries rightly asked for protection, mindful of the Bear's legendary claws, while Western guilt grew over past betrayals: Munich, Yalta, Hungary, Prague . . . The Baltic and Polish communities in the United States were putting pressure in crucial electoral areas. Clinton's White House played dirty: It initially dangled the prospect of a peace partnership with eastern European countries, even Russia; then it drafted a proposal for cooperation with NATO. Finally, it went ahead with the "spinach treatment," as Kozyrev calls it. Thus, between 1999 and 2004, Poland, Czech Republic, Slovakia, Hungary, and other eastern European countries joined NATO, along with three former Soviet republics on the Baltic. Kozyrev remembers the conditions in which these historic events occurred: Boris Yeltsin negotiated missiles with Clinton over the phone, completely plastered.

Not unlike the time Polish President Lech Wałesa got Yeltsin drunk on a very hot night in August 1993, when the Russian president was visiting Warsaw. Unaware of diplomatic intrigues, Wałesa was more used to the world of dockworkers and rough union negotiations in the Danzig shipyards. He suggested that he and Yeltsin meet up alone, as two survivors of Communism: He knew a *tawerna* that would guarantee discretion and a home-cooked meal. They began their meal at eight o'clock in the evening. When the phone rang in Kozyrev's room, it was almost two o'clock in the morning. "The president wanted me to join him in his quarters immediately," Kozyrev told me. "When I got there, he couldn't stand up and was barely able to speak. I gathered that he'd approved a new paragraph to a previously agreed-upon statement that was due to be signed the following morning to great fanfare. The new paragraph, jotted down in the tête-à-tête in a trembling hand, committed Russia to supporting Poland's intentions to join NATO." According to Kozyrev, similar alcohol-fueled ambushes had occurred in Kazakhstan and Ukraine.

"But with the Balkans, Clinton handed Russian nationalists their new enemy on a silver platter," Kozyrev explained. "The USSR saw NATO as a tool of the American imperialist aggressor. Now, after the

Cold War, the West's enemies in Moscow considered NATO a tool of American world domination."

The Balkan crisis of the 1990s, which caused the breakup of Yugoslavia, was the first true clash between Moscow and Washington since the fall of the USSR. NATO's unilateral raids—carried out without consulting Moscow—revealed Russia's fragility and dealt a serious blow to its sense of dignity. "We had to find a way to send the Americans a signal without ignoring our nationalist opponents," Kozyrev confessed. "Because of our common Slavic roots, Russians came out on the side of the Serbs. But only on paper, because in truth, Yeltsin had not forgotten Milošević's support for the 1991 coup [against Gorbachev]. Plus, we were standing by the West. Bosnia was supposed to be our chance to showcase a new reformist and communicative Russia. Unfortunately, the Clinton–Christopher administration seemed to stand in our way. Clinton became shortsighted and arrogant." Kozyrev got riled up just thinking about those days. "This made NATO an internal Russian problem and allowed our Communist and Orthodox opponents to turn public opinion against Yeltsin's government, whom they saw as democratic traitors. I wanted to keep anti-NATO sentiment from rising inside Russia and leading to conflict or a new Cold War. Unfortunately, I wasn't heeded, so here we are. Much of the responsibility for the current conflict between the United States and Russia lies with Clinton, Christopher, and their cronies."

America's decision to bomb the Balkans and launch Operation Deliberate Force—without notifying Moscow—proved fatal. "We learned of the decision from the press. It was a deliberate snub," Kozyrev said. "The United States wanted to combat Karadžić and Milošević's nationalism, but it ended up fueling Russia's. That was when the clock of history turned back, where the democratic process was nipped in the bud. From that moment on, the idea of avenging our humiliations took hold. Note that at the time, Putin was still vice-mayor of Saint Petersburg. Let me be clear: We weren't against the use of force—we were on America's side, no ifs, ands, or buts. But we also needed to let our internal enemies come to terms with the idea of a Western-led military operation before it occurred. If the bombing had been advertised as a Yeltsin invasion, and not just an American one, it could have dealt the decisive blow to the Cold War. It could have put Russia on the right side of history."

But this was just the beginning—there was still a lot of spinach to swallow: NATO's 1999 bombing of Serbia, Russia's longtime Slavic Orthodox sister, without the approval of the UN Security Council, of which Russia is a permanent member; American and NATO support for Kosovo's independence, a dangerous precedent for Russia; the United States' unilateral withdrawal from the ballistic missile treaty and the threat of establishing missile-defense bases in former Warsaw Pact countries; and the invasions of Iraq and Afghanistan after September 11, which, according to Moscow, confirmed that NATO wasn't just a defensive force after all.

"Mind you," Kozyrev said. "Putin had just come to power, and he was the first leader to call President Bush after the attack on the Twin Towers. He offered the support of the UN Security Council and authorization to set up a temporary base in Kyrgyzstan—in the former Soviet sphere—as a bridgehead for American troops in Afghanistan. Moreover, he allowed American military cargo planes to stock up on food in Ulyanovsk, Lenin's birthplace on the Volga. To highlight his pro-Western politics, he voluntarily closed Russian bases in Cuba and Vietnam. And what happened? The Americans still occupy that temporary base in Kyrgyzstan, even after withdrawing from Afghanistan. Not only that, but they're also in Uzbekistan and in half the Caucasus. In 2002, Putin called Russia a European nation, which was unpopular among nationalists; and on NATO he simply held that expansion to the Baltic states would be a red line for Russia."

By 2005, when Putin declared that the fall of the Soviet Union had been a colossal geopolitical disaster that had left tens of thousands of Russians stranded abroad, echoing Hitler's words in the 1930s, many things had happened in the meantime. For one thing, that red line had been summarily crossed with plans for NATO's expansion into Ukraine.

HEADLIGHTS IN THE NIGHT

So what to do? We wait on the beach reflecting on our situation, which seems precarious no matter which way we look at it. We speak in whispers, even though we're alone by the dock and no one can hear us. But it seems best to be prudent. We decide to get out of Dubna as soon as possible: It is not an ideal place to be foreigners in Putin's wartime Russia, without permission. Last night at dinner, Andrey told us of a few newly built strategic centers in Dubna, like MKB Raduga, a massive aerospace company that manufactures next-generation missile systems designed for antisatellite nuclear rockets. Just having heard that information, though probably exaggerated, makes us feel like a target.

Moreover, that suspicious car had still been there with its engine on, after Andrey left on foot. After driving out of the parking lot, before we turned onto the street leading to our hotel, we noticed that the headlights had been turned on and the car was moving. I felt a rush to the brain, a mixture of adrenaline and paranoia. Even Vlad couldn't reassure us anymore: He said it was a strange coincidence and didn't downplay it, as he usually did in confusing situations, when he'd describe apocalyptic scenarios before bursting out laughing. Instead, he turned off the radio and kept checking his rearview mirror. Katya, drunk, kept sliding off her seat, slurring curse words in Russian at Vlad, or at us, while she peeked out the window, frowning at the dark void outside.

At the hotel, Vlad told us the van rental was in her name. He wasn't authorized to drive outside greater Saint Petersburg. "We could put her on a train, but then it'll be a headache for all of us if we get stopped," he said. He was unusually serious and pale: He seemed to share our anxiety and anger. This trip was turning out to be more challenging than expected. "Shit, we can't afford trouble," he exclaimed, looking like he could have downed a bottle in one gulp. Perhaps that very thought steadied him, because then he smiled and hugged us. "Come on, everything will be fine tomorrow. We'll get up early, go for a swim, and hightail it before they stick a nuke up our asses!"

But here we are, just me, Ale, and the atom brainiacs in their underwear. The scent of pine fills the silence as we wonder, in vain, about what's to come.

The sun is high in the sky when we spot Vlad and Katya hobbling across the sand. We suspect their sunglasses are hiding dark and swollen eyes, but they both seem in high spirits. Vlad bites into his first Eskimo of the day. He takes off his shirt and pants and dives into the river. We follow him. The current is imperceptible; it feels like swimming in a lake. The Volga has its emergency brake on here, because we're just upstream of the largest artificial hydroelectric basin in the world, built by Stalin between the 1930s and '40s, at the cost of forty-eight flooded villages. It is one of our next stops.

5
The widow's *izba*

"Damn you, Pavel"

THE SANITATION EFFECT

Heavy rain has kept us stranded under an awning outside Andrei Kovalev's bakery in the Red Square in Rybinsk, a city of about two hundred thousand people. We have somehow gained the trust of the effusive baker, who is forty-four years old and popular among locals. He hands out samples of his black bread made with ancient grains, sporting a well-kept beard artfully covered in flour, a white tunic, baggy pants, and a pair of *lapti*—traditional shoes in woven birch raffia. He's a marketing wiz.

Rybinsk was once called the fishery of the czar because it used to send some of the best sturgeons on the Volga to Saint Petersburg. Now it's no longer possible to fish here at all. Instead, the city has reinvented itself as Moscow's oven. Every day, trucks set off for the capital full of warm loaves. Bakeries abound, each one competing to be more authentic than the next, displaying hand-painted signs that recall the rustic shops of the old *derevnya*, the Russian countryside. Wheat and rye production has grown by 40 percent compared to the prewar period.

Our new friend was one of the first to fire up an oven in the Red Square. Kovalev tells us that he found his way after struggling to earn a living for years. "I saw the growing interest in local products. And now we're in a war economy, so we have to make the best of what we have. Russians, even here in the provinces, became spoiled over the years—we have a sophisticated palate. But I learned to use *zakvaska*, a traditional yeast that keeps bread fresh for ten days, and then I discovered flours that had been falling out of use." He also sells curative oils made from hemp, sea buckthorn, grape seeds, and Siberian cedar at a rather high price. He sees opening a bakery as a political act, a way to salvage "rural Russian values and counter the consumerism imported from the West. Over the past thirty years, people grew to hate Russian bread," he continues. "They thought it was beneath them. They wanted baguettes, the little sirs! Mine are old recipes, from before the perestroika, from when we were happy."

The Red Square reminds me of Campo San Polo in Venice. It has recently been restored with an eighteenth-century layout and the soft Venetian shades of color that Catherine the Great loved so well. A statue of Lenin stands in the center, with pigeons gathering on his head and shoulders. He is not depicted in mid-speech here, but on his own, with one hand under his coat, like Napoleon.

It was erected in 1920, on the same pedestal that used to host a statue of Alexander II. You can still see how the old inscription was chiseled away hastily to make room for Lenin, the man who had just put an end to three centuries of the Romanov dynasty by ordering (via telex) his Bolshevik forces to carry out the massacre at Yekaterinburg, where Nicholas, his wife Alexandra, his five children, his four servants, and their dog were executed by firing squad and bayonet.

The square seems like a movie set: the restaurant, the general store, the haberdashery, Mr. Kovalev's bakery, the cutesy aesthetic and retro graphics of the signs, all evoke imperial Russia—if you can overlook Lenin's dystopian presence. I've noticed this in many recently restored city centers along the Volga: an apparent attempt to strip away any residue of the gray Soviet sadness that used to envelop even the liveliest baroque buildings; a regime makeover inspired by the idea of a new Russia. The result is that nothing looks ancient or contemporary, traditional or modern—just fake. The sanitized beauty suggests a reassuring, peaceful rebirth of community while giving the square a Disneyland or outlet mall effect, where the streets and squares just smell like french fries. This is not so different from what has happened in our historic centers in the West.

BATTLESHIP MIKHALKOV

This square is closely tied to the great history of film. On one side, a light sage building where the brothers Nicholas and Joseph Schenck lived before they emigrated to the United States and founded Metro-Goldwyn-Mayer; on the other, the pink manor of the Mikhalkov dynasty, which goes back to the sixteenth century, and of which filmmaker Nikita Mikhalkov is the last famous descendant.

Since the days of the imperial government in Yaroslavl, the Mikhalkovs have sided with whoever was in charge. Nikita Mikhalkov, who won an Oscar in 1995 for directing *Burnt by the Sun*, is now one of the president's men, nicknamed Putin's Eisenstein, even though the real Eisenstein, who directed *Battleship Potemkin*, ended up being censored and sidelined for his trilogy on Ivan the Terrible. Stalin considered the film to be critical of Ivan, to whom he liked to compare himself. Mikhalkov is head of the Russian Cinematographers' Union and polices every upcoming film on behalf of the Kremlin. He accuses the West of trying to destroy Russian civilization and Orthodox ethics. Sanctioned by the EU for his support of the invasion, he is in the process of starting the Eurasian Academy of Cinematographic Arts to counter the academy in Los Angeles, which, according to him, has killed film "through a dictatorship of the politically correct."

Various still shots of Mikhalkov's films are displayed in Kovalev's bakery. Kovalev proudly shows us a recent television interview with Mikhalkov, saying, "The maestro loved Europe, but now he says it has become a cesspool." In the interview, Mikhalkov says that Europe once exuded a "spirit like the smell of coffee permeating the streets of Rome in the morning, but now you have to close the windows on Europe to keep out the stench of shit. Western culture can no longer make anything like American films of the 1970s with Jack Nicholson, for instance. Europeans have debased themselves trying to stay in America's slipstream. They've developed, sure, and are rolling in dough, but they've lost their identity. They're boring, derivative, and hide their cowardice and impotence behind the concept of tolerance. Look at Sweden: The crime rate was close to zero and now the head of police is asking women not to go out after dark. The head of the Catholic Church tries to be trendy by kissing the feet of an African." Mikhalkov then boasts of having introduced Putin to Ivan Ilyin, though Kovalev says he doesn't really know who this Ilyin guy is. I explain he was an intellectual who lived in the first half of the twentieth century, a rather obscure and marginal figure. Russian history never really had philosophers—only great writers with a philosophical vision.

Ilyin is the only philosopher Putin has mentioned publicly, and he fits Kremlin ideology like a glove: Provocative ideas, such as Ilyin's, are Putin's bread and butter, so it makes sense that he would coopt the philosopher's *avant la lettre* antiglobalization writings to give meaning to his vision for Russia. Mikhalkov had guessed Putin would love Ilyin, who is also popular among the priests. As a fervent patriot who called for Russia's renewal and rebirth during his exiles in Nazi Germany and Switzerland, he is considered the heir to Dostoyevsky. He believed that modern Russia has been infected with an "anti-Christian virus" imported from the West. "After losing our ties to God and Christian tradition," he wrote in the essay most cited by Putin, "Russia was morally blinded, seized by materialism and nihilism. . . . To overcome the global moral crisis, we must return to eternal moral values: faith, love, conscience, family, homeland, and nation but especially faith and love."

Ilyin hoped for a strong government in line with Russian autocratic tradition. He was kicked out by the Bolsheviks in 1922, but he hated the Western bourgeoisie just as much, saying, "It has withered human souls and wants de-Christianization." An apocalyptic, melodramatic, mystic, and reactionary conspiracy theorist, Ilyin comes off as Putin's ghostwriter, especially when he prescribes *smuta* as a way to achieve an even stronger Russia through repression. "The day will come when Russia will rise from its disintegration and humiliation and begin a new era of development and greatness." Ilyin described the Russian people as "the nucleus of everything that is Eurasian and, therefore, of universal balance." He believed Russia incorporates Christian Byzantine culture and Mongol political strength, an idea akin to Gumilev's *passionarnost*, in which one must sacrifice oneself for an independent Russia that is neither European nor Asian.

In the 1950s, Ilyin published "What Will Russia's Dismemberment Do to the World," an essay where he predicted the fall of the USSR and explained how Russia could be spared from the corrupting influence of the West. "We have to start by purifying our brains, giving sovereignty to the conscience," he wrote. He was obsessed with Ukraine and saw it as a threat to Russian integrity, calling it the Trojan horse of the West—in short, he was a prophet of the Putin doctrine.

On Mikhalkov's request and by order of the Kremlin, Ilyin's remains were repatriated from Switzerland in 2005 and interred at the Donskoy Monastery in Moscow, where the Soviets had turned the cells of the monks into *kommunalka*, shared abodes, and a crematorium for the victims of the Bolsheviks. Putin, Mikhalkov, ministers, bishops, Cossacks, monarchs, and ex-Communists attended the ceremony. "This is the real end to the civil war," Mikhalkov declared. Indeed, the rite seemed to represent the repairing of the rift between imperial and Christian Russia and Soviet Communism.

COURT SONGWRITER

Kovalev knew Nikita's father, Sergey Vladimirovich Mikhalkov, a poet and author of satirical fairy tales. Shortly before dying at almost one hundred years old, in 2009, he'd returned to Rybinsk to see his family building. "A wonderful welcome. A band, fireworks, speeches. But do you know what I think?" Kovalev says. "Sergey was a sellout." Indeed, he wrote anthems for three different, successive regimes. First under Stalin, when in 1942 he was given the delicate task of replacing "The International" with lyrics to the music of Alexander Alexandrov. The USSR needed a more patriotic anthem, able to inspire soldiers facing the Nazis. The workers of the world could wait: The infantry came first. It was an ode to Stalin, who "taught us to dedicate ourselves to the people / inspired us to work and accomplish heroic feats!" The Man of Steel appreciated this, as he'd created the Soviet Union in his image.

With de-Stalinization, the anthem fell out of favor until 1977, under Brezhnev. Sergey licked those boots too and was asked to write a new version of the Soviet anthem. In his free time, he also helped the KGB plant undercover spies in compromising positions with Western diplomats, such as French Ambassador Maurice Dejean, who was lured into a honeytrap. Even Sergey's younger brother Mikhail, a writer, was an active agent with the KGB. But when the USSR fell, the Soviet anthem was discarded. One of Putin's first decisions was to replace the one from Yeltsin's era, deemed too submissive and not evocative enough: He asked around and learned that old Mikhalkov, at eighty-seven, was still active. And who better than he could write Russia's new anthem without renouncing the USSR? Putin decided to give new life to Alexandrov's Soviet composition and trust the court songwriter to capture the Putinist mood:

Russia—our sacred country
Russia—our beloved land
. . . From the seas of the south to the polar circle
Our woods and fields are vast

You are unique in this world, inimitable
Native home protected by God.

Kovalev sings it to me. Then he tells me about the time some guy said to Mikhalkov: "You wrote such an ugly anthem." To which Sergey allegedly replied, "Yeah, it's terrible, but you'll have to listen to it standing up."

THE PRIEST'S SCALPEL

We first hear about Pavel from a taxi-driver friend of Mr. Kovalev, as we discuss war casualties from Rybinsk. He was an ethnic Romani who died in Ukraine in the fall of 2022. The taxi driver tells me they'd been colleagues, but that the poor guy, really a great guy, had died after stepping on a mine, only forty days after enlisting. Almost every week the baker's friend drives buses from Rybinsk to Donbas to bring help and comfort to the boys at the front. He tells us that Rybinsk is a gathering point for supplies and volunteers from throughout the region. It takes him more than a day to drive to the front, but that's about all he is willing to tell us. "Only those with an unshakable faith can face such a slaughterhouse."

The expeditions are led by a young priest, Father Ioann Perevezenkhov, a spiritual guide at the Cathedral of Transfiguration in Rybinsk and a former surgeon. He goes to Donbas to stitch up the wounded and give mass in the encampments. Everyone here speaks of him with deference, like he's a saint, and the taxi driver and baker have a long, secret meeting to decide whether they should give me his phone number: They look clumsy and bewildered, perhaps fearing trouble for connecting such a prominent figure with Western strangers. In the end, we get the number and call the priest. Vlad speaks to him at length and says we can meet him in Kalyazin, on the Uglich basin, where he will be leading a procession. It is two or three hours away. Meanwhile, we insist on getting Pavel's address. "What the fuck are you doing with fucking gypsies?" the baker asks. Katya agrees, or so we guess from her poorly stifled giggle. She has started to disassociate from everything and seems eager to get to Mari El, in the land of the Chuvash, where she's planning on meeting up with the mother of a musician friend of hers who recently drowned himself in the Volga. Vlad thinks he was one of Katya's old flames from when she sang in the nightclubs of Saint Petersburg.

THE SQUALOR STRATEGY

So we head out of town with a map sketched on a napkin and a good dose of bread "made like old times, before the perestroika."

Every time we leave an urban center, we're seized by a strange knot in the stomach and a sense of impending doom rises within us, especially in bad weather. Any excitement we may feel for what lies ahead is immediately extinguished, like a match, amid the oppressive uniformity of the countryside. One feels a similar sense of distress when crossing American suburbs or the outskirts of European cities, which always make me wonder: How did destiny lead people to settle here, of all places? But here on the margins of Russian cities, the distress is compounded by the fact that some kind of plan lies behind so much squalor: a deliberate attempt to discolor cement, clothing, and lives to make everything—streets, Soviet and post-Soviet buildings, bus shelters, supermarkets, gas stations, and even puddles—submit to a single aesthetic. It must have always been like this if even Gorky wrote that the squalid suburbs "love to distract themselves with pain. They play with it, like children, and rarely do they feel ashamed of being unhappy. In those interminable weekdays, pain is a party, fires a distraction; even a scratch can look like beauty on a plain face." In this gaping void, the regime places, as a distraction, bright twenty-by-ten-foot signs of strapping young soldiers calling for recruits and promising "a real man's job," contracts for 650,000 rubles upon signing, and buckets of money once at the battlefront—just call 117.

When I visited the former Soviet Union in the early 1990s, I thought the sadness that pervaded roads, buildings, and faces from Tallinn to Vladivostok revealed the end of an empire: what Orhan Pamuk calls *huzun*, or "comforting melancholy," referring to Istanbul's sense of inadequacy after the sudden fall of the Ottoman Empire. Not a private feeling, but a communal depression, an internal darkness shared by all. I thought that those tattered and poor places represented grief for a departed empire, good or evil as it may have been. "*Huzun* is like nourishment and can only be seen from the outside," Pamuk writes. The decrepitude of the former Soviet world seemed beautiful to me, a foreigner. I liked that desperate decadence, thinking it would pass. But it hasn't.

Outside the cities, after the last block of houses, is space full of nothing. In this region of the Volga, it spreads across a monotonous alternation of bland birch and pine forests and unkempt plains where no cow or sheep would ever go, empty landscapes like Gorky's faces, adorned with a few scratches, crows, gas pipes, pylons, and high-voltage lines that bring electricity to the villages.

In western Europe, the border between city and countryside is now nonexistent. Urban and rural economies are integrated. In Russia, villages exist alone; their horizon ends at the edge of the village. It is a subsistence economy, where people produce no more than what they need, and the little money they earn through excess produce or odd jobs is used to pay for basic services. Rural districts that host agricultural industry are an exception where everything revolves around that, like in the days of the *kolkhozy*. Life in the Russian countryside is a closed-circuit system, opportunities for personal development are not even contemplated, education is of second or third order. Even the language is different. Vlad tells us that city folk often don't understand country folk, who don't open their *o*'s, who break off the end of adjectives, and who muddle their consonants. "It's called *kolchoznoe proisnosenie*, *kolkhozy* speak," he says. But he's a patient translator. He might curse if he doesn't understand something, but he always finds a way to communicate even with the most reticent people.

Until the end of the 1970s, farmers in the collectivized agricultural cooperatives, almost 50 percent of the Soviet population, didn't have the right to an ID card or to leave town without permission, so they couldn't even imagine making a life for themselves somewhere else. They left only by order of the state, which could mean a faraway destination, or conscription. Mistrust of development remains strong, because it could lead to an even worse situation. Any interest in change is viewed with suspicion, as a form of arrogance, while hope for collective transformation is perceived as a harbinger of turmoil. A warning down through generations.

These are the people Putin addresses and that vote for him in large numbers. It's not a medieval world, as the West believes. Even the United States has vast pockets of human stagnation and social erosion that Russia does not experience. But in America, it's a matter of sectors of society that have been left behind because of economic or racial injustice, victims of social cyclones that kill off entire cities. In Russia, the prospect of mass isolation pushes people together in the face of those wide-open spaces, harsh winters, or tragic turns of events. The *Homo sovieticus* was not created in a lab. All Communism did was violently rage against an era of widespread collective apathy, an inertia and resignation that has led many Russians to blindly entrust their lives to whatever regime, or despot, happens to be in charge.

At a 1929 dinner, after Stalin had just been promoted to head the party in Leningrad, he remained silent as his comrades spoke animatedly about the best way to lead the party, which had been without Lenin for five years at that point. Stalin suddenly stood up and started to pace, then said, "Don't forget we live in Russia, the land of the czars. The Russian people love having one man at the helm. Of course, this man must apply the collective will."

Stalin became the czar of Bolshevism and now Putin is the czar of neo-imperialism. The world he is addressing may not be the most advanced, but it is of this world. It's a brutal police state, but Russians also take cleanliness seriously. Waste management in urban centers and remote villages alike is impressive, perhaps comparable only to that of Japan. Garbage cans are constantly being emptied, even at truck stops in the boondocks, and toilets are always being scrubbed. In a country of die-hard smokers, tossed cigarette butts are conspicuously absent from the sidewalks, and smoking is not allowed at exterior restaurant tables. Society is also very digital. In cities and in remote rural areas, payments are mostly contactless—the wild strawberries babushkas sell along truck routes can be bought by typing in a phone number, and speeding tickets arrive a second after the fact and can be paid in one click. There is less cash in circulation than in Europe and internet connection is excellent almost everywhere.

Even so, suburban and rural dwellers experience contact with the outside world only through state TV channels. "Russia can manage modernity because it's not a democracy," a young computer engineer told me in Moscow in the first months of the war. He'd worked in London for many years, but he could no longer stand to hear people talk badly about Russia, so he returned, despite having to take a large pay cut. "In the West, democracies are overwhelmed by modernity, which is very different from previous eras. Now the West is dominated by two dogmas, profit and technology, both of which are virtual realities. For Russia, the only dogma is unity, with everything that comes with this concept, including the willingness to give up freedom and truth. This may seem like Putin's invention or obsession, but it's a feeling rooted in reality, it permeates the air Russians breathe when they're together. Because deep down, we know what disintegration looks like. So even though our technology is on par with the West's, or more advanced, it will never be our creed. If there is a new revolution, it won't be made of technology but of flesh and blood, like the others. It will take only a few hours to go from indifference to apocalypse, but it won't happen on YouTube or Telegram."

Outside cities, people don't look for truths to complicate their lives, but for certainties to simplify them. If a hospital closes, if it's raining in the schools through leaky ceilings, or if the roads are impassable, it's not Putin's fault, but that of the fall of the Soviet Union and the Communism that provided it all. Or of the West, which hates and threatens Russia. An indifferent population sees Putin as a sure bet who can fight to regain lost grandeur, who opposes the Western aggressor in Ukraine, and who chastises regional governments on live TV for not filling potholes. Where Putin's TVs don't reach, you'll be sure to find the priests and their beards, or apathetic officials who oppose change because it could threaten their positions.

A STREET WITH NO NAME

Yet, upon entering a village, the sadness disappears and is replaced by awe—as quickly as you can change the channel with a remote. The oppressive void instantly turns into a chaotic and lively bustle of wonders, color, and form, like in a Pieter Brueghel painting. There's a sense of self-management and anarchy: Dogs, chickens, goats, and cows seem to belong to everyone and no one. Kids play ball in the square dominated by a faded red hammer and sickle painted on cement, tractors are parked outside the bars, the bus takes off with a salute of three honks. Plum and apple trees are bursting with fruit, while property boundaries are marked with flower arrangements or intertwined branches. The most recent dwellings are the least appealing, just like in Western neighborhoods where surveys have supplanted planning.

There are still some *izby*, the traditional cottages around to lend charm to the scene: Some are in ruins, as if bombed, others were blackened by fires, but many have been rigorously remodeled and fixed up. Vlad says people like to turn them into dachas, little vacation homes for city folk. Vasily Grossman was right when he wrote that no two are identical, even though the structure, in larch, is always more or less the same, with its 150 required beams. The variety comes in the number and shape of the windows, the molding, the curtain lace, the inlays on the sloping roofs, the pastel colors, or the addition of a sauna or shed. They are small, almost like burrows, a Russian remedy for the primordial fear of the great void. Grossman saw the izba as the antithesis to the German work camp, where human savagery was expressed through perfect symmetry. "There are millions of them, but there cannot be—and there are not—two that are perfectly identical. What is alive," he wrote, "has no copies. Two people, two rosehip bushes cannot be the same—it's impossible. And where violence tries to erase variety and difference, life fades."

We leave Katya at a village bar. She doesn't want to have anything to do with Romani people. "They pretend to be Russians, but I know them. Watch your wallet, they'll steal your underpants if you let them, but you won't notice until you're taking a shit." As we set off for Pavel's izba, I can't stop worrying that we're traveling with a dangerous racist alcoholic—and Ale and Vlad seem to be harboring similar concerns.

We get directions from an old woman pulling a cart of kindling. Pavel's izba is at the end of a street with no name, a road of wide puddles shaded by two rows of elms. It's a faded light blue, surrounded by a dangling, rotting fence.

Two women come to the gate: Valentina, Pavel's widow, and Zarina, his eighteen-year-old daughter. It's not easy to convince them to let us in: They firmly but politely decline our offer to pay them for the inconvenience. But Zarina is curious and intrigued by the camera. Vlad tries to put them at ease and tells them of how fondly people spoke of Pavel in Rybinsk. Eventually, they let us in.

The yard is overrun with skeletal hens and car carcasses repurposed as chicken coops. The women excuse themselves and come back dressed up and wearing makeup. Valentina is wearing a long silk gown typical of Russian Romani people of the mid-Volga, who originally came from Belarus. Zarina, with big upturned copper eyes, looks at us in awe. She is five months pregnant. She's sitting on the burgundy couch next to her mother, who looks weary. The ceiling is low, in plexiglass, with clouds and swallows painted on a sky-blue background. Vlad ducks as he paces around nervously, gathering his thoughts and energy to prepare himself for translating in such an unexpected situation. The linoleum floor wobbles under his steps. Hanging on the wall, behind the couch, are various photographs: the children swimming in the Volga with their father, Pavel beaming with his new Weedwacker or with his elbow resting on his taxi door, the steering wheel lined with a plush cover that looks like Trump's comb-over.

They tell us Pavel had gone into debt to pay for his taxi license. One night, he came home drunk. "I signed," he told Valentina, staring at his soup. "What did you sign, Pavel?" "I'm going. To Donbas." "Are you out of your mind? Do you want to get yourself killed? Did you think about us? You're almost an old man, Pavel, it's not up to you. Your hip hurts all the time, you're always saying that. You have to fix the fence. . . . Damn you, Pavel." Then he showed her the contract for enlistment: He would earn almost $3,000 per month, while as a taxi driver he made $600 at most, and some months almost nothing. "He was a good man, respected," Valentina says. "I couldn't stop him. Maybe I should have flung myself to the ground, kissed his feet. He did it for his three children, to pay off the mortgage," Valentina tells us. "I begged him, don't do it, Pavel, fuck the money, think of Zarina, Cristina, and Stanislav. People are dying in Ukraine, and for what?" But Pavel got angry. "I'm Russian, it's my duty, I want to show those fuckers how much Gypsies love Russia," he said. One week of training and he left.

Zarina brings up the mine. "They sent him ahead to check out the terrain, but we'll never really know." She sniffles and bites her lip. She says that several boys from the clan had escaped to Georgia, while others enlisted for the money. "They tell us one truth and another one to the Ukrainians, but why kill each other? Here in our village, there were two Ukrainian families, good people like us. I grew up with their children, and months ago they just left, from one day to the next. They left a cow tied to the fence and a letter thanking everyone." The war has become a sort of public subsidy, according to Zarina, but Pavel had his convictions. "He thought the United States had infected Ukraine, like a tumor that would destroy Russia," Valentina says.

Then one Sunday, two military officials came to deliver a form letter from Putin, and a medal. The vice-mayor of Rybinsk stopped by to offer his condolences. Valentina assures us their neighbors were there for them. Even people she hadn't spoken to in years came by with bread and plum liqueur.

She and Pavel had loved each other, she says, but they were never married. And now Valentina is suing Pavel's mother for the $60,000 the state provides to compensate the families of the fallen. She wants to buy an apartment in Rybinsk for her children. "What was Pavel thinking?" she says. "He had his ideas, and said it was time to stick it to everyone who had left the Soviet Union. For some reason, he had an even bigger grudge against Estonia than Ukraine—he really hated Estonia. His family there had had a hard time after the fall of the Soviet Union. But he left only to make a few bucks, that's what I think, his ideals didn't have anything to do with it. In the end, my Pavel was a mercenary, right?"

Zarina reiterates that poor people enlist for the money. It's big money for most Russians, and if you come out alive, you're set for a while. But she also knows people who got injured on purpose, to get the $20,000 owed to the wounded and come home. "We know this guy who blew it all in one week. Now he doesn't even have a house. He lives in a barn."

In the southern corner of the izba, a space typically reserved for icons, next to the stereo and CDs, tea lights illuminate a small shrine flanked by the Russian flag: It contains Pavel's accordion, his straw hat, fake sunflowers, images of the Madonna, whom Pavel worshipped, and stuffed animals he bought Zarina. And then, smiling like a kindly uncle, there's Stalin. "His beloved Stalin," Valentina says.

MULE-MEN

Pavel's ancestors, Valentina tells us, were *burlaki*, or boat towers. In the nineteenth century, during the "big waters" of spring and autumn, the burlaki would tow boats against the current where the Neva joins the Volga, using a series of ropes, and haul them onto the banks. In 1929, the Soviets officially banned the use of the "slaves of the Volga," as Lenin called them after having seen them as a child in Simbirsk, also because Russia had long since been using steamboats. But the mule-men remained yoked to their ancestral labors. They were used in emergencies on Volga tributaries, and during World War II, they helped supply troops at the front.

Until the 1930s, Pavel's grandfather had pulled barges along the Sheksna River, which joins the Volga at Rybinsk. He was one of the last river slaves: He hauled boats for small landowners from the interior, the kulaks, and was freed during the forced-collectivization period, when the state rounded up "class enemies" in the countryside, executing people en masse or deporting them to Siberia, and requisitioning grain. Stalin's picture in Pavel's shrine, according to Valentina, is thus a sort of votive offering, a tribute to his burlak grandfather's emancipation brought about by the slaughter of the kulaks.

Before starting our journey, we stopped at the Russian Museum in Saint Petersburg to see an Ilya Repin painting. *The Boatmen of the Volga* was a symbol of worker exploitation in czarist Russia, but it also represents the revolutionary fervor that dwells in the hearts of the exploited. In 1870, Repin moved to Rybinsk, where he lived with the burlaki for more than two years. This total, hyperrealist immersion yielded one of the most powerful paintings in Russian art history. Historians believe there were about a million burlaki in those years, working barefoot and hunched for ten hours a day: mule-men with ropes tied around their waists, toiling through wind and weather along the banks of the Volga. They were often serfs on the run from a previous owner or army deserters; in any case, people who were desperate. Those who tried to escape were beaten and forced to work for free for the length of time they'd been on the run. They were given nothing but slop made with cabbage and black bread.

Maksim Gorky, a river boy like Mark Twain and autodidact like Jack London, learned to write at twelve years old, from the galley cook, as a scullery boy on the Volga. As a child in Nizhny Novgorod, Gorky had heard his grandfather's stories of life as a burlak, when he'd sink his bleeding feet into the stones, burn his back under the scorching summer sun, feel his head "melting like molten steel" and his chest creaking under the vise of the ropes, "until I couldn't see where I was going. Blinded by sweat, my soul cried and tears stained my cheeks." He'd traveled the river for hundreds of miles, "from Simbirsk to Rybinsk, Saratov to Nizhny Novgorod, Astrakhan to Makarev . . . I would ask the Volga how a mother could cause her children so much suffering."

Repin's painting depicts eleven men awash in moonlight who seem to be collapsing forward onto the sand, exhausted by the heat as they pull an elegant vessel, their hands swollen with veins. The strongest are in front, capable of superhuman effort; only the last one has given in. He's still standing because he's tied to his miserable companions, like a dog tied to a team of dogs. It's a sequence shot in which some look straight at the viewer, as if to reclaim their human dignity and spirit, each man's face a silent cry for their plight and a condemnation of their exploiter—almost a violent threat.

They all look defeated, resigned, yet sustained by a stoic will. Except for one man, standing in the middle of the line and at the center of the great canvas: His tattered clothing is bright, he holds his head high, his face is not soiled or foul like the others. As he looks proudly at the horizon, he struggles to free himself from the ropes as he assumes the heroic stance of a man ready to rebel and die for humanity. The Russian flag hoisted on the mast of the vessel is upside down, signifying injustice, an omen of smuta. In the background is a steamboat, symbol of hope in industrial progress.

Even Dostoyevsky was moved by this documentary on canvas. He'd read about it in the paper and expected it to be another sentimental piece of limited social value. But, "to my delight, all my fears turned out to be unfounded. . . . Not one man screams from the painting saying, 'Look how unlucky I am and how much you owe us.' . . . I saw the transporters, the real transporters, and nothing more. . . . One can't help but think we owe them, that we really are indebted to the people."

This was precisely the underlying idea behind the populist movement, which came about after the abolition of serfdom and led avant-garde realist painters like Repin to leave the academy and set out to walk among the dispossessed. They wanted to bring art to the countryside and challenge the system of oppression. These roving artists, the Peredvizhniki, or Wanderers, descended the Volga exhibiting their work in villages and painting the inhuman conditions of farmers. Their impact and visibility were greater abroad than in Russia: Repin's painting met with immediate international success at the Universal Exhibit in Vienna in 1873, and was purchased by the son of a czar, ending up in enemy hands.

The Volga itself was mythologized. Between 1850 and 1900, some forty books were published praising it as a patriotic destination: A popular guide described it as having "a wild grandeur impossible to find in any other river in Europe." It became an exhibit unto itself, a mirror of the Russian soul, and an artistic counter-cliché. The novelist Ivan Goncharov, born in Simbirsk like Lenin, couldn't help but set the famous idyllic and pastoral dream of *Oblomov* on the banks of the Volga. It became fashionable for artists, real or presumed, to go on cruises on new steamboats to make an impression or to show off. Anton Chekhov subtly teased them in his short story "The Grasshopper," in which the entourage of the beautiful Olga convinces her she possesses immense talent as a painter, writer, and musician. On a steamboat trip with her lover, Ryabovsky, she stands on the bridge entranced, believing herself to be immortal as she watches the gray waters of the Volga, thinking they look turquoise.

ON THIN ICE

As we leave Pavel's izba, Ale and I offer our hands but notice that Vlad does not. Hygiene-related fastidiousness? Is he revealing a bias we didn't notice during our meeting? But then he holds back, lingering on the threshold. Suddenly, he squeezes both of Valentina's hands in his and leans over to kiss them. It's not a fleeting kiss, nor the ritual kiss of an icon as a sign of respect—Vlad has little familiarity with churches. No, these are full-on kisses, given freely and passionately. Valentina looks uncomfortable and covers her face. Vlad then whispers something unintelligible he refuses to translate for us later. But Valentina's cheeks become damp with tears, while Zarina uses her sleeve to dry her big copper eyes.

Perhaps Vlad feels the need to confer solemnity to the moments experienced in Pavel's izba. They've clearly affected him: This was his first time meeting people with whom he never would have had contact, had it not been for us, without violating some taboo. We were all emotional in that room with the plexiglass sky, sitting on tattered rugs and besieged by a litter of kittens. Valentina and Zarina brought us the war and the intense intimacy of its pain.

Later that evening, at the hotel in Rybinsk, Vlad strikes again. As we sit down to dinner, he orders a beer in our presence, for the first time on the trip. Several beers, in fact, which he drinks in quick succession. With each glass, I see his face transform and become increasingly drawn and pale. He seems to be calming down, in his speech and in the puffs of smoke he blows toward the sky when he goes out to light a cigarette on the terrace. His expression is completely serene, that of someone who knows they're about to enter familiar, if dangerous, territory. He seems younger, terribly young.

Earlier, after returning from Pavel's village, he and Katya had a harsh argument in the van, probably linked to Pavel's story. Vlad spoke to her in brief, harsh sentences. She was upset and nervous and didn't talk to us, as she normally did after a few drinks, but instead tried to stir things up with Vlad: At times she tried to caress him, other times she tried to kick him from the back seat.

By the time we retire to our rooms, we are again lost and worried, our minds cluttered with questions. What kind of relationship do they have? Vlad told us he's known her for only a few months. I run through a mental list of risks: Katya reporting us to the FSB as revenge; or our continuing the trip with only Vlad, who doesn't have a license to drive outside the Saint Petersburg area. We don't feel safe, but we also don't want to cut the trip short, at least not yet.

THE VOLGA BELL

The next morning, Vlad and Katya wake up late, with swollen red eyes, like in Dubna. But they are both ready to meet the surgeon-priest at the Uglich basin—one of the symbols of Stalin's great leap forward—whose reservoir covers almost one hundred square miles.

We are on time for our appointment in Kalyazin, and Batyushka Ioann is waiting for us in his long cassock and thick beard, sitting on the edge of a fountain in what was once the town's central square and is now its dock. Much of Kalyazin ended up underwater, along with another fifty villages and settlements, some thirty churches, and two seventeenth-century monasteries, in order to create the hydro-canal basin and build huge hydroelectric power plants to feed the Soviet industrial revolution: perhaps the most exorbitant endeavor, in terms of human cost, in the history of modern progress.

Father Ioann is extremely thin, like a marathon runner, and swift: He seems more ready for action than for the altar. A driver is waiting for him in the shade, leaning against his vehicle and watching over the *batyushka* protectively. The procession he mentioned on the phone was canceled because the guest of honor, an important general, couldn't make it. It was going to be a sort of holy regatta dedicated to Saint Nicholas to bless a bell for a new church in Luhansk, in Donbas—which is due to be transported in the next convoy led by Father Ioann. This is just conjecture, since he has no intention of talking about his work as a surgeon-priest in the field. He doesn't ask us any questions or show any curiosity about us whatsoever. At forty years old, he already has nine children, two of whom are disabled. "God has given me this opportunity to save my soul," he explains. "God tests us to make us better. Like this war. It's not a punishment, but our last chance of deliverance. Russians are ready to sacrifice their lives for their brothers."

It's easy to picture him dressed in camouflage and with a muddied beard: This really is an assault priest, someone who doesn't know uncertainty, and we represent his chance to preach to some Westerners who have happened upon him. "The entire world is witnessing the success of our mission," he says, reaching into the fountain to brush his fingers along the surface of the water. "When a small group of people tries to plunge the world into the abyss of sin, vice, and malice, Russia will stand against it and state the opposite—that God created men in the purity of truth and righteousness." He adds, "European culture didn't start to dissolve yesterday. Saint Nicholas of Serbia wrote about it a hundred years ago and even then, he claimed that European culture was over. Russia rejects the shame of sin that runs rampant in your countries."

"Is it a fight between good and evil?" I ask.

"That's exactly it. The final battle. Where evil will feed off its own evil until it succumbs. Even in Apocalypse, John the Apostle spoke of these last days as a terrible test for the human race, when everyone must choose to either stay with God or head for eternal pain and torment."

The situation is complicated. I know Father Ioann has ties to power, to the army and the secret service—he is someone who could easily get us in trouble. I've met many Russian priests: They tend to be curt and diffident with strangers, they won't easily open up without the authority to do so. But Father Ioann has prepared talking points. "Everything that's happening in Ukraine is leading to great pain and suffering. Our country experienced this situation in 1991 with the fall of the Soviet Union. We knew that the next step would be the destruction of Russia. Our fears were confirmed in 2014, with the coup in Kyiv. All right-thinking people know this war was not started by the Ukrainian people. Ukraine is not what is at war with Russia. It's the West."

The bell destined for the new church in Luhansk is to be taken from Saint Nicholas, a seventeenth-century cathedral submerged in the waters of the hydro-canal basin, six hundred feet offshore. Father Ioann says it has a symbolic meaning in the defense of Christianity "in this time of disorder." It's like a rib plucked from the sacred river, a link between the blue of the water and the blue of the sky.

The bell tower pokes out of the water like a sharp two-hundred-foot spear with four tiers, each with arched windows on four sides, so the eye can pass through the tower to the sky on the other side. Unusual architecture for these latitudes and for Orthodox tradition, which is closer to Sicilian Romanesque. The symbolic impact is remarkable, as if the original builders somehow knew this bell tower would be the sole survivor of a Communist flood. The cathedral itself was taken apart in 1939 before the sluices were opened: The bricks were used as levees and the bell tower, reinforced with a cement island that doubles as a dock, became a lighthouse and then a radar station.

I ask Father Ioann what he thinks of this desecration. "In those days, the mystique of big industry dominated," he says. "As it did in the capitalist world, right? In Russia, we knew that industrialization—the state ownership of vast means of production—would create socialism. That ideology played a cruel trick on everything that had been dear to Holy Russia for centuries. But God cannot be erased from the hearts of our people, and when it was time to ask for help, Russians asked God, not Stalin. Now this belfry is the symbol of an unsinkable Russia."

AND THE FLOODGATES BURST

During the second and third *piatiletka*, the Five-Year Plan for national industrialization, the Soviets tried to mark the triumph of socialism over nature with canals and dams on the Volga and inverting the flow of some tributaries.

Boris Pilnyak, a half-Tatar and half-Volgan German (the community imported by Catherine the Great), in his book *The Volga Flows to the Caspian Sea*, writes that "the generation that killed God replaced eternity with courage and the constructive effort of proletarian collectivism." In the novel, a father asks his son, a hydroelectric engineer, if the rivers will really flow in reverse. The engineer responds that "what was before no longer is. This is the true aim of the revolution. The children of the revolution don't drown in hope, they march toward socialism and remake nature."

A new world governed by terror and the laws of science. The state used the labor force from the gulags to build huge hydraulic plants in Uglich, Rybinsk, Saratov, Cheboksary, Togliatti, Stalingrad, and Gorki—which later returned to its former name of Nizhny Novgorod. They also dug canals, such as the one connecting the Volga to Moscow and, in the south, the Volga to the Don, which flows into the Black Sea. The Belomorkanal, between the Volga's northern basin and the White Sea (Arctic Ocean) was one of the most brutal. It took twenty months for 226,000 forced laborers to dig 140 miles by pick and shovel in freezing polar conditions. According to American journalist and historian Anne Applebaum, more than twenty-five thousand workers died. The regime's top brass, including Gorky and Aleksey Tolstoy, arrived in Belomorkanal in August 1933 to extol the accomplishments of the Soviets. Stalin declared that Moscow had become the port of the five seas because, through the Volga basin, it could be reached from the Arctic Ocean and the Caspian, Black, Azov, and Baltic Seas. Thanks to Stalin's slaughterhouses, Putin can now use the Volga to circumvent sanctions, import and export, arm the country, and build an alternative economic bloc with Iran and the other BRICS.

"Men must be pushed forcibly toward history, because everything that is rational is real," wrote Pilnyak. He was an enthusiastic supporter of the *piatiletka*, even though he, too, ended up in a mass grave during the great purges of 1937–38. Along with more than a million others: Accused of spying for Japan and sent to Siberia, he was executed after confessing under torture.

In his 1991 novel *Siberia, Siberia*, Valentin Rasputin illustrated the dangers of the race to the top. It features a similar story to what happened in Uglich on the Volga, but in a town set on the Angara River, in his native Siberia.

There, too, the flood took everything but the village bell tower and there, too, progress overwhelmed everything, ousting the dead from the cemeteries and eradicating all trace of humanity.

A FIGHT TO THE DEATH

The mystique of big industry, as Father Ioann defines it, represented a new civil war. "The days of the capitalists and the kulaks are numbered," Stalin told the Central Committee in April 1929. Within two years, he had set up giant iron and steel plants in Ukraine, the Urals, and Siberia, creating a 40 percent increase in output from the entire czarist industrial era. Plus petrochemical plants, mines, hospitals, and schools. Russia is such a frighteningly large country, taking care of all this was like an act of Creation. In 1927, Russia counted 12,000 cars and trucks while India had 100,000. The Soviets made a deal with Ford to build a massive plant in Nizhny Novgorod and make 150,000 cars per year. Ancient wooden plows and oxen, whose slow progress made them emblematic of traditional Russian indolence, were being replaced by tractors, of which the country had only 457 in 1925, but 3,000 in 1930. This was still too few, which is why state agricultural conglomerates were importing German tractors: Rivers of money were often wasted because without proper maintenance and parts, the tractors broke and were left in the fields to rust. Planning costs rivaled those of a war economy because, then as now, priority went to heavy industry, while consumer goods got peanuts. As Stalin put it, he had to upend a backward and untamed country to rouse the "ancient and dormant Russian energy."

The plan included training 8,000 engineers, 150,000 technicians, and 800,000 qualified workers tasked with increasingly ambitious goals: In 1930, they had to increase industrial production by 25 percent; in 1931, by 45 percent. "We're completing a project that, if successful, will upset the whole world and free the entire working class." Stalin hoped to drum up Russian pride to stamp out resistance. He spoke of the old Russia, which "was constantly being beaten for its backwardness. It was beaten by the Mongol khans, it was beaten by the Turkish bey, it was beaten by the Swedish feudal lords, it was beaten by the Polish-Lithuanians, it was beaten by the Anglo-French capitalists, it was beaten by the Japanese barons, it was beaten by everyone for its inferiority. Military, cultural, industrial, and agricultural inferiority.

It was beaten because there was no risk to challenging it. Remember the words of the revolutionary poet, 'You are miserable and opulent, you are strong and helpless, Mother Russia.' Do you want our socialist homeland to be beaten and lose its independence?" The clash with the capitalist world would be a fight to the death: "We're fifty or a hundred years behind the most developed countries. We must bridge this gap in ten years. We must succeed, or they'll crush us."

As in the days of the smuta of Ivan the Terrible and Peter the Great, the peasants paid the highest price. Many resisted the forced collectivization in the countryside. The kulaks hindered the seizure of grain surpluses, especially in Ukraine, positioning themselves as an enemy that needed to be exterminated. "It's no use dwelling on the expropriation of kulak lands. When they cut your head off, you don't miss your hair," Stalin said. Hell soon broke loose in the countryside, but for Pavel's burlak grandfather, hell was the path to freedom.

6
Among mercenaries

"Now let's take care of the Poles"

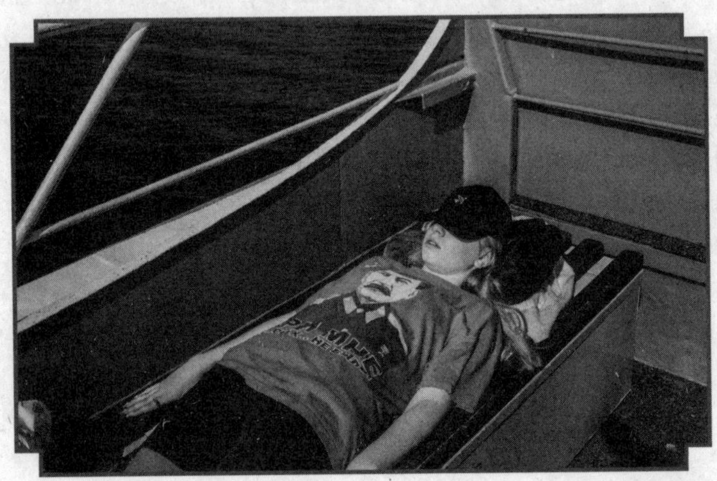

BABY SOLDIERS

We board a boat in Yaroslavl and spend a long day exploring the river. Yaroslavl is a UNESCO jewel brimming with basilicas, monasteries, and citadels, all shiny and clean. Twinkling golden cupolas bear witness to a thousand years of history and a past as a capital, in 1612, when Moscow was occupied by Poles and Russia seemed to be on the brink of extinction. Yaroslavl shows no sign of being on high military alert, yet ordinary urban normality remains equally distressing, because it can be due only to the normalization of the idea of war, which in Putin's Russia is an idea like any other.

The old town is clogged with public works, building restorations, repairs to sidewalks and pipes. Teams of town gardeners are hard at work in the parks and along the beautiful riverwalk alongside dozens of high schoolers, who must contribute to urban improvements for two weeks over vacation. The war is a background noise, like an air-conditioning unit or a boiler; the only visible conflict is etched in the marble monuments that commemorate a long tradition of bloody revolts, the last of which was in August 1918. Then, answering the most tenacious and violent resistance the Bolsheviks ever encountered, Trotsky's Red Army razed the city almost to the ground, bombing it from the river and the sky, annihilating the anti-Bolshevik stronghold on the Volga.

We blend in with some Russian tourists. Cops, including undercover agents, patrol the streets in large numbers—we notice them asking people for papers, especially individuals wandering around alone. Not far from the Church of Elijah the Prophet, one of the few that escaped the bombings and demolitions of the 1930s, we look out over a sports field surrounded by a track. A bare-chested instructor barks orders at forty kids in camouflage, combat boots, black bandannas, and shaved heads who have paired off to fight each other. We take a seat on some steps without getting too close. It looks like a military training session, but what stuns me, aside from the recruits' ages—they must be between fourteen and seventeen—is their inadequacy. They are simulating boxing moves in a very awkward way, punching the air with skeletal arms and bouncing around in jackets a size too large. We wonder who they are: Did they come from juvenile prisons, a penal colony, or some asylum? Or did they go hungry in the villages of Donbas? As in Rzhev, we can't investigate: It's the curse of a semiclandestine trip to one of the most off-limits and dangerous countries in the world for journalists. Even from afar, Ale is able to shoot some videos and snap some fairly close-up pictures as the kids practice in eerie silence. Not once do they look our way. They remind me of prisoners doing forced labor in Angola, the infamous maximum-security prison in Louisiana: Inmates, almost all of them Black, serving life sentences, chained and held at gunpoint by guards on horseback. No one looked up from the turnips they were gathering, no one dared make eye contact with a guard.

We're distracted by the yellow crest of an airborne division and forget to pay attention to the instructor, who is no longer barking orders but seems engrossed in a conversation on his cell phone. "Let's beat it," Vlad hisses. "Move your asses right now." It's strange to see him so alarmed, so frantic: Just a moment ago, videochatting with a friend, he was pretending to be interviewed, with an Eskimo ice cream as a microphone.

We review our plans and decide to leave Yaroslavl separately. Katya goes ahead with the van, while the three of us take a ferry south. We will meet again just after Kostroma, to visit the philosopher Tichomirov V.

It's a good opportunity to finally be *in* the river, and a relief to leave Katya behind.

THE LADY IN THE PANAMA HAT

On this section of the Volga, the boat acts as a Venetian ferry: It stops on both sides of the river, even in deserted places without a port. The gangway is simply extended precariously onto the riverbank, where passengers clamber off with bags, strollers, and backpacks before heading up a little road or dirt path into the woods, an orchard, a sunflower field. A young woman in high heels with a wheeled suitcase is greeted by a young man on a dirt bike parked among the birch trees. Mooring can be complicated by the waves, and passengers sometimes have to cling to the gangway to avoid toppling into the water. But everything goes smoothly, without anxiety or curses. We are delighted by these diversions: We're expecting someone to end up in the river, but even if they did, they'd probably chalk it up to bad luck, like slipping on ice or scraping an elbow.

The Volga here is several miles wide and rather busy—barges, several hundred feet in length, line up one by one. Aside from those transporting coal, scrap metal, or grain, most are covered in tarps, probably to cover military equipment or material imported illegally to circumvent sanctions. Tugboats, tankers, and cruise ships sail by—some come so close to us we can see the passengers dancing and drinking on deck.

No recreational or fishing vessels in sight—private navigation has been suspended.

The sound of the boat's engines muffles our voices, so we talk freely among ourselves. Other passengers include elderly people, families, and schoolgirls, but one woman in particular stands out. She's sitting alone at the stern, in a short sheath dress, a tobacco-colored Panama hat, Gucci sunglasses, and Capri sandals. She seems to be listening to music through her headphones, gracefully keeping time by tapping her fingers on the railing, but maybe she's just eager to arrive at her destination. We send Vlad to break the ice—he tells her we're tourists.

Her name is Tatiana, and she looks much younger than her fifty years. She speaks English well and seems to hardly believe we're here. "I'm overjoyed," she exclaims, beaming. "I'm tired of being among only Russians. We've run out of trivial things to talk about to avoid talking about what we really want to talk about. I haven't seen foreigners since the start of the war." Tatiana runs a chain of grocery stores around Yaroslavl and is heading south, to the same dacha where she spent her summers as a girl. "My boat has been docked in Mykonos for three years. I wonder if I'll ever see it again," she says, showing me a photo of herself on a forty-five-foot Beneteau. She's pictured topless, with the same Panama hat, engrossed in a book. "The West doesn't want us anymore. But I'm getting to know my river again," she says in a slightly amused tone. "I'm running into friends I haven't seen in thirty years, people who come from all sorts of backgrounds. Everything feels a bit unreal, but also carefree. An interesting vacation. I brought wine and meat for tonight. We're having a party."

We're at the confluence of the Tunoshonka River, and Tatiana tells us of the great tragedy of Lokomotiv Yaroslavl in 2011, when a plane carrying the city's entire hockey team crashed shortly after taking off for Minsk. All fifty-five passengers died—Tatiana knew some of those kids. There were a hundred thousand people at the funeral in Yaroslavl and Prime Minister Putin, a great hockey fan, even cried. "I think that was the first time we ever saw him moved," Tatiana says. "He didn't even flinch in 2000, after the Kursk submarine sank and 118 sailors died like rats."

Tatiana now looks dejected: Despite her initial euphoria, our meeting seems to have upset her. I ask if she's thinking about the war, of how quickly everything has changed. "Russians have been sad and resigned for a thousand years. It's how we stay resilient," she says, smiling almost mischievously. "I'm against this fratricidal and self-destructive war, but there's nothing I can do but wait, like everyone else. You saw how they've flooded Yaroslavl with Russian flags, patriotic manifestos. It's because they know it's not a passive and aligned city like the others. They've arrested a lot of people there. They manipulate us with artificial ideas. Garbage. But the West has been humiliating us for too long. Don't we have the right to be whoever we want without having to feel like barbarians? I'm not religious or married. My friends are not religious and few of them are married. I steer clear of the priests, but I can assure you that on the matter of gender identity, for example, or overcoming biological sex, as you call it, we're all 99 percent in agreement: We'll never accept it. It's not a matter of propaganda or bigotry. The culture is incompatible with ours. Russians remain true to biology," she says with the scornful smile of someone who has no doubt that they are right.

Two girls are sitting at the stern with us, on the opposite bench. We haven't given them much thought, engrossed as we are in our conversation with Tatiana. But we notice that the girl lying in the sun is wearing a red T-shirt bearing Stalin's face. We wonder how we missed it—it's the kind of thing that stands out. "She just put it on, I saw her go change," Tatiana says. "She wanted to shock the Westerners. She must have been listening to us." We see the girl make furtive glances in our direction under her baseball cap, which partly obscures her heavily made-up face, satisfied that her punch has landed. "You'll see plenty of those T-shirts. They're trendy with the kids this summer. They always come with a Stalin quote, like, 'If I were here, there wouldn't be all this shit going around.' It's scary. My nieces' and nephews' history books don't even mention Stalin's crimes. And our family knows a thing or two about those."

Tatiana doesn't want to tell us about them, because we're almost at her stop, a small dock nestled between the silver river and a yellow sea of sunflowers. Before bidding us goodbye, Tatiana takes off her sunglasses as if she were doffing a hat, leaving us with an unexpected flash of intense dark eyes.

As we proceed south, we notice that the green wall of trees lining the river is becoming increasingly sparse. I look over the railing and past the villages, imagining that beyond the horizon, east of the endless plains, lie the terrifying Asian steppes.

Meanwhile, the ceaseless current drags us onward.

BRISTLY PONIES

The Volga saw the birth of Russia. It watched it suffer and grow for more than a thousand years, silent witness to unspeakable violence. It has flowed past bands of warriors, massacres, vengeance, lands conquered and governed by terror. Few places on earth have undergone so much pressure: The Volga, like a fault line of history between two continents, is a slow, grueling tectonic shift of peoples. Events that have unfolded along these shores still emit an oppressive energy that hangs in the air, in the water, in the memories of the people—ready to explode again.

"They are the most lurid and primitive pagans I've ever met," wrote Persian philosopher and explorer Ahmad ibn Fadlan shortly before the year 1000. "They drink like demons, don't bathe after defecating, and have sex with slave women while their wives watch."

He was talking about the people of the Rus of Kyiv, the future rulers of Russia. He'd sailed up the Volga on behalf of the caliph of Baghdad. He was part geographer, part spy. Back then, the Volga was still known as the River Idel, but it was already the main trade artery between north and south: honey, wine, hides, spices, slaves, weapons, silver coins. During his trip, ibn Fadlan explored the realm of the Khazars, who ruled a land that stretched from the central region of the Volga to the Caucasus. Present-day Kazan was a crossroads of caravans coming from China and Persia and inhabited by people who spoke Turkoman. Their society was religiously tolerant, with many elites ascribing to Judaism imported from the Levant. It is believed that the Khazar refugees who headed west after the fall of this empire were the ancestors of the Ashkenazim. The other regional power on the Volga was the kingdom of the Bulgarians, Islamic Turkish tribes of ancient Scythian descent. They were merchants who traded between the Baltic and the Caspian, middlemen for all types of merchandise—mammoth tusks, wheat, wax, falcons—coming from Europe, Siberia, Asia, or the Middle East. In the tenth century, the Bulgarians turned the Volga into the biggest commercial hub between Europe and Asia.

The "primitive" Rus of Kyiv were the last to settle between Ukraine and the Novgorod region in the northeast, but they were already the talk of the town. Ibn Fadlan noted their reputation as ruthless warriors when he said, "They're not done until the last enemy has been massacred." They fought the Khazars for control of the Volga, and in 969, they leveled the old capital on the river delta and adopted present-day Astrakhan as their new capital.

But soon, new and old societies vying for supremacy over this slice of earth discovered that their greatest enemy would come from very far away. Straight from hell, according to a Russian reporter of the time, a devout Orthodox Christian: "Because of our sins, pagan strangers arrived that summer. We call them Tatars, and nobody knows whence they came or who they worship. Only God knows that, and maybe some wise man who learned it from a book."

In those days, Tatars, more widely known as Mongols, were seen by the Slavic people of the East as demons, children of Satan. In the summer of 1223, the Mongols descended on the Slavs, emerging from the great nothing of the steppes and raising clouds of dust with their bristly ponies. Twenty years later, they crushed the Rus of Kyiv, and for almost three centuries the only remaining Russian powers—the Northeast, Novgorod, Tver', Moscow—continued to pay taxes to the Mongol rulers and their khanates on the middle to lower Volga.

To survive, the Russians drew inspiration from the despotic tactics Genghis Khan used to rule the Golden Horde, the name given to the western part of the Mongol Empire. Even though naughty children still see the Mongols as their bogeymen, many Russians—and foreigners who psychoanalyze Russian history—believe that Mongol domination left indelible traces in their psyches: an Eastern heritage branded in their characters, destined to loom over events through the centuries, from despot to despot. Which brings us to Putin, who now threatens to unleash his atomic warheads like the bristly ponies of the Mongol horde.

We're talking about the most formidable war machine in the history of humanity. It took two centuries for the Mongols to expand their empire from China to the Sea of Japan, India, Myanmar, Vietnam, Europe, Persia, the Caucasus, and the Levant. No civilization has ever conquered so much, although the Mongols' objective was not to occupy but to pillage, extort, and trade. Wherever they ruled, traders could travel safely from Europe to the Pacific, availing themselves of services like efficient postal systems and Chinese scientists and surgeons. There have been more than a few scholars—such as Edward Gibbon in the eighteenth century—who have believed in the need to revise our unflattering views of this chapter in history. Unlike modern Russian generals and their willingness to sacrifice many lives on the battlefield, Mongol leaders were haunted by losses, making them precursors of the Powell Doctrine, which prioritizes minimizing American deaths. But if the enemy didn't surrender at the first dark rumble of the Mongol cavalry, or if it turned out to be annoyingly tenacious, the Mongols would erase cities and villages from the face of the earth, leaving behind smoldering ruins and shredded bodies: what we now call the "Grozny model" as applied by Putin in Aleppo, Mariupol, and the rest of eastern Ukraine.

The Cuman nomads from Crimea were the first to fall under Mongol rule. They warned the Rus of Kyiv, their worst enemies, using the same argument Ukrainian president Volodymyr Zelensky used when alerting Europe to the Russian peril: "These barbarians are trying to take our land, and tomorrow they will take yours if you don't support us." But the Rus, arrogant as ever, paid no heed: They killed the Mongol ambassadors when they arrived to propose neutrality with Moscow. The first battle took place in 1223 on the Kalka River, present-day Donets:

All twelve Russian princes were massacred and only one in ten soldiers returned home. This little training match helped prepare the Mongols for their main objective: the conquest of Europe. They pulled back to regroup and returned ten years later with 140,000 men. They wiped out the Volga's Bulgarian civilization forever, then made their way up the river until the Rus of the Northeast were entirely under their thumb. They attacked in winter, when the freeze was their strongest ally: Accustomed to blizzards, their ponies crossed frozen rivers and swamps at a gallop. Napoleon and Hitler must have been unaware of the adage "Never attack Russia if your name is not Genghis Khan." The Mongols sacked Moscow in 1238 and practically leveled Kyiv in 1242. It had been one of the most developed and beautiful cities in Europe, but when the pope's envoy arrived six years later to meet the Mongol khan, he found it in ruins. "Skulls and bones blend in with the stones," he wrote.

Kyiv ended up outside the Russian world and under the control of the Turks, Hungarians, Poles, and Lithuanians. For Russia, that was the moment of great fracture, when it uncoupled from Europe and began its geographic and existential unmooring.

After the Volga, the Mongols took the Don and the Dnepr. Batu Khan, grandson of Genghis Khan, tested the mettle of the Polish, Hungarian, and German forces but then, for reasons that are still debated, the Mongols spared Europe and returned to Asia. But Batu Khan stayed behind. Lands under Mongol control gradually shifted from shamanism to Islam, and authorities began to tax subjugated principalities. Those who rebelled were tamed with iron and fire, as in Yaroslavl in 1262, when Mongol khans repressed an uprising by killing anyone who looked Muslim, and in Moscow, when they massacred thirty thousand people in a city of just fifty thousand.

Rus cities bled out and became poorer and poorer, but they didn't cease to exist: Their identity was bolstered by Orthodox language and ideological strength. The church and its bishops became increasingly political, replacing a secular power weakened by Mongol retaliation or by fearful and corrupt regents. The patriarchate thus took up their scepters for the preservation of the nation.

The khans continued to harass the Russians with the threat of extinction. They had come to dominate trade among Asia, the Middle East, and Europe, establishing their Silk Road hub in Sarai, present-day Astrakhan, on the Volga Delta. It was a Mongol city, but an international one: In the fourteenth century, Sarai boasted a population of almost one hundred thousand. Moroccan explorer Ibn Battuta described it as a cosmopolitan center of paved streets, beautiful mosques, madrassas, caravansaries, Orthodox bishoprics, and Armenian, German, and English trade companies—a frenetic mosaic of cultures and nationalities, each with its own neighborhood and stock exchange to negotiate the price of salt, fabric, silver, and caviar.

Often hostage to the boyars—feudal lords and large landowners seen as secular obstacles to the emancipation of Russian society—Russian princes fought among themselves. Some obtained a degree of autonomy and privilege from the khans by submitting to humiliating servitude. As the Mongols guarded the eastern and southern borders from incursions by nomadic tribes, the princes and boyars had to contend with Polish pressure, predatory Lithuanian campaigns, the growing power of the Swedes, and the aggressive and bigoted Teutonic Knights.

Alexander Nevsky, prince of Novgorod and Vladimir, led the legendary ambush on the Neva River, where he routed the Swedish invasion of 1240. Two years later, he became a venerated hero (as well as the future patron saint of the military and secret police) when he beat the Catholic Teutonic Knights, the so-called Northern Crusaders, in the Battle on the Ice, the first clash between Orthodox Russia and the Catholic West. Nevsky established a strong alliance with the Mongols, who were called to restore order to Novgorod and guarantee the prince's rule over the kingdom of Muscovy, the embryo of the future Romanov empire.

But the warriors of the steppes had softened over time, and the thirst for blood from the days of Batu Khan had dissipated. They were decimated by the plague as it traveled down the Volga on trading ships. The intercontinental corridor of the Silk Road began to break apart under the constant threat of raids from Tamerlane, the great emir of central Asia. The ambitions of glory of the frightening Mongols had dissolved, generation after generation, into the temperament of the Russian population, the only people left to put up a fight. The decisive moment came at the Battle of Kulikovo, on the Don, on September 8, 1380. The Russian army was inferior, but better organized and more disciplined than the troops cobbled together by Mamai, the last khan of Sarai. The prince of Moscow, Dimitry, won the clash and became Donskoy, the hero of the Don, a new icon in the nationalist pantheon.

But the battle for sovereignty was not over yet. It took another century for Russia to emerge from Mongol rule, when Ivan III, or Ivan the Great, finally refused to pay taxes once and for all. In true khan-style despotism, he forced other Russian princes to pay Moscow the taxes they had previously given to the Mongols. It marked the start of a system of domination within the Russian world: Moscow used the revenue to expand, form a great army, and establish collective taxation in the villages, a system the Bolsheviks were still using in the twentieth century. Ivan III became the great unifier of Russian lands, quadrupling the expansion of Moscow, crushing rebellions, exterminating entire boyar families, deporting dissidents. He reigned for forty-three years, longer than Stalin and Putin—even though the latter seems determined

to set a new record. He also transformed the Kremlin from a spartan fortress into a regal palace, proclaiming himself czar, from "caesar," as a way to put the past aside and launch a Russian state, the Third Rome, as a new player on the stage of history.

THE PLAGUE-RIDDEN PATRIOT

Did the Mongols really leave such an indelible mark? Can those 250 years of occupation explain regimes of terror, brutal repressions, Moscow's autocracy, and the arrogance of Putin's neo-imperial comeback?

I ask Tichomirov V., a former philosophy professor, who welcomes us to his rundown studio on the outskirts of Kostroma, where he lives in the company of five thousand books and a blind cat. He introduces himself as plague-ridden, meaning he ascribes to the "Turgenev party" and is a Western sympathizer like novelist Ivan Turgenev, who openly opposed Dostoyevsky's Slavic nationalism. Tichomirov is the first to talk to me about Putin's turn to the East. "They call me a traitor because I'm claiming my place in European civilization," he says. "But I'm a true patriot. I don't want Russia to end up swallowed by this *Russkiy mir* nonsense. It's as artificial as the idea of the 'mysterious Russian soul' that has so fascinated you Westerners. Mystery has been used to legitimize cruelty, the annihilation of the individual, the cult of the despot. Even the West has mythologized Communism using the same notion that fuels Russian ideological fervor: the willingness to give one's life for an absolute cause, the collective instinct to burn it all down. If Putin and his court start to appear weak, we will burn for a century. Russia will either live as Russia or die as Russia—there is no middle ground."

The remains of smoked fish lie on the table next to a manuscript on the curse of the steppe. "I write for myself, because I don't have the strength to be a hero," Tichomirov says, giving me a vague, watery look. "The priests push us to the brink," he claims. "In church they worship Alexander Nevsky, who chose the Mongol horde over compromising with the Catholic Antichrist. The Mongols didn't interfere in religious affairs, so they were seen as more acceptable than the Germans or

Poles." He believes it was inevitable that the traumatic Mongol occupation would lead Russians to use myths to explain who they are and where they come from. Mongol rule has often been used to explain old behaviors, shortcomings, and voids never filled by the West. There's a word, *aziatčina*, or "Asianism"—he tells me—that suggests incivility, cultural backwardness, cruelty. It's a pejorative term that Yasha, the servant in Chekhov's *The Cherry Orchard*, uses to describe workers in the countryside.

Liberation from Mongol rule in the Battle of Kulikovo was for centuries seen as the inception of an independent and unified Russia. Kulikovo became a symbol of Russian nationalism even before the fall of the USSR: The six hundredth anniversary of the battle was celebrated throughout 1980, when the Communist Party wanted to foment Russian patriotic spirit against Solidarność trade union threats from Poland and in support of the Red Army struggling in Afghanistan. That year saw the publication of 150 books on Kulikovo, including one by Lev Gumilev, who elevated the Russian super-ethnos of nomadic peoples of the steppe compared to Western democratic civilization. But Gumilev, now a reference for Putin and Dugin, didn't see Kulikovo as a battle between Russians and Mongols but as a civil war within the Mongol Empire, because commander Tokhtamysh Khan, rival to the defeated Mamai Khan, was on Moscow's side. "Kulikovo wasn't a clash with the Mongol horde, but against Mamai's Golden Horde, which was bankrolled by the Catholics—especially Genovese merchants—and had deployed Lithuanian and Polish troops," Gumilev wrote in 1980. A common refrain since the time of the Romanovs was that Russia had saved an ungrateful Europe from the Mongol invasion. But Gumilev's anti-Western nationalism, which is popular in the Kremlin today, and which Beijing probably doesn't mind either, holds that Russia survived a religious and capitalist European aggression thanks to the Mongols. "Genghis Khan over NATO," Tichomirov says sarcastically, picking at his herring with the same hand that holds his cigarette.

POSTCARDS FROM VIŠEGRAD

The only accommodation available in Kostroma is a hotel on the edge of the park. It's a strange park, surrounded by semi-abandoned buildings from the early Soviet era. Art deco pavilions emerge from the linden trees along with a dilapidated open-air theater and neoclassical statues, all brutally mutilated and suffocated by the ivy. It's the perfect landscape for a photographer, and Ale uses the last opaline light of the evening to hunt for decapitated statues. Despite everything else in town being fully booked, we're the only guests at this newly updated hotel. But it's quiet here—we're in a city, but it's like being in the middle of a forest, amid the trill of the goldfinches. We will spend only one night here before leaving early the next morning for Nizhny Novgorod.

As we're about to head off to find a restaurant in town, loud music emerges from an adjacent building: It sounds like rehearsals for a concert, and a strong male voice starts singing into a microphone. We peek into an internal courtyard where a few tables have been covered with red-and-white linens. The singer is standing on a small stage in a corner of the courtyard by a disused fountain, the cherub covered in yellowish moss and surrounded by empty beer cans. There's no one else here yet—it's obviously early. But Katya doesn't mind: She positions herself in front of the singer and starts to sway, snapping her fingers, eyes closed, hair over her face, still damp from the shower. She looks younger in a silk yellow top. She's also been driving all day, so she hasn't been able to drink. "It's a love song—actually, a war song. I mean, stuff to make you cry," Vlad says dismissively. A good smell wafts out of the kitchen and we decide to grab a table. We can go to bed early and leave at dawn the next day. We order a few beers and Katya receives hers in a margarita glass, with a straw. "We treat women like women in Kostroma!" the singer exclaims. His name is Artur, he's sixty-five, tall and slender with a chiseled physique. He's dressed in black and his hair is dyed black too, with purplish reflections that shine under the spotlight. He roots for the Red Star Belgrade soccer team—I notice the sticker on his amp, and he confirms it's a passion he's had since his youth, when he was in Višegrad, Bosnia, in the '90s.

I don't share my memories of Višegrad with him, but I know what he's talking about. I was there around the same time he was, reporting on the massacre the Serbs had carried out in the Drina valley, site of a mass grave for thousands of Bosnian Muslims, most of them civilians. We had heard rumors of Russian volunteers, but we didn't know, until later, that there had been three thousand of them, fighting on the border with Serbia. On a hill near Višegrad, a few years ago, Bosnian Serbs erected a large cross to celebrate fallen Russian Orthodox combatants. They showed even more loyalty when thousands of Bosnian Serbs volunteered to support Russia in Donbas.

In Bosnia, the Russians fought with the Tigers, a Serbian paramilitary unit responsible for some of the worst crimes of the war. Their leader, Arkan, had been the ringleader of a group of soccer hooligans rooting for the Red Star Belgrade: His responsibilities had evolved from whipping up die-hard soccer fans to massacring entire villages in eastern Bosnia. Given that these were the people Artur supported, we steer clear of details. But he doesn't seem reticent at all: He tells us about how he fought in the hills of Sarajevo and is thrilled to share the photo albums he painstakingly archived in his phone. He also has photos from Chechnya and Dagestan, where Artur appears in his guerrilla gear: macho-man pics in his Cossack mustache, bodies lying in the streets behind him. He belonged to the SOBR, a rapid-response unit in the national guard also used in the dirtiest operations of the past twenty years, mostly by the FSB. SOBR is suspected of carrying out a spate of strange terror attacks attributed to Chechens in the first years of Putin's rule: probably false flag operations to legitimize the use of force and make Putin look like an uncompromising new leader sent by providence to end years of chaos.

Artur lives off his veteran pension and karaoke nights. But tonight is special—it's a reunion of sorts. Artur's son is also a former SOBR who worked in Syria and Ukraine, where he was injured in an ambush near Irpin. It was one of the first and most resounding failures of the Russian army: The SOBR company ended up isolated and without ammo. Few survived. After that episode, Artur's son immediately switched to the Wagner Group, "out of anger toward the high command," according to Artur. "But now he's back. Almost everyone left after the mess Prigozhin made. He's waiting to see how things turn out. He said he'd be here tonight, but I'm not sure. He's not so well in the head."

Suddenly, we're no longer alone. Some off-road vehicles have arrived. The rest of the tables in the courtyard are now occupied by men between the ages of thirty and forty, all bearded, thick like Molossians of the Caucasus—they're Wagner mercenaries. Two waitresses run back and forth to the kitchen, supplying the men with a constant stream of soup, meat, vodka, and beer. The men attack their quarry with hands and teeth, downing frightening amounts of food and alcohol. Their collective slurp is so loud it's as if it were coming from Artur's amps. The hotel manager has joined them, and within half an hour, the evening has descended into a mad vortex of loud music, cheers, shouts, songs, and stomping that make the courtyard pillars shake.

Katya has been sucked into the turbine by the magnetic force of the mercenaries, especially the youngest, with the largest stomach—his nom de guerre is Ezzor. They look thick as thieves, as if they've known each other for years. Katya places a hand on Ezzor's and he pulls her in close. He's the only one who seems to take notice of us—he orders a rapid fire of drinks for us. Vlad seems increasingly uncomfortable—his drinks go untouched. I can't tell if he's ashamed, contemptuous, or jealous: He has put on a stoic front and won't let anyone in. Meanwhile, Artur, microphone in hand, divides his time between the Wagner front and our table. His boy's not coming, he says, he's sorry to disappoint us, but he suggests setting up a meeting for the following day, to which we agree, despite our previous intention to leave early. He then intones what sounds like an anthem to Kostroma:

> Beautiful and proud Kostroma
> where those who disagree with you are wrong
> even the Polish enemy got lost in Kostroma.

What do the Poles have to do with anything? But Artur has already moved on to Katya and her warrior. They have confiscated Artur's microphone and are singing cheek to cheek. A song by Katya Lel, I learn, a pop star from the early 2000s who used to sing in Chechnya to support troop morale. She is a favorite of Prigozhin, according to Artur, who makes a lewd gesture that alludes to a physical relationship. Two mercenaries listen enraptured, standing with their arms over each other's shoulders, gently swaying.

By now, I've become inured to the threatening absurdity of the situation: These moments of great intensity seem memorable, so I start to document them with my phone. I, too, end up in the vortex, subsumed into Wagner territory. When I turn back toward our table, Vlad and Ale are gone. I get a message from Ale a moment later: "We're at the hotel. Vlad asked me to go with him. He's so pissed off it's scary. It looked like she was ignoring him on purpose, didn't it? Maybe he's jealous? I have no fucking clue. Watch out. Who knows what she said about us. Shouldn't you come up?"

SUSANIN THE LUMBERJACK

But just then, Ezzor hugs me. He's strong enough to crush me like a mouse, but he says we're brothers and assures me that foreigners have nothing to fear in Russia. That our trip will proceed without issues. It's a different story with the Poles—it's time to even the score with them, he says.

We communicate via automatic translator: Bent over our phones, we speak in turns and then read. This helps us focus on the words without straying from the topic at hand, especially given the circumstances. Despite all the drink, Ezzor is lucid and tells me about Ivan Susanin, the lumberjack hero of Kostroma, when the Poles ruled Moscow at the beginning of the seventeenth century, in the darkest days of the *smuta*. Russia was practically done for, but Susanin quickly chased out the invader and rebooted the empire. The resistance started right here, in this section of the Volga. Kuzma Minin, a merchant from Nizhny Novgorod, recruited a battalion of mercenaries and kicked out the Poles, who burned the capital to the ground as they left. The most plausible candidate for czar was sixteen-year-old Michael Romanov, a distant relative to the last reigning dynasty. He'd been hidden away in the Ipatiev Monastery, near Kostroma, with his mother. A contingent of Polish militants came to eliminate him. Unable to find the monastery, they asked a passing lumberjack for directions. That lumberjack was Susanin, who offered to show them a shortcut. But he led them into a fatal trap—a spot where the forest was so dense they could no longer find their way out. Susanin was tortured to death, but did not collaborate. And Michael was able to reign for thirty-two years, founding the Romanov dynasty.

Ezzor tells me that their company is named after Susanin. "We're all SOBR veterans. We've known each other for a long time. We're waiting to see what happens, then jump back into the fray. We'll bring Ukraine home and then we'll settle the score with the Poles once and for all," he guarantees.

In January 2022, shortly before the invasion, a delegation of entrepreneurs from Warsaw came to Kostroma—or so Ezzor tells me. They were ferried around the city, but the guide did not bring them to the monument to Susanin, erected by the Bolsheviks in the center of the city. So when the Poles caught sight of it, they wanted to know who it was. "He was in charge of the first Polish delegation to Kostroma," their guide said. We laugh, and I feel a pat on the back that takes my breath away. Katya is now sitting at the console with Artur, singing something requested by the mercenaries. Ezzor wants me to know that Russia was saved by people like him, soldiers of fortune from the Volga. "We have internalized the lesson of the smuta: It's no coincidence that Putin mentioned it after what happened with Prigozhin. And he's right. If Russians are not united, we'll end up being humiliated, defeated, and occupied, maybe by the fucking Poles, like after Ivan the Terrible. And to keep Russia united, we need the Volga to be united. And we need our spines," he says, landing another heavy pat on my back.

IVAN IV THE COMPASSIONATE

Ivan IV, known as Ivan the Terrible, was obsessed with the Volga becoming the artery of his empire. Before him, Moscow had controlled it only up to Nizhny Novgorod. Under him, in the sixteenth century, the entire Volga became Russian. Kazan and Astrakhan fell after a series of wars that included the destruction of all mosques and conversion to Christianity. A process of assimilation was forced upon ethnic groups living along the river. Ivan IV built fortifications around the new colonies that followed Islam or traditional shamanism: Kremlins and Orthodox churches had to appear monolithic, in deliberate and ideological architectural uniformity. He formed mercenary companies known as the *streltsy*, royal guards not unlike the French musketeers or the Ottoman janissaries—highly paid special units deployed to garrisons in subjugated territories (they were replaced by the Cossacks under Peter the Great, who transferred them from the Don to the Volga). But the most reliable watchmen turned out to be the monasteries, which the czar compensated with land and funds. Entire districts, dozens of villages and their inhabitants, became the property of the *vladika*, the bishop-monks, who governed people, crops, Volga fishing, and the salt trade along the river.

Sergei Eisenstein's *Ivan the Terrible: The Boyars' Plot*, featured Nikolay Cherkasov as Ivan IV. In a striking scene in the second part of the trilogy, the Ivan character, chin held high, long pointy beard thrust toward the sky to challenge fate, bursts into the throne room. A long close-up ensues, constructed to the smallest detail, as in all of Eisenstein's films. It is a brilliant depiction of the man who guided Muscovy with a brutal hand, bent the Orthodox Church to his will, fought the feudal lords, created an absolute monarchy, and adopted the double-headed eagle, symbol of the new Rome, heir to Constantinople, which at the time was in the hands of a Turkish sultan.

In the translation that favors the brutal side of the character, Ivan IV is known as Grozny, the Terrible. But for many, including Tichomirov, the philosopher from Kostroma, "it is best translated in less negative terms, like Turbulent, Furious, or Threatening. The population may have feared him, but it also adored him for ousting the despised slave-owning tax barons."

But Ivan was also a paranoid sadist. As a child, he tortured dogs, cats, and birds, before moving on to torturing and raping his peers. His youth had been deprived of joy: Crowned at only fourteen years old, alone—his father and mother had both been killed in a palace plot—he was at the mercy of two powerful courtiers. One wanted to see him bend to the Teutonic Knights, and the other to the Hanseatic League, which controlled trafficking routes in the Baltic. Ivan soon had his boyar regents slaughtered by his faithful mercenaries. "He might have been one of the most complex characters in Russian history," Tichomirov told me, as I sat in his book-lined studio. "Able to effortlessly combine blood with holy water in an obsessive and superstitious religiosity: Those who disagreed with him would be arrested and tortured before morning prayers were over. He had no doubt that God approved of his violent acts and even encouraged them. But Ivan also loved and understood Russia more than any other czar. He ruled for the people and not for power."

Gifted with a savage intuition for plots against him, Ivan IV behaved erratically. On December 3, 1564, he left Moscow with his family and servants for the village of Alexandrov, coat of arms and court treasures in tow. On January 3, 1565, he sent Bishop Atanasio a letter in which he denounced the boyars for criminally degrading the country, indicating an intention to abdicate—a desperate but clever move to challenge the overwhelming power of the boyars. He then ordered his henchmen to read two of his proclamations in the streets of the capital: One where he accused the nobility of mistreating the people and announcing his departure from power; another where he denied his rejection of the crown and stated that it had been just a threat, or a test. Confused, a delegation of boyars (who feared accusations of treachery), merchants, and bishops went to Alexandrov, asking the czar to return to power. "It was a bogus exile and a coup against his own state: tactics Kremlinologists have been studying for centuries, including under Stalin, Gorbachev, and Putin, who knows how to disappear and reappear to weed out perceived enemies. Yesterday the boyars, now the oligarchs."

When Ivan returned to Moscow, he was a different person. He had deep wrinkles, a threatening gaze, sunken, ghostly eyes: He had become Ivan the Terrible. In Eisenstein's film, his return is epic and his revenge on the boyars is lucid and implacable. "Here I am—what, you weren't expecting me? I name you all governors. Take the land you want. I've been widowed, so I get the widower quota, the borderlands."

This split the realm in two, between the feudal nobility and the *oprichnina*, "my part," where the czar had absolute power. He unleashed terror through the political police and his personal army, the *oprichniki*, a caste of killers who executed blacklisted people. Ivan's henchmen roamed the countryside on black horses, dressed in black and wearing the emblem of a dog's head with a broom, a representation of their mission: sniff out and sweep away the prey. They executed generals, their families, and their clans. All relatives suspected of plotting against the throne were eliminated. As were any nonaligned members of the church.

"Ivan IV was a master of evil for the good of the people, but also a master of geopolitics," Tichomirov explained. Ivan turned a group of loosely connected medieval states into the foundations of a modern empire that stretched from the Baltic to the Black Sea and the Pacific. Ivan's expansionism was physiological, dictated by fear: Mongol invasions and the aggressive ascension of the Polish-Lithuanian Empire had shown him how a lack of natural land barriers exposed Russia to external threats. Since then, Russian leaders have upheld the idea that Russia must dominate its borderlands to survive.

Ivan Grozny could also be enlightened and progressive. While Muscovy's economy was based on agriculture, the czar opened new frontiers for commercial development. He built the port of Arkhangelsk in the western Arctic to reach northern European markets and bypass Baltic routes, which were complicated by unfriendly relations with Lithuanians and Poles. He used customs taxes to strengthen the military, fund the church, and build Saint Basil's Cathedral in Moscow to celebrate the conquest of Kazan and Astrakhan.

But Russian power was about to be dealt a nasty reputational blow. Ivan Grozny's purges did not spare any important centers. In 1570, it was the turn of Novgorod, the most ancient, Western-leaning, and politically developed city in the realm. "I think Russia would have been fully integrated into Europe and experienced social and democratic progress had Muscovy adopted the Novgorod model," said Tichomirov, who identifies as "a hopeless old liberal." But Ivan hated Novgorod more than anything. He suspected its boyars of being aligned with Polish and Baltic Catholics. He ordered the *oprichniki* to eliminate anyone who breathed—he wanted to erase Novgorod. Ivan demanded a list of their victims so he could order the priests to celebrate requiem masses for them. The figures of the bloodbath vary, depending on the source, between fifteen thousand and thirty-five thousand dead. Then Ivan changed course and turned on his henchmen. About one hundred *oprichniki* were tortured and killed in the Red Square, some with their wives and children. Ivan participated in the slaughter: After four hours, soaked in blood and exhausted, he walked into Saint Basil's to kiss the icons and pray. Pushkin's verses render the horrific moment Ivan returns to the scene of the crime, in the moonlight.

"Was he a psychopath? Perhaps. He had the traits, for whoever wants to reduce Russian history to a crime novel. But his legacy does not coincide with his biography. The extermination of the landowning nobility allowed Ivan to usher Russia into a new era, not yet modern, but no longer medieval. It was a war of liberation that marked a new beginning," Tichomirov pointed out. Ivan's absolute power determined the destiny of the people of the land in between: It didn't guarantee peace, but it created the conditions of possibility for a new world between Europe and Asia. Ivan turned out to be tolerant toward non-Christian communities and allowed them a modicum of religious and cultural freedom. The Muslim Tatars, for instance, could be members of the court and hold high-ranking military positions. Meanwhile, something big was happening in the Far East: The colonization of Siberia was almost as historically important as the westward expansion in America. Siberia changed the geography of the empire and the very idea of Russianness. It made Russia not only vast—the vastest country in the world—but also extremely rich in natural resources: The region became the personal vault of the czars, and today it is the credit card Putin uses to finance his war economy and fuel the creation of a world bloc opposed to Washington and Brussels.

Siberia shifted Russia's center of gravity east. "Siberia magnified the Russian ego," Tichomirov said. "Eastward expansion triggered the sense of grandeur that has always driven Russia to want more land. But it also raised fears that all that vastness would be its undoing."

Expansion into Siberia magnified Russia's poetic imagination, but that land of savage freedom turned out to be its opposite: a cage of ice, the land of the gulag, paradigm of repression and inhuman torment. From an economic standpoint, it ended up becoming a true Eldorado, full of iron, gold, copper, oil, gas, and rare minerals. And was therefore a curse. As Siberia filled state coffers, it also inhibited the development of a modern economy and encouraged social apathy and autocracy.

Ivan IV's forty years in power upended Russia forever. As his regime came to an end, and the country slipped into chaos, Ivan spilled his own blood: He first beat up his pregnant daughter-in-law for having worn indecorous clothing, causing a miscarriage; then, in a fit of rage, he killed his beloved son, Ivan Ivanovich, with the steel tip of his staff. Overcome with fury, he ran through the hallways of the imperial palace, banging his head against the walls, screaming that he could no longer be the czar of all of Russia.

Yet the people seemed to disagree. In fables, which mirrored popular sentiment, he was the good czar: Ivan the Compassionate, the friend of the people, who hated the extortionist boyars; ally and protector of the oppressed against the common enemy—the slave-owning, famine-causing nobles. He was the emblem of the class war.

Stalin saw himself as Ivan's natural heir, according to Oxford don Robert Service's acclaimed biography of the Russian dictator. Stalin owned a biography of Ivan IV, where he jotted down a few notes reprimanding the czar for not being ruthless enough with the boyars. "You should have killed more, Ivan Vasilyevich: Russia wouldn't have suffered such torment after your death," Stalin wrote. "He was a great ruler full of wisdom," he once told Eisenstein. "He didn't let foreigners into his country. He was extremely cruel, but he had to be. He made the mistake of sparing at least five big feudal families. He'd kill someone and then pray and repent. God was a hindrance for him. You have to be more determined than that."

NEW AND OLD BOYARS

Three-quarters of a century later, *Ivan the Terrible, Part II* remains prophetic. Especially when the oligarchs were called to the Kremlin, on February 22, 2022, to the great hall of Ekaterininsky, named after Catherine II. That list of thirty-six rich guys summoned to hear Putin's will and mission represents the economic power that fuels the political and military establishment. Although the Kremlin signed a pact with these billionaires in the late 1990s, creating a winning partnership for thirty years, this pillar of post-Soviet Russian power can become an Achille's heel at any moment. So at that meeting, on the eve of the invasion, many wondered why some of these modern-day boyars were missing, including Boris and Arkady Rotenberg, Putin's judo and hockey mates, lords of banks and construction; Yuri Kovalchuk, Putin's dacha neighbor and owner of the Rossiya, Putin's private bank; Gennady Timchenko, a former colleague in Saint Petersburg and present-day oil and gas broker; former lord of aluminum Oleg Deripaska; and Chelsea FC owner Roman Abramovich, whom the British secret service wanted to participate in negotiations between Russia and Ukraine. Perhaps Putin considers them plot proof.

But the fact is, dozens of the oligarchs at that meeting have ended up in the great beyond. Andrey Botikov, the scientist who invented Sputnik, the (failed) Russian Covid vaccine, was found strangled in his home. Sergey Grishin, known as Scarface, the banker who sold Meghan and Harry their villa in California, was also killed. Pavel Antonov, one of the richest politicians in the Duma and a critic of the invasion, fell from the balcony of a hotel in India. Ivan Pechorin, CEO of the Far East and Arctic Development Corporation, was found drowned in Vladivostok. Ravil Maganov, vice president of Lukoil, fell from the sixth floor of the hospital where, that same day, Putin was due to pay tribute (if reluctantly) to the corpse of Mikhail Gorbachev. In a residential neighborhood in Saint Petersburg, Yuri Voronov, head of Astra Shipping and maritime contracts for Gazprom, was found floating in his swimming pool with a gunshot wound to the head. The bodies of Vladislav Avaev, Gazprombank vice president, his pregnant wife, and his thirteen-year-old daughter were found in a Moscow apartment, killed with guns of different calibers. A similar slaughter occurred at a villa in Lloret de Mar in Spain, where Sergey Protosenya, former head of Novatek, was found dead with his wife and young daughter. A high death toll of magnates, high-ranking bureaucrats, and generals; a grim list of Russian billionaires—many in the energy industry—who have ended up dead in unusual circumstances.

The key word of power is *bespredel*, or "by any means necessary." In the first twenty years of the millennium, brutality and violent deaths were so common, most Russians ignored them. "Successful Russian leaders have always possessed the qualities of criminals as well as of statesmen," Tichomirov said. "We're inured to it; we continue to accept this dark side of Russia. Death by assassination is just part of the tradition."

Were the deceased bigwigs plotting behind the scenes like the boyars against Ivan the Terrible? The CIA and other Western agencies certainly hope for disloyalty from the oligarchs. That could make them Trojan horses in the Kremlin or useful in a post-Putin Russia. Putin has allowed them to prosper as long as they don't get in his way, but now he fears them and has sent them a clear warning.

"The last czar in the footsteps of the first?" I asked Tichomirov.

"A tumultuous succession of czars followed the fall of Ivan Grozny, until Peter the Great. Meanwhile, the boyars oversaw wealth and power," he told me. "I also put my hope in the oligarchs, at least the ones with villas in the West. I thought they'd rebel, not so much for love of the West, but for the sake of their nice villas. But I was wrong. They chose loyalty to the Kremlin and Russia's Eastward drift. Those who dissented or wavered were offed by Putin's henchmen. Does history repeat itself? In the West, sometimes. In Russia, often. Putin, like Ivan Grozny upon his return to Moscow, reminded his oligarchs that they can 'go ahead and get rich, but I'm in charge. Step out of line and you're dead.' "

In 2017, Putin commissioned a statue of Ivan the Terrible in central Moscow. It immediately became a pilgrimage destination. According to a survey conducted that same year, 71 percent of Russians see the czar in a positive light. Putin first among them: "He didn't kill anyone, I promise you. The story of him killing his son is also false. It was invented by a papal emissary. The usual distortion of Russian history."

History books approved by Putin as recently as in 2015 depicted Ivan the Terrible as a reformer alongside "modernizers" like Peter the Great and Stalin.

To understand what Ivan IV represents is to understand the "Russian question." But beware the risk of oversimplification, or of equating the Russian people with their first great tyrant. He was a model for Stalin and today he represents Putin's patriotic ideal, and while he can't take all the credit for how recent dictators have chosen to wield their power, the mark Ivan left on Russia is upsetting because of its eternal relevance: He has passed his legacy down through the Kremlin, almost like a gene, in an uninterrupted sequence of autocracy. The terror he unleashed among his people sowed the seeds for the smuta to come.

THE SILENT TREATMENT

The long shadow cast by Ivan IV over Russian power also covers the matter of succession. By killing his son and only heir, Ivan IV created a succession crisis of fundamental importance not just in Russia's history but also in its imagination.

In 1825, a few months before the Decembrist revolt against Czar Nicholas I was crushed, Pushkin wrote an epic play on a period of political upheaval that resembled his present circumstances. *Boris Godunov* was inspired by what happened after the death of Ivan Grozny, a nightmare that has become part of the national myth. The plot revolves around the *samozvanec*, the "aspiring czar," a recurrent figure in Russian history. He appears during periods of chaos to challenge the established order. In many ways, Prigozhin was a modern *samozvanec*. A few years after Ivan's death in 1584, the Poles occupied the throne, an offense that has never been forgotten, as evidenced by Ezzor's comments. The collective trauma of that event led Russians to believe that questioning their leaders' legitimacy creates social conflict and exposes the country to foreign occupation. Czars, Soviet leaders, and Putin have exploited this belief to justify autocracy and impose unity. As Hannah Arendt said, autocratic regimes offer the carrot of stability while perpetuating the threat of instability. Even though this tactic no longer seems unique to autocrats: It may be time to ask ourselves whether this perverse system has now been adopted by Western democracies, which seem to create a constant state of tension to avoid losing consensus.

Pushkin describes the *narod*—the Russian people—as "amenable to the conditioning of the moment, deaf and indifferent to the truth, a beast that feeds on fairy tales." In the last lines of *Boris Godunov*, as the people face the consequences of their actions, Pushkin writes that they "are silent with horror." When called upon to sing the praises of their chosen heir to the throne, "the population is speechless." Even today, Russians use silence to deflect reality. According to English historian Orlando Figes, "Autocracy in Russia since Ivan the Terrible can be explained more through the weakness of society than the strength of the state." This dynamic continues to shape the course of national history. "The principle of power has not changed in the least over the past five centuries," wrote playwright Vladimir Sorokin three days after the invasion of Ukraine. "This is the greatest tragedy of our country."

THE ORDER OF THE VETERAN

"Why do they call you Ezzor?" I ask the Wagner captain.

"It's where I fought the Marines," he says, a cigarette in his teeth, his little eyes, blue and clear as vodka, squinting at me. He's standing an inch from my nose. I smell the alcohol and smoke that have seeped into the hairs of his reddish beard. He switches off the automatic translator on his phone and opens a photo album. Photos and translation: We've been going on like this for a while. Ezzor has fought in quite a few wars with SOBR and Wagner. "February 7, 2018, in Syria," he tells me. "We had to take Conoco's oil rigs, near Deir Ezzor, controlled by the Marines and [US Army] Rangers. There were 500 of us, almost all Russians, supported by Syrian T-72s. The battle lasted four or five hours. They were shooting everything at us, even Javelin missiles, but we kept advancing. Then the US Air Force joined in with fighter jets, AH-64 Apaches, even Lockheed AC-130 bombers. We asked the Russian base for help, but those fuckers didn't come: They were afraid of a direct confrontation with the Americans so they left us in the mud. The planes were pounding us, going back and forth, and then they retreated because they were low on fuel, and the battle became almost hand to hand. We left 250 men on the battlefield. I'm called Ezzor in their honor." The images from the Syrian campaign are frightening, though Ezzor doesn't give me time to take a good look at them—he keeps scrolling through, to the next battles, which include Libya, Crimea, and Ukraine.

Ezzor is thirty-eight years old, but he's already spent a lot of time in special operations, almost always covert. "You talk about NATO provocations and American wars, but in thirty years, how many wars have you guys started?" I ask, referring to wars declared, secret, masked, by proxy, or by neo-imperial decree to quash ethnic clashes, protect Russian minorities, or install puppet governments.

"Russia has only two allies, the army and the navy," Ezzor says with a booming laugh. "We're Russian. We can't let anyone bust our balls."

Indeed, Russia's recent conflicts have been warnings to an expanding NATO. The 2008 war in Georgia was brief, but it showed the world that the Bear was absorbing the shock of dissolution. The 1992 Moldo-Russian War, or Transnistria War, was a clash between the Moscow-armed Cossack militias and the fledgling Republic of Moldova. Both conflicts signaled an era of resurging ethnic cleavages, religious sectarianism, and democratic aspirations. The Kremlin's military operations were mostly meant to extinguish embers of hatred that Soviet repression had banked under ash for more than seventy years. As in the 1992–97 civil war in Tajikistan—Moscow's first open conflict in supporting the old post-Soviet guard against Islamist movements emerging from neighboring Afghanistan—which left almost 50,000 people dead and led one in five Tajiks to leave the country. Then there was Chechnya, Russia's Vietnam. Its first round, in Yeltsin's day, ended in harsh defeat—up to one hundred thousand civilians killed along with ten thousand Chechen soldiers and just as many Russian military personnel. In the second round, with Putin, it turned into a resounding victory. When he came to power, Putin's first order of business was to end conflicts with Chechnya, Dagestan, Ingushetia, and anyone else undermining imperial pride. The second Chechen war was a wasteland that Putin calls peace: a ruthless, pounding firestorm so devastating the UN called the Chechen capital, Grozny, "the most devastated city in the world."

But the place Putin mentions most in his speeches is Kosovo. He brought it up to justify his support of the Russophile republics of Donbas, and in 2008, before invading Georgia. In the Kosovo war of 1998–99, the Russians were the first to enter the capital, Pristina. They planted their flag and declared a victory that was not theirs to claim. But Kosovo has always been a sore spot for Moscow, which objected to the NATO bombing of its Serbian brothers and to the Washington-brokered peace agreement. "We're in Georgia to support Russophones," Putin said in the summer of 2008. "Just as NATO intervened in Kosovo to help the Albanians." The 2008 war in Georgia was extremely quick—Russian shelling began on August 1 and the Georgian military responded by bombing South Ossetia, a breakaway region Russia recognizes as a sovereign state. Meanwhile, a rise in hostilities was recorded in Abkhazia, another Georgian breakaway region. By August 12, French President Nicolas Sarkozy had brokered a ceasefire that stopped the Russian tanks a few miles outside the Georgian capital of Tbilisi. But this did not stop Russia from unilaterally recognizing Abkhazia and South Ossetia—and Transnistria, while it was at it—as autonomous republics. "I copied the Kosovo solution," Putin concluded.

Then there was the war against ISIS in the northern Caucasus, which caused almost four thousand deaths between 2009 and 2017 and the dismantling of the emirate that wanted to import anti-Russian jihad from Azerbaijan. In Syria, where Ezzor's Susanin team was deployed, Russia stood by Assad, first with air strikes and then with boots on the ground. Eleven years of war, four hundred thousand dead, eleven million refugees. But thanks to Putin, Assad was able to change his fortunes at the front and push back rebel factions and jihadists, at least for a while. Moscow deploys people like Ezzor, men without flags or badges, anywhere in the world so the Kremlin won't have to declare losses and defeats. Meanwhile, they lay the groundwork for more substantial interventions. Putin used them in Ukraine in 2014, for instance. Ezzor was there when they invaded Simferopol' and Sevastopol without firing a shot, before the invasion by the regular army.

As Ezzor shares his photos with me, I begin to sense a strange tension, a sudden distance or distrust, even though Ezzor still stands here, his beard practically rubbing against my nose. Now, behind his comradely air as a drinking buddy, I sense a dangerous individual, an uncanny unfamiliarity born of the space that exists between someone who has never fired a shot and someone who has killed profusely. After all, Ezzor was showing great pleasure in displaying his trophies from a life of violence. Or did I express too much interest in them?

He hugs me again, at length, more tightly than before. "We're brothers," he says. "Do you see how welcoming Russians are? Foreigners are welcome here. You'll see—nothing will happen to you. Don't worry."

"I'm not worried. Why should anything happen?"

"It'll be fine. Russians are good people. Maybe not everyone likes it when you go around asking questions, looking at pictures . . . You know, we're at war. It's normal." He insists on giving me his phone number. "If you have any issues, call me, okay? When are you leaving?" he asks.

"We were supposed to leave tomorrow morning, but maybe we'll stay a bit, to meet Artur's son," I say.

"No, you will leave tomorrow morning," Ezzor says abruptly, after a long sip of beer that soaks the hairs under his nose.

I'm confused—was that an order? "Yes, we'll leave tomorrow after meeting Artur's son," I repeat, feigning innocence. I look around, but Artur is gone. The music has stopped, and Katya is drinking at one of the Wagner tables, where the conversation seems heated.

"Artur went home, he was tired. I'll tell him you said goodbye," Ezzor says.

"Right, I'll see him tomorrow anyway, with his son."

"There's no need to meet Artur or his son, right? So tomorrow morning you will leave Kostroma, right?" This time Ezzor hugs me hastily and barely taps me on the back.

Now it's obvious that Ale's fear was well founded: Katya must have told Ezzor about us while they were whispering and singing. Who knows what she said. Suddenly, no one is giving me the time of day and I decide to return to the hotel. I hear the voices of the mercenaries and the sound of clinking glasses behind me. In the park, the decapitated statues stand in the dark, white as bones against the black earth.

We decide to leave immediately. We get ready and wait for the *oprichniki* to leave their lair and for their headlights to disappear down the road. When Katya comes back, we heave her into the van and leave.

PART THREE

Na grani

■ ■ ■

At the edge of the centuries
On the cusp of two worlds

—VLADIMIR GILYAROVSKY,
MOSCOW AND THE MUSCOVITES

■ ■ ■

I do not need much.
A crust of bread,
A drop of milk,
And this sky,
And these clouds

—VELIMIR KHLEBNIKOV,
47 EASY POEMS AND ONE HARD ONE

7
The sausage oligarch

"Thanks for the sanctions!"

SOVIETLAND

At a lonely intersection in the steppe, we come across a massive electoral poster showing Duma member Sergey Kazankov next to Lenin and Stalin—a surreal image of Soviet revival. Using a VPN to protect my online searches, I learn that fifty-three-year-old Kazankov was reelected to the State Duma in 2021 as a Communist, that he was sanctioned for supporting the invasion of Ukraine, and that his father, Ivan Kazankov, has been a Communist power broker since the 1990s, right-hand man to General Secretary Gennady Zyuganov. Sergey himself had been the director of a meat-processing plant and agricultural combine in the Zvenigovsky District, owned by his father.

We are on the eastern flank of the Volga, in the Mari El Republic—some ninety miles from Kazan, the capital of the Republic of Tatarstan. More specifically, the Zvenigovsky District, which lends its name to Kazankov's company. We stop at a gas station for directions and are guided toward a *sovkhoz*, a large-scale collective farm created in the forced collectivization of the 1930s along with the *kolkhozy*, an agricultural cooperative. We assume the gas station attendant is using a verbal anachronism left over from the twentieth century to refer to an agricultural business. But in truth, we are about to walk into an idyllic Communist past, rebuilt without the burdens of the Communist state and with the aim of making a profit. "When you see the monument to Marx, you're practically there," says the gas station attendant.

As we approach, the van becomes a time machine and we are transported to a place forgotten by history—a sliver of surviving reality, frozen in time in the twentieth century.

THE STACHANOV PRIZE

This is no gimmick for nostalgic tourists. It's a real agro-industrial business, complete with the smell of manure and slaughtered cattle. A stench that floods the brain and turns everything red.

The red flag of the USSR flutters above the white-and-yellow complex, swelled by the wind from the Urals. According to the company, the flag is the same size as the one lowered from the Kremlin on December 25, 1991, when Communism fell.

The walls of the nearly two-hundred-thousand-square-foot plant are covered in red inscriptions marked by the exclamation points the Bolsheviks had so loved to use: "Honor and glory to the workers of the Zvenigovsky combine!"; "Comrades, let us fight for our village, let us fight for Russia!"; "Now and forever, war on Fascism!"

The road to the entrance is lined with photographs of employees who have received Stakhanovite awards, traditionally given to Soviet workers who exceeded production norms. Among them are Ivanovna

Lidya Vasileva, best sausage stuffer; Nikolai Zinoviev, best tractor driver; and Nikolai Vasilievich, best agronomist.

Trucks and vans marked with a hammer and sickle and the slogan "Traditional, for the people" pour out of the gates. A statue of Stalin presides over it all, his pants tucked into his boots on a four-tiered pedestal. Off to the side, a metallic Lenin stands on a two-tiered pedestal, his brow furrowed, partially obscured by the branches of a birch tree.

The entrance to the management building, a solid modernist structure, is dominated by bronze letters reading CCCP. The burly security guards at reception are in fatigues but they seem meek and annoyed at having to deal with Westerners. We encounter a similar disbelief, sometimes accompanied by awkward smiles, among all the workers we meet at the plant.

IVAN'S PANTHEON

I soon realize this is one of Russia's most successful agricultural producers, delivering tens of thousands of tons of meat and dairy to the market each year. The business, established in 1995, well after the USSR was dead and gone, identifies as a Communist-Stalinist enterprise.

When we ask Ivan Kazankov's office if we can speak to him, we have little hope. But they tell us to wait, so we do, for two hours, staring at the Stakhanovite pictures with growing apprehension, fearing we've pushed our luck too far. Why didn't they bark a dry *nyet* in our faces right away? Is it worth waiting, or should we make a run for it in the event our request has triggered a series of dangerous calls?

As I've been doing since the start of the trip, I present myself as a historian gathering material on the history of the Volga. After that, I try to redirect the conversation toward present-day Russia as much as possible, despite not always being able to speak freely. Ale and I take what we can get. This is not a normal trip: We are here to bear witness, to gather voices, thoughts, and images from a land that has suddenly become a world apart, mysterious and alien, almost fantastical—while a nuclear superpower on a warpath. We remain aware of our vulnerability: A quick online search would reveal my extensive reporting on Russia in the past few years for the international press, especially on sensitive topics like the Arctic, where "journalist" and "spy" are considered synonymous. Not really an ideal profile if you want to stick your nose (and Ale's lens) into an industrial complex strategic to the war economy.

There is a Russian expression we've started to adopt: *na grani*, which means "on the brink." We think of it often as we try to interview people about the Russian psyche without arousing the suspicion and patriotic zeal that could land us in an FSB field office. There is a fine line between freedom and prison in Russia today. No manner of precaution will help us if fate has an off day and decides to sympathize with the secret police.

But Ivan Kazankov welcomes us without reservations: His face is inscrutable, but you can tell he's a real boss, one who doesn't answer to anybody—the top dog at this agrarian empire on the Volga, paradoxically inspired by the greatest peasant exterminator in history. Kazankov is eighty-one years old and has a gray, wolflike gaze. He's tall and robust and as he speaks, he caresses a wide red tie that rests on his protruding belly. He, too, is intrigued by our unexpected visit.

His office seems to have been designed with the express purpose of disorienting anyone hoping to understand contemporary Russia: busts of Stalin next to Russian Orthodox icons; a portrait of Nicholas II looming over a Soyuz statuette; a picture of Vladimir Putin hanging next to an image of Saint Andrew, the patron saint of Russia. The chaos of this pantheon is compounded by a general sense of opacity about the nature of the company, which at first is presented to us as a "state-run agricultural coop, exactly like in the days of the USSR," but has turned out to be a private family holding. Ivan handed it down to his daughter after his son left for his role at the Duma. "What matters is that it runs as before, as a Communist, anticapitalist business," he explains. "Profits are used to increase the salaries of the four thousand employees and grow the business."

Later, in Kazan, I learn that amid the robbery and corruption of the 1990s, when hardened racketeers pilfered oil, Soviet industrial equipment, and strategic nuclear material, Kazankov, a Duma member and son of Chuvash farmers, took his own modest cut. He got his hands on a rundown farm and got to work. After the system crumbled, *sovkhozy* and *kolkhozy*, which employed entire villages or districts, cut back on manpower by 90 percent just to stay afloat. In 1995, Kazankov fired three thousand workers—two-thirds of the total workforce, at the time—and started gradually to rehire as the business grew. In so doing, he deftly transformed his farm into an industrial colossus that can help Putin turn Russia into an agricultural superpower through large-scale public financing—just as Stalin had intended.

Kazankov was able to harness a widespread hunger for restoration. People wanted to return to a planned economy, so he adapted the socialist combine production system to the wild post-Soviet market, drawing his workforce from the surrounding area, as in the days of party land seizures.

Kazankov, the sausage oligarch, knows just how much Russian consumers still suffer the loss of state collectivism, but also how in the countryside, large-scale private land ownership continues to evoke memories of exploitation and revolts. So, he has fashioned himself as the comrade president of a *sovkhoz* that survived the neoliberal catastrophe of the 1990s: a sort of old-school apparatchik who prioritizes the well-being of the collective.

THE SILENT WEAPON

At lunch, Ivan highlights the quality of the food—which is in fact our best meal of the trip. He eats in the same cafeteria as his workers, though at a private table behind a purple curtain. A dedicated waitress—the youngest, with the lowest-cut top—serves his food alongside a bottle of excellent Georgian red.

Kazankov waxes poetic about his assets, which seem to have ballooned in the war economy. He has earned a spot on the War & Sanctions blacklist, a database on the Russian *nomenklatura* deserving of sanctions. He is a great fan of international sanctions and Russian countersanctions: bans on imports and exports of goods, technical equipment like fertilizers, agribusiness machinery. "They've been an incredible developmental tool for Russia," he says, digging into a plate of beef and cabbage rolls. "We're at our best when backed into a corner, isolated and hated. If this commercial war had occurred in the '90s, we'd be the engine of the world by now. What a shame! Russia is just too rich—so rich we haven't been able to steal everything yet. We have to get over the oil curse and start to invent and produce, plow and sow." For Kazankov, the sanctions are pure adrenaline, which he underscores by explaining how his combine has copied Italian, German, and Israeli means of production. "We doubled processing in one year and we supply almost a thousand supermarkets in all of Russia."

Kazankov reveals an aspect of the war we haven't yet considered in detail, calling agriculture a silent weapon. When Russia annexed Crimea in 2014, the Kremlin held meetings with agro-industrial bosses like Kazankov to plan the offensive. Already, they decided to halt many imports from Europe to launch the diversification of industry and invest in finished products. "Since 2019, our net worth has increased by $60 billion a year. We've begun almost six thousand new projects, funded with $30 billion a year from Rosselkhozbank," he explains. "Putin wants Russia to build 80 percent of its own agricultural and processing machinery. We're switching quickly from being net importers to net exporters. And we're aiming to export $50 billion worth of agribusiness products per year." According to Kazankov, the boom has already occurred in the dairy industry. "Russia was importing 60 percent of its cheese from Europe—France, Italy, the Netherlands—and now it has started to export. The state fully subsidizes logistics: We don't pay anything to export to China, Turkey, or Arab countries. The next target is pork, because the internal market is saturated, while China now wants to substitute American pigs with Russian ones. We're raising more livestock for the Chinese market," he says, while attacking his incisors with a toothpick.

Wheat, barley, sunflower seeds, and maize production are all growing. "Wheat is the new oil," he explains, and Russia is already the top producer and exporter in the world, with 220 million cultivated hectares yielding a value of $100 billion a year—20 percent of global production. Kazankov claims Russia could feed two billion people on its own. Indeed, wheat exports have increased by 70 percent in four years. "We took out Ukraine, halved their production and export of wheat, and undercut European and American farmers. We've entered new markets in Africa, South America, and Asia. Like in the days of the USSR, we help our friends: North Korea, Southeast Asia, Cuba, Venezuela. For example, we sell wheat to Mexico at below market price, which drives the Americans crazy, as if we were exporting missiles."

GRETA WHO?

There is one other thing Kazankov likes as much as sanctions: climate change. "The rest of the world despairs, but for Russia, it's a great ally, a blessing: You won't hear anyone here complaining about global warming." I express my agreement on this point. Russia seems to be on a different planet in this matter, or a different geological era. "More Greta Garbo's era than Greta Thunberg's," I say, but Kazankov doesn't respond—perhaps he's never heard of either of them.

"In the Arctic, the more ice disappears, the better off Russia is, because energy sources and new maritime commercial routes become increasingly accessible, allowing us to export oil and gas to Asia without going through the Suez Canal. But for agriculture we see a bright future, which will turn us into the breadbasket of the world," he says, while stuffing his napkin into his collar. "In addition to the fact that we don't have much extreme weather, like typhoons or severe heat waves. Here on the Volga, the growing season is longer and the harvest is better. Have you seen our black soil? It's the most fertile in existence. They used to say that having so much wealth, but a shitty climate, was a punishment, but now we are doubling production, and we are getting state and private investors. The agricultural field has become strategic for national security, just as heavy industry was for Stalin before World War II. After the '90s, fifty-six million hectares remained uncultivated. Now I think it's just about thirty million. A more favorable climate increases the amount of arable land, including in the Urals and Siberia."

RED RESCUE

Kazankov finally comes out with what he's been implying all along. "The West fears our grain silos more than our missile silos. They know food is the most powerful political weapon. Have you wondered why more and more countries are joining the BRICS? This is why!" he exclaims, poking his fat finger into the last slice of black bread.

This sanctions fever is infecting many other sectors too, producing figures that, for now, point to the defeat of the West. Not only has the Russian economy, the most sanctioned in history, withstood the blow, but it is growing faster than the global economy, more than double the rate of the Eurozone. It seems to be subverting all reasonable financial logic, with a performance that has allowed Sberbank to distribute dividends of more than $8 billion to shareholders. Unemployment has plunged to below 3 percent, and international analysts say that inflation—usually a weakness in war economies—is heading for stability, fully supported by the military-industrial complex.

Kazankov has his theories. "They wanted to reduce Russians to beggars, but it's the same old story: The West doesn't get us, it doesn't understand our adaptability and spirit of sacrifice. It assumes we're like them, think like them, react like them; that we have the same priorities and expectations. So now Europe is bearing the brunt of the sanctions. The West blocked 58 percent of our exports to Europe, so in response, we increased exports to Asia by 78 percent. It blocked imports by 61 percent, so we increased our imports from Asia, Turkey, and Iran by 68 percent. The Caspian-Volga corridor is an essential artery to screw the blockade."

But for now, oil remains Putin's biggest source of financing. The G7's imposition of a $60-per-barrel ceiling on the sale of Russian crude oil to third-world countries simply did not work. Russia continues to export between $5 and $6 billion worth of fossil fuels per week, including $3 to $4 billion in oil. About two-thirds of the crude material is transported or insured by European or G7 companies that are not subject to sanctions if that fuel is then sold to China, India, or Malaysia, violating the limit of $60 per barrel. European shipowners sell oil tankers to mysterious Russian entrepreneurs or their intermediaries. With this oil revenue, Moscow can inject the economy with public subsidies and support military spending (and a system of police repression) with more than a third of the federal budget.

It's too early to say whether Putin has won the bet. But the trade war is already enriching a new generation of oligarchs. Ivan Kazankov is a small fish compared to those who have jumped on the spoils left by Western companies that abandoned Russia after February 2022, with Kremlin approval, in the greatest pillage of resources since the privatizations of the 1990s. "We made it very difficult for Western companies to leave—they're practically held hostage," Kazankov says. "To leave, they have to sell at half the value and pay a 25 percent tax on what they made in the past year." Fewer than 10 percent of companies fully left Russia after the invasion of Ukraine—all those who did leave had their assets nationalized. Alexander Varshavsky and Kamo Avagumyan of Avilon—an automotive company—spent a mere $135 million—a twelfth of the market price—on a Volkswagen plant that generates over $4 billion a year. It bought the Hyundai plant for the paltry sum of 108 million euros. Andrei Olkhovsky of the automotive company Avtodom made away with a Mercedes-Benz factory for 74 million euros, along with all its commercial and insurance activities, which generate profits of 3 to 4 billion euros a year. Arsen Kanokov and Alexander Govor raked up 850 McDonald's restaurants literally for free and bought 130 Starbucks for a pittance. Finnish company Fortum and its German subsidiary—which in Russia generated more than $2 billion in 2021—were transferred, free of charge, to Rosneft, a group owned by Igor Sechin, a former KGB operative and Putin ally. The Italian company Ariston, an appliances colossus, went to Gazprom.

No one was unaffected, not even the profiteers of old, not even those who have already enriched themselves by swearing fealty to the Kremlin. It doesn't take much to have everything taken away. A critical comment on the invasion was all it took for oligarch Oleg Tinkov to be forced to sell his bank to Interros Group. The former governor of Chelyabinsk, who was not considered loyal enough, was accused of corruption and his Makfa Group, the country's largest pasta producer, was expropriated. Not to mention loyalists who are paid in kind. A Dannon subsidiary was expropriated and given to an associate of Chechen leader Ramzan Kadyrov. "Often, a business is requisitioned because someone important wants to get his hands on its resources, that's all," Kazankov says on our whirlwind tour of the dairy department, where they package cheese and raw milk that reminds me of Brie. Kazankov guesses the direction of my curiosity. "European groups have large agricultural holdings, especially livestock, here in the mid- and lower Volga. Sooner or later, someone is going to take an interest in them."

He finds this more than reasonable. "We're at war! If the West wants to freeze $300 billion in Russian central bank assets, obviously we're going to have to make that back." Then, with a frankness, or bravado, that continues to surprise me, he adds, "We couldn't make it without China." He's referring to Beijing's "red rescue," which has replaced the technology that used to come from the West, like smartphones, cars, or semiconductors. I note that we did see a lot of Chinese Havals on the roads. "That's junk," he says. "But we need to sell them for political reasons, to show the Chinese we appreciate their cars, which is obviously bullshit. Even the Ladas that Fiat used to make in Togliatti, on the lower Volga, were better than these."

Kazankov explains that almost all the goods arrive by way of Turkey and central Asian republics. "My new Mercedes just got here from Kyrgyzstan, and I only had to pay an extra 5 percent for it."

I ask Kazankov whether the *sovkhoz* is some kind of provocation, a marketing move to drum up nostalgia for the USSR. He says he runs an "end-to-end Communist business. Workers participate in profits and the whole system of production involves the collective, spanning the fields to the farms, the land to the finished product." He sees it as the way "to rebuild a Soviet-style autarchic economic system and guarantee Russians access to healthy local food born of their lands at prices set by the state and not the competition."

I express confusion at this, saying it seems like a game of smoke and mirrors where the past gets deformed and current realities become muddled. "Our history is circular," he says. "It always comes back to the same point. In Russia, what seems to be gone will come around again. Albeit in new ways." I ask what role farmers can play today compared to the Stalin era, when they were seen as an obstacle to Soviet progress. "I think that now, the sickle is more important than the hammer," he says. "The solidarity of the Russian people is felt in the countryside more than in the factories. Every day I see evidence of patriotism among my workers, my farmers."

THE LOW OF THE COW

Kazankov offers to show us his newest stable, about ten miles away, where he has copied Israeli dairies. The herd grazes in large, well-defined clearings that have obviously been carved out of the forest. A driver ferries us around in the illegally imported armored Mercedes. Kazankov dons a red baseball cap, with CCCP stitched in white on the front and a hammer and sickle on the sides. He says he's thinking of branding the cows in the same way—given his inscrutable gaze, it's hard to know if he's joking. He chews on toothpicks as he speaks, like a trucker. "We grow fodder and cereal on thousands of hectares of land," he explains, watching his property from the tinted window. "We raise dairy cows and pigs and take care of them all the way until the packaging of the finished products: meats, cheeses, and kefir. Even ice cream, good like the ice cream from my childhood. Gorbachev and Yeltsin ruined ice cream, the cowards. In the USSR, the *sovkhoz* could raise 600 pigs. Now, we have 220,000 pigs and produce sixty thousand tons of meat per year."

Comforted by the intimate environment of the luxury vehicle, I ask him about the war in Ukraine. "Obviously we'll win," he says, without looking away from the fields, as if he's been waiting for the question. "Because we know how to fight and because we can't lose. If we must, we'll use atomic weapons, we'll destroy the earth, we'll destroy everything."

For Kazankov, the war means a mountain of rubles. He wants to talk numbers—I see that I represent a world he wants to impress. "Cheese production has grown 80 percent," he says. "We're making up for lost French and Italian cheeses. We're still buying cows and now have 120,000 Friesians."

The stables are so quiet you could hear a pin drop. Workers shovel manure without looking up, and even the cows low quietly. "We milk them three times a day, like in the Netherlands," he says. I think of the crisp emerald landscape of the Leiden or Utrecht plains—but without bicycles, whose existence seems to have escaped the attention of the locals. Kazankov sighs, tells me it hasn't been easy to build all this. The fight for power was brutal and violent. "Leonid Markelov, the previous president, tried to stop me—he tried to kill me twice. With a car bomb even. Then he was arrested for corruption, and they took everything

from him: villas, sixteen cars, and a chest of gold bullion. He's serving thirteen years in a penal colony."

Later, in Kazan, I will learn more about those unusual square pastures: The same prosecutor that sentenced Markelov in 2017 stripped Kazankov of his immunity and seat in parliament because he was found "guilty of large-scale deforestation for the purposes of illegally taking possession of new grazing lands," according to court records. That is, of creating his own little Donbas on the Volga.

THE FINAL CLASH

As we make our way back to the farm, I ask Kazankov how, as the son of farmers, he can abide by the Stalinist cult. "He was a clever, practical man, and I'm a clever, practical man," he says, stroking his red tie. "Stalin knew that if he didn't annihilate the opposition in the countryside, the revolution would have been nothing but an experiment. The Bolshevik Revolution came from the head before it came from the heart," he says. "Stalin was in a hurry, but the farmers were not: They were waiting for failure, counting on the fact that without them, no one could claim ownership of Russia and so Communism would fall. They never imagined that Stalin would attack their lands. I know farmers. It's why I fly the flag of the Soviet Union and put Stalin at the factory gates. Communism changed farmers: Their lands are no longer their assets—Russia is their asset, and Putin is their czar. But that's no reason to let our guard down."

Kazankov proceeds to tell me the story of the old peasant caught praying on the steps of a church, wrapped in a sheepskin coat. An atheist Communist agent interrupts him with a kick. "What are you doing? Confess!" "What do you mean, what am I doing? I'm praying," says the peasant. "Who the hell are you praying for?" "I pray for the Soviets." "Fine. But who did you pray for before the revolution? Be honest." "I prayed for the czar." "And didn't you see where he ended up?" "That's why I'm praying for the Soviets."

In Lenin's time, factory unions garnished a quarter of each laborer's salary to pay British workers on strike. Factories were supposed to be the engine of the revolution, in Russia and in the world. Industrial development was necessary for Soviet victory "over the forces and traditions of the ancient peasant society," Lenin said. When Stalin arrived, he cracked down on the "revolt of the earth." He leveled resistance in the countryside to ensure the success of his great leap forward. He needed grain to support urban workers, who were dutifully propelling his industrialization plan. But everything seemed to be working against his ambition to transform a Communist ideological experiment into a successful economic system. He wanted the proletarian dictatorship to become the "engine of the world"—the same words Kazankov used to describe the potential beneficial effects of the sanctions on Russia, had they been imposed in the 1990s.

A series of famines ensued, and the countryside refused to respond to Soviet demands. Lenin's new economic policy had created a problem when it allowed kulak landowners to reclaim control over agricultural production: The state couldn't force them to plant more wheat when milk or butter yielded better returns. And it couldn't force them to sell grain at political prices, causing a freefall in cereal stockpiles: Ukraine delivered 15 percent of its previous total yield in 1929 after an already meager 40 percent in 1928. The same went for the Volga, Caucasus, and Crimea.

The kulaks were amassing cash, the workers suffered famine, and industrialization trudged along—or so the party thought. The kulaks responded to requisitions with further reductions in planting and by hiding goods, causing additional famines. They butchered cattle as an act of sabotage and didn't hesitate to take up their muskets against the political police. The result was a new civil war: The kulaks were the class enemy, the capitalists, and as such, they needed to be punished and returned to slavery through forced collectivization. The goal was outrageous, regardless of the human element or the backwardness of the agricultural system: Increasing productivity with a smaller workforce would have meant asking for a leap in centuries, not decades, and broken the backs of millions of peasants. The job was entrusted to local commissioners: They compiled a list of kulaks to be expropriated or deported. From November 1929 to the end of 1931, 50 percent of farms were collectivized. The Volga region, as crucial then as it is now in grain production, was among the hardest hit: Between 1938 and 1940, in present-day Mari El and Tatarstan, 96 percent of farms became *kolkhozy* or *sovkhozy* (Zvenigovsky's collective farm was founded in 1939).

Kazankov brings up the Soviet mindset. "The kulaks continued to abuse their positions, like in the days of the czar. Poor peasants supported collectivization and encouraged the war against their overlords, accusing them of enriching themselves on unpaid labor, hiring workers from outside the village, speculating on prices, and keeping a stranglehold on the means of production." He quotes Kalinin: "One of two things: Either we win, or the kulak, meaning capitalism, wins." Kazankov has no doubts: "Communism is antithetical to the traditional peasant, who is by nature reactionary. The rural revolution meant changing habits, personality, the nature of the Russian peasants themselves. It was a final clash against the real enemies of progress."

Collectivization thus settled the score against small landowners who'd never accepted the Bolshevik Revolution or joined agricultural collectives but who weren't exactly rich. If compared to European or American farmers, they would have appeared destitute (in 1928, more than half their harvest was reaped with a sickle and almost half of the threshing was done by hand). But amid the general state of misery in the Russian countryside, they appeared as islands of privilege.

Anyone could end up on the list of kulak targets, including former Red Army soldiers. Party and secret police officials had imposed quotas on local commissioners, who fulfilled them by attacking anyone who so much as owned a cow. The worst affected were the Volga Germans, the descendants of immigrants brought in by Catherine the Great in the eighteenth century: Given the amount of wealth circulating in their villages, they were automatically seen as capitalists. Among the Mari and Chuvash ethnic minorities, the poorest peasants in the region, owning a single nice item of clothing, a pair of raffia shoes, or a sled for children, was enough to land someone on the list. Kazankov does not want to tell me about his family of Chuvash farmers, but he admits that Russian officials showed minorities no mercy. Research published after the fall of the Soviet Union—now unthinkable in this climate of Stalinist rehabilitation—documented how in the 1930s, the middle and lower Volga was the epicenter of the peasant revolt against Soviet policies: These uprisings also had religious roots, because along with land expropriation, churches were demolished or turned into barns and stables.

As we drive in Kazankov's armored Mercedes, I get a better understanding of the stories I heard two days before as we strolled through the crowded streets of Nizhny Novgorod with Artem, a scholar of twentieth-century Soviet cinema. He was telling us about a film that had never been shot, on the horrific torments endured by the peasants of the Volga.

8

The Tatar merchant

"Allah roots for Putin"

COSSACK WARRIORS

Clean-shaven and with very short hair, Artem Fomenkov may look like an army recruit, despite his almost fifty years. His green beret and Maoist coat lend him a militaristic look, yet the man has a peaceful nature that transmits calm, even though he was anxious about being on the streets of his city talking to a stranger about Russia.

A political scientist and historian who specializes in the USSR and avant-garde Soviet cinema, Artem knows I'm not interested in avant-garde film. I've asked him about peasant insurrections in the mid- to lower Volga. "People in the countryside saw collectivization as proof that Communism was the Antichrist," he says. We're near the Nizhny kremlin, which dominates the old town with its thirteen towers. As in Yaroslavl, I notice a slew of public works and stunning public engagement: furniture showrooms, art galleries, and bookstores full of people, throngs of students in parks, young people lying on the grass soaking up the sun. It takes a lot of imagination to reconcile these images with a war-mobilized country, whose sons and daughters are dying at the front. It seems even more absurd when we turn onto Pokrovskaya Ulitsa and see a six-story building covered in a flag with the letter Z, a symbol of support for the war. The incongruities are making me dizzy. "Priests are preaching that we must fight the demons from the West," Artem tells me. "But in the '30s, when peasants were believers, they professed eternal damnation for anyone who accepted the *kolkhozy* and warned that the Cossacks would come and slaughter those possessed by demons. In villages around the Volga, the myth of the Cossack bandit and defender of the people has never died. Even though we haven't seen large revolts since collectivization, this part of Russia has retained an atavistic predisposition for antiestablishment violence. Prigozhin's mutiny immediately brought to mind names like Stenka Razin and Yemelyan Pugachev. Cossack warriors of old who inspired peasant revolts against the Soviets in the '30s."

Artem explains that the Cossacks had been at once the guardians and enemies of the empire, at least until the start of the nineteenth century, when they became the czar's most ferocious repressors of dissent. They had helped patrol the southern borders against the Mongols and Kalmyks. They were formidable in battle, but also an eternal source of unrest. Just like the Wagner Group, I think, remembering Captain Ezzor in Kostroma. I wonder if Prigozhin will ever get his own statues, streets, and squares like folk-hero revolutionaries such as Razin and Pugachev—the Russian version of Spartacus, Robin Hood, or Che Guevara.

POPULIST HEROES

In 1667 Stenka Razin left the Don with some one thousand men, mostly deserters and former prisoners, and wreaked four years of terror on the Volga and Caspian Sea. He led pirate incursions against convoys of ships loaded with riches, pillaged forts, and set czarist prisoners free. To reinforce his leadership, he sacrificed his beautiful wife, a Persian princess, by throwing her into the Volga—a legend that has fueled generations of poets and folk musicians. Then he turned his attention to the heart of power: He played the role of the revolutionary standing up for exploited peasants, the defender of the people against the rich and privileged, leader of persecuted ethnic minorities. He sailed up the river from Astrakhan to Nizhny Novgorod, massacring governors, boyars, traders, and their families. Wherever Razin went, peasants rose up against landowners and crucified priests that did not join in the Church of the Old Believers. Hunted by the imperial guards, he escaped back to the Don, where he was captured by loyalist Cossacks and delivered to the Kremlin. According to Artem, Razin's execution explains the power of his legend. Carted into the Red Square in chains—as happened to Vercingetorix with Caesar in Rome—he was publicly drawn and quartered, his head displayed on a stick, his torso thrown to the dogs. Dimitri Shostakovich dedicated opus 119 to his dreadful death. The Kremlin's retaliation hit tens of thousands of Razin's rebels: Entire villages were razed to the ground, and barges loaded with bodies flowed down the river.

Pugachev's turn came in the eighteenth century. "His was a true attempt at a revolution," Artem specifies. "He had political objectives. He wanted to subvert the established order and counter pro-Western religious reforms Catherine the Great had inherited from Peter the Great—such as the manner of doing the sign of the cross and the requirement for peasants and priests to shave their beards. It was a failed attempt at a populist, antiestablishment revolution."

According to Artem, Pugachev belonged to the Church of the Old Believers, which was born of a seventeenth-century schism with the official Orthodox Church—when anyone who opposed 1667 Western-style reforms of Patriarch Nikon were deemed *raskolniki* (schismatic). It remains a powerful force in the lower Volga. To give legitimacy to his destabilization project, he declared himself the true czar, passing himself off as Peter III, who was overthrown by his wife, Catherine the Great, and died soon after in unusual circumstances and who, in his telling, evaded an assassination plot.

In *The History of Pugachev*, Pushkin wrote that "in these turbulent times, an unknown vagabond wandered from Cossack yard to Cossack yard. . . . He stood out for the insolence of his words; he insulted the authorities, instigated Cossacks to flee." He described Pugachev as an impostor, short and gaunt, who wore a peasant caftan in camel skin, crossed himself like a heretic, and said he was the emperor. He'd roused a rabble of Tatars, Bashkirs, Kalmyks, rebel serfs, escaped convicts, and vagabonds.

In 1774, Pugachev occupied Kazan and sparked a revolt against the boyars and officials on both sides of the Volga, from Saratov to Nizhny Novgorod: More than three million peasants participated in the raids against landowners, according to Artem. The imperial army, which had been distracted by a war with the Turks, decided to make an example of them. Pugachev was betrayed, captured, and taken to the Red Square in a bear cage. Catherine the Great spared him the torture inflicted on Razin and simply decapitated him. The crowd raged against this disappointing spectacle, of which Pushkin wrote, "Dear Lord, save us from the Russian mob, so senseless and merciless!"

Artem says some country folk still associate Pugachev with Jesus. They pray to him and hope for his return. Old Believers worship icons of his bloody sword. When Napoleon entered Moscow in 1812, he asked for accounts of the Razin and Pugachev revolts. He wanted to know how to win over the souls of Volga peasants. Revolutionary anarchist Mikhail Bakunin cited them both as precursors of the socialist revolution.

But the Soviets did not have an easy time turning them into heroes. They could hardly include Razin's and Pugachev's peasant revolts in the class-struggle category, given their religious and conservative nature. Plus, glorifying revolts against the state could set a dangerous precedent. This may explain why Soviet director Vasily Shukshin's attempt to make a film about Razin in the 1960s failed spectacularly.

THE SICKLE AND THE FURY

But no one could protect Volga peasants from the massacres of the early 1930s. About three million people died in the Volga region alone from extermination, mass deportations, and famine caused by collectivization policies, according to an analysis of documents that were declassified in the 1990s. Between seven and fourteen million people suffered violence, famine, and sickness in the Caucasian and Ukrainian countryside. Census records reveal an estimate of the death toll: There were thirty-one million Ukrainians in 1926, but twenty-six million in 1939.

Artem tells me villages on the eastern shore near Kazan were among the hardest hit. Less than a hundred years ago, thousands of starving families wandered the roads we walk now, like dead souls, heading for faraway lands of forced labor. Or they migrated to industrial cities on the upper Volga. As in the days of the civil war, orphaned or abandoned children gathered in packs, eating tree bark. There were even cases of cannibalism. The red militias tipped cartfuls of bodies into the river as they requisitioned wheat down to the last grain: In addition to feeding urban workers, it was exported to fund the import of machinery for the new factories. One in three deaths was a child or infant—some were buried alive in mass graves. The heads, legs, and tummies of starving children would swell up to monstrous proportions, and the little ones screamed like animals. Their mothers ran away so as not to hear them. Cities were cordoned off so peasants couldn't shelter there: They had to be punished for opposing Stalin's plans.

In Ukraine, the consequences of this extermination endure to this day, forming the base of anti-Russian nationalism in Kyiv. The grudge has been passed down through generations and continues to grow, along with the sunflowers. In those lands of legendary fertility—Europe's breadbasket—men, women, and children dropped like flies: twenty-five thousand a day, seventeen per minute—at a rate four times higher than in Verdun. It was the first time in history people experienced extermination by food seizure, so Ukraine had to invent a new word for it: *holodomor*, meaning "man-made famine."

Stalin declared war on peasants, whom he believed to be the foundation of the Ukrainian national movement, and continued to eliminate the political and cultural elites. The national deconstruction that followed imposed a sanitized version of Ukrainian culture, though it stopped short of eradicating it. It's impossible to understand Kyiv today without looking at what happened in the '30s: Nazi sympathies that persist in Ukrainian society took root in that era, when much of the country welcomed Hitler as a liberator.

DURANTY SYNDROME

These days, it would be inconceivable to carry out mass starvation without the rest of the world finding out. But back then, Stalin's USSR enjoyed a complacent, if not complicit, Western press. Capitalism was too distracted by the 1929 crash to pay attention to the evils of Communism. And Roosevelt, newly elected, was busy negotiating diplomatic recognition for the USSR and its entry into the League of Nations. Those few who escaped the famine and made it to the United States were faced with distrust and incredulity. Then, after the war, Communists in England, France, and Italy simply denied its existence. Millions of famine victims were thus ignored due to bias, realpolitik, and bad-faith ideological journalism. Walter Duranty, the Pulitzer Prize winner whose *New York Times* dispatches from Moscow acted as Stalin's megaphone, was a handy Kremlin tool to suppress, minimize, or cover up political machinations, the backwardness of Soviet society, and deaths by collectivization.

Duranty was posthumously found to have known the truth—he'd admitted as much to the London Foreign Office—but in the conformism that reigned around the Soviet Union, it was inconvenient to step out of line or sow doubts. When a young Welsh reporter, Gareth Jones, attempted to investigate, he was dismissed as not credible, and struggled for a long time to publish his reporting on events in Ukraine. Intellectuals and colleagues dismissed him as a sensationalist. Almost all of them sided against him. George Orwell was among the few who believed him.

This type of conformism resembles how media outlets—especially in Europe—now censor, ridicule, and marginalize anyone who does not align with the dogmatic and propagandist narrative on the war in Ukraine and the Zelensky phenomenon.

The theme comes up often in my conversations with Ale: We'd started our journey with many questions about Russia, but as we made our way down the Volga, we ended up asking just as many about ourselves, our world, our freedom.

Ale was last in Russia in 2019—he even entered with his American passport. Putin was already the same ruthless leader we know now, but to Ale, a European living in America, life in Saint Petersburg still resembled life in Paris, Copenhagen, or Warsaw. "There were moments when Saint Petersburg reminded me of a Nordic version of Miami—same Bentleys, Lamborghinis, restaurants," he said. "As long as you ignored what was beneath the surface." This time, though, he had to watch what equipment he brought: a compact camera, for tourists, or just a phone. He had to consider what shirts he packed: maybe not the one that said "Peace" on the front. And to think for a moment of using his American passport instead of his Italian one? Madness. This time, it was a whole different story because Russia had become a dangerous place. A complex one. But we can't stop questioning Russia just to avoid facing our equally complicated—and unpalatable—responsibilities.

Since the start of the war, the American press has proved to be far less Manichean than its European counterpart, publishing reports that have been devastating for the reputation of the CIA and NATO, who bear plenty of responsibility for the Ukrainian conflict. In Europe, the press depicts Russia as evil, with a George W. Bush or Rocky vs. Ivan Drago sectarian approach: a hysterical Russophobia that has burned bridges at a critical moment in European history. It is unforgivable that the European press has painted such a historic junction in terms of black and white, good and evil. Even though Putin did attack Ukraine and rules his people with terror. European democracies may pay dearly for this attitude.

In Europe today, it's inconvenient to look back on the events that led to the Russian invasion. Those who doubt that this global dumpster fire could be handled like a Netflix script are automatically branded Putin sympathizers; those who suspect the West may not be in the best position to lecture Russia are seen as antidemocratic.

In Europe, NATO is now the object of media praise, just as Stalin's USSR was: an irrefutable, almost supernatural entity perceived as a just and modern force for good that wages war peacefully and defends Western Civilization against the barbarian peoples of the steppes. To raise doubts about its imperious and unchecked role, despite its often nontransparent, dangerous, and illegal strategies, is seen as heretical and pro-Russian.

A code of silence has been instituted, Duranty style.

OSHARSKAYA ROAD

Night falls as Artem and I stroll along the streets of Nizhny Novgorod. It's Friday, and young people are out in force. We soon get sucked into the hubbub of drunken revelers. Bars are overflowing, with many people dancing on the sidewalks grasping colorful drinks. The girls seem to be holding up better despite their heels, which are as high as their necklines are plunging and their skirts are short. Some are holding hands with their fingers intertwined, perhaps a nod to a subversive intimacy in a country that calls itself gay-free. Maybe it's their way of waging war.

Katya drags Vlad to a bar where the techno music is so loud, I feel my guts shaking just standing outside it. They dance, glasses in hand, a neon sign in the window reading, "To be, not to appear."

I ask Artem why these kids seem to be having the time of their lives when many of their peers are up to their elbows in mud at the front. "Those fighting aren't from the big cities," he says. "They're from small, disadvantaged communities in destitute areas. They join up only for the money. Collectivization is to blame for this, too: Rural and metropolitan areas are like separate hemispheres now. Depending on which one you're from, you'll end up in Donbas or on a dance floor. These posters in heroic Socialist Realist style, which the government uses to offer hundreds of thousands of rubles to volunteers, are directed at those who are desperate, who've already sold their children's gold necklaces and have only their lives to give. Most of the urban population is not directly affected by the war. They go on with their lives, laugh and have fun. What else can they do?"

Was this fatalism? Indifference? Or arrogance, as Piotrovsky had implied back at the Hermitage? I struggle to find meaning in this bizarre July evening on the Volga. I tell Artem that in 1991, I wrote about the first summer of conflict along the beaches of Yugoslavia. I remember an orchestra of elderly musicians playing the foxtrot just for me, the only guest at a grand hotel on the Isle of Pag. Mortars were falling and people were dying just a few miles from the Dalmatian coast. Here along the Volga, the only danger I see is alcohol poisoning.

But only a few hundred feet from the crowds, reality comes crashing in. Artem takes us to Osharskaya Road, which is still known as the brothel street because of its reputation in Gorky's day—in one of his short stories, he calls this corner of the river "desolate and black, like a cold death." A building that once served as a prostitution hub now supposedly hosts military police and FSB offices. Anyone dragged in there at night has a high chance of being sent to a training camp the next morning. "The kids you saw are actually terrified. They drink much more than before," Artem says. "They know not to be found in certain places alone, drunk, and without a solid alibi, or at least an important last name."

PICNIC TIME

As the night draws to a close, we manage to convince Katya and Vlad to halt their hard work of drinking and dancing, and return to our hostel. Along the way, Artem insists on stopping by his house—he wants to give us something. He parks in a yard surrounded by Khrushchevka buildings, popular housing from the 1960s. These are well maintained and inhabited by bourgeois families. He goes up to his apartment and reemerges with a wicker basket. "Lunch for your journey tomorrow:

I hope it will be better than my boring speeches," he says, wiping his forehead, which is covered in sweat from the rush and the emotion. "I wanted to prove my friendship like we did in the old days: The journey is always long in Russia, and it's nice to have some nice food to remind you of who you've met along the way."

We proceed to our lodging as a quiet piano sonata plays on the radio. As we cross the center, near Minin Square—Kuzma Minin was a hero of the war against the Polish invaders Ezzor had mentioned in Kostroma—we come to a traffic jam.

A young woman is lying on the ground, surrounded by a crowd. She has just been run over and she's dead. We are told a drunk driver was responsible. As I close in on foot, I trip on a green high-heeled sandal. There is a frightening silence—even the ambulance's sirens have been turned off. Everyone is standing still around the body, which is half covered by a man's coat. Only the girl's long bare legs poke out, barely a scrape on the ankle of her bare foot. Some girls are sitting on the ground, looking at their friend's body as if it were a blank screen. One, a redhead, is covering her face with her hands. They seem overwhelmed by their inability to cry, but it's as if they all share the same indecipherable feeling. Are they acting this way because of a familiarity with pain? Is this how Russians face death? I wonder whether this small crowd is representative of Russian submissiveness in the face of events—whether its reaction is indicative of the tightening grip of the regime, a seemingly unending war, or a commonplace occurrence—a girl killed on the street on a normal Friday night.

Artem, Katya, and Vlad are just as silent as the ambulance's siren, but soon after leaving the scene, they resume the conversation that had been so abruptly interrupted in the car.

BEE HEAVEN

After leaving Nizhny Novgorod, Gorky's city, we descend on the region of Cheboksary, the land of the Chuvash, a flat land of expansive linen and grain crops, woods, and lakes, where we search for the cemetery where Katya's friend is buried. The area is dotted with peasant villages with thatched roofs. A few minarets announce the presence of a Tatar community. The grass is dark and thick, and the earth is black as tar.

For the first time, we see cattle grazing: Cows belonging to the agricultural collective farms have a large build, while those loitering around peasant stables are as skinny as calves. The landscape is orderly, almost manicured. We drive along a white fence for several miles, beyond which we can see herds of golden horses with slim snouts and big eyes—a breed popular among the Cossacks of the Don, Vlad explains, who famously fought Napoleon's cavalry. Whenever we slow down to photograph them, they run off at a gallop and meet up with us farther down the road, just to tease us again. Vlad finds it extremely amusing and praises the great sense of humor of Russian horses.

Luckily, during this half day of traveling, the road is almost like a walk in the park, without too many killer potholes. Normally, our drives impose a state of hypervigilance that is theoretically incompatible with driving under the influence of alcohol—potholes here are so deep, you hold your breath as you pass over them and forget anything that doesn't have to do with the fate of your tires. It is no trivial matter: The only war scenes we see on this trip are vehicles left in ditches along the side of the road, as if felled by drones.

The likelihood of crashing on a Russian road, especially because of potholes, is sixty times higher than in the United Kingdom, with an average of eighteen thousand deaths per year despite a very limited road network (the United States has ten times more paved roads than Russia). A whole hour can go by without coming across another vehicle, but when it does happen, there is no solidarity between drivers as in the American hinterland, where a honk and a knowing smile mark a return to civilization, a deliverance from solitude and nature, both of which can be immersive and meditative but can also become alienating and oppressive.

We traverse the plains and villages destroyed by forced collectivization. Looking out the window, I can imagine rows of desperate people, their carts stuck in the snow—it's hard not to associate great Russian suffering with the implacable freeze that rages against the most vulnerable. But today, the countryside is flooded with light and farmers are bare chested on their tractors. We pass by hops plantations and vast expanses of scorpion weed—a blue-violet sea that emits such a strong scent we have to roll up our windows to avoid getting high. Each village comprises a handful of little prefab homes and a few *izby* overlooking the only road that cuts southwest as the river veers east, toward the Urals. Geese and chickens roam the few feet of grass that separates each home from the dirt road.

We reach Katya's friend's childhood home, where his mother still lives. A mangy blind dog on a chain stares at us, its vacant eye sockets colonized by swarms of flies. We wait as Katya sits on the steps with the woman, talking and chain-smoking. Then we head to the cemetery. Vlad asks Katya something multiple times in Russian, but only receives annoyed, monosyllabic replies. She continues to smoke. Every so often, she bangs the nape of her neck against the headrest, accentuating the shocks from the van. We are now driving off the main road, onto a path that runs along the scorpion weed, a pure drug for millions of insects.

The graveyard appears out of the field like an atoll in the ocean.

Katya asks us not to enter. "I have to be alone!" She sticks her ear buds in and walks through the wrought iron gate, which squeaks as she opens it. Vlad has a plan (by now we know that when tensions boil over, he pulls out the ace up his sleeve): He places Katya's suitcase on the ground, lays out a towel, and prepares a picnic with the food Artem gave us—smoked pork, black bread, cheese, sweet-and-sour pickles, gooseberries, a bottle of homemade vodka, and four little glasses with silver embroidery. "To the living!" Vlad exclaims in the direction of the tombs. "To the living!" we repeat.

An old man in a wifebeater and heavy wool military fatigues exits the cemetery: He seems friendly, and we offer him a drink. He tells us that the scorpion weed has grown on the abandoned lands of a *kolchoz*: a sign of degradation, but also providence. It's a phenomenal plant, he explains, that feeds on its own flowers because when they fall off, they become a natural fertilizer. This is bee heaven, because here they make the best honey in the world. "We practically live off honey here," the man says. "And there's no need to interfere—the flowers and the bees take care of everything. The villages have emptied out since they closed the *kolchoz*. At the time, the Russians wouldn't let us speak our own language—you could end up in prison if they heard you speak Chuvash. Then, once they allowed it, in the '90s, they closed the *kolchoz* and now we don't have anyone to speak Chuvash with." He tells us the cooperative had been in business since 1937: fourteen villages, each with two hundred houses. They grew hops. Each household was allowed to keep one cow and six thousand square feet of land for a vegetable garden. But what about Stalin's rationing and deportations? The old man shrugs, but not out of carelessness. It's the futility of speaking of the past. "He was the man for the moment," the man says. "He didn't kill anyone personally, right? Russia owes him for everything it is today. Putin couldn't do any better than that." We ask him about Katya's friend. He shrugs again, as if this, too, were in the distant past. "I think he should have stayed in Saint Petersburg. He was a singer there, I hear. There's nothing left here. Only this," he says, pointing his stiff, arthritic finger at Artem's bottle of vodka.

BULL TESTICLES

After leaving the cemetery, Katya downs two cans of beer and starts to talk incessantly with her usual aggressive excitement. Until she falls asleep.

The road to Kazan is long, so we spend the night in Cheboksary. I usually like arriving in a city after dark, expecting to be surprised when I wake up, when a place's true identity emerges in the light of the day. But when we wake up in Cheboksary, that sensation turns into a frightening urge to escape: The receptionist's breath reeks of booze and the air outside smells of industrial chemicals emanating from the local machinery production. The city is doubly depressed because it's no longer Soviet, despite its appearance, but neither has it benefited from the boom of public investment that has rained down on its heavy industry since the war machine took off: tanks, cannons, bulldozers, tractors, threshing machines. The only open restaurant we found for dinner last night served only bull meat, testicles included. Once we'd had enough, we left Katya and Vlad there to finish their drinks.

We wait a long time for them to wake up before we can leave for Kazan. Finally, they appear, with red eyes and groggy voices but also the usual optimism that dissolves our dark sense of foreboding. Yet the ticking of the bomb doesn't go away: Sooner or later, it will go off.

Na grani, on the brink, the condition of relying on a timer.

GREAT EXPECTATIONS

Amazingly, for a few days now, I've been communicating through an encrypted channel with Farid Khairutdinov, a Tatar businessman in Kazan who was described to me as "a very influential Tatar in town." He promises to arrange some interesting meetings for us and to fulfill practically any request. It seems like a great stroke of luck, because Kazan is marked in red on our map: It plays a crucial role in Putin's Russia, it's a political mecca for Russian Islamism, and it acts as a counterweight to the irredentist Caucasian Islamism hostile to Moscow. Rustam Minnikhanov, the governor of Tatarstan, is the Kremlin's shadow negotiator when dealing with Muslim countries in central Asia, the Middle East, and North Africa. He manages the exportation of grain across the Black Sea and traffics with Tehran to circumvent sanctions through the Volga and Caspian Sea. Iranian drones are assembled in Tatarstan. He's also a close friend of Viktor Orbán, who asked Brussels, unsuccessfully, to remove Minnikhanov from the list of individuals sanctioned for supporting the invasion of Ukraine.

Kazan is also home to a prominent university. In 1844, Tolstoy studied Oriental languages and law. That same year, he lost his virginity to a prostitute, which led to an existential crisis, so he packed his bags for Yasnaya Polyana, his estate in Tula. Then came Lenin, perhaps planning on starting a career as a provincial lawyer. But after starting law school, he was expelled for having taken part in a protest, a charge that came after his brother was sentenced to death for trying to assassinate Alexander III.

Kazan is also where Gorky baked bread for a living, and where he decided that after nineteen years of a miserable life, he ought to end things then and there. He tried to shoot himself in the heart on the banks of the Volga but missed and got his lung. At the hospital, he tried again with acid, but he survived that too. His suicide letter ended up in the hands of the local priest, who gave him a good talking to. Gorky agreed that if he decided to hang himself, he'd do it in church.

Kazan awaits us with a host of ideas and stories. Great expectations are confirmed by a message I receive from Khairutdinov while I'm in Kazankov's Mercedes talking about kulaks and Friesian cows: He wants to take us to Tatarskaya Usad'ba, the best restaurant in town.

PUTIN'S EMIRATE

In Kazan, we have just enough time for a brief spin around the city before meeting with Khairutdinov. I'm still experiencing that *na grani* feeling, but this time in the sense of "border."

No one asks us for our papers and we don't pass any barriers, but we've obviously crossed a threshold, as if there were a before and an after to our trip. Even the sky—cluttered with clouds to the west and blue like a Kandinsky painting to the east—tells us we've left the West behind: This is the start of imperial, multiethnic Russia, where the Volga acts as cultural fault line between Europe and Asia. Half the population speaks Russian and the other half Tatar, but there doesn't seem to be any separation between the neighborhoods.

The city outskirts are clean and neat and dotted with wide gaps where the old Soviet apartment blocks were torn down. Traffic flows easily along the wide avenues. The city is undulating, with steep inclines like in San Francisco, modern without looking like a McCity. University areas wend into Islamic alleys, signs are in Cyrillic and Arabic. The vibe is that of an ancient and consolidated community, an amalgam we see in young people, women's clothing, shop windows, street music, architecture. The Orthodox Cathedral of the Annunciation oversees Russian millenary power near the turquoise cupola and four two-hundred-foot minarets of the Kul-Sharif Mosque, the largest in Europe outside Istanbul, built with funds donated by Saudi Arabia and the United Arab Emirates. It's a symbol of a centuries-old Islamic presence in Europe: To make a political point, the mosque was built on the site of the original, which was burned down by Ivan the Terrible. Its imposing structure is a symbol of transcontinental Russia and of its ability to swallow other worlds—the empire was not built overseas, like the British one, but as a physical extension of itself, on the Eurasian plains, steppes, and mountains. Islam is no stranger to Kazan; it's at home here and has been for centuries.

Catherine the Great was invested as empress of Russia in Kazan. In May 1767, she sailed down the river in a four-galley fleet—the *Tver'*, the *Volga*, the *Yaroslavl*, and the *Kazan*—with twenty other vessels containing food and two thousand courtiers. She sent daily reports to Saint Petersburg, describing the people of the Volga as "wealthy and welcoming" and the river as "more beautiful than the Neva." Each stop was a great party, complete with fireworks. Despite being secular and enlightened, she participated in Orthodox processions, met with Islamic and

Orthodox leaders, and denounced the persecution of Old Believers. Despite being a foreigner, she shaped the identity of modern Russia on the Volga. "My friend, I'm in Asia!" she wrote to Voltaire. "There are at least twenty different peoples in this city. None of them look like the others, yet they are one people."

Today, Kazan is a metropolis that seems to have barred the elderly. From what we see in the pedestrian zone between the central Bauman Ulitsa, Tukaya Square, and the kremlin citadel, the median age of the population is below forty. In a country that is facing a dramatic decline in birth rates, including among its Slavic Christian majority, the non-Slavic Muslim community in Kazan and Tatarstan goes against the flow, making it a rising demographic worthy of political courtship: While the median birth rate among Slavic Russians is 1.3 children, it's 2.3 for Muslim Russians. This may be why Putin is so keen on Kazan: If this is the future, he wants to keep a tight grip on it. He knows that Orthodox Slavs are not the only face of Russia and that without an alliance with Islam on the Volga, his plans to rival European and Asian power are destined to fail.

TATAR LAMB

Khairutdinov's welcome at Tatarskaya Usad'ba immediately contrasts with the tone of his messages. He's clearly trying to keep his distance.

He's in his fifties, stocky and square faced, with giant ears and the hands of a child. He leads us into a private room, where we sit down with Mansur Hazrat Jalaletdinov, a mullah at the Marjani Mosque, the only one active in Kazan until 1990, after which about a hundred more sprang up. His secretary, Alina, translates—she speaks excellent English. Khairutdinov tells me that just a few days ago, at this very table, he and the mullah lunched with Governor Rustam Minnikhanov and Dimitry Medvedev—former prime minister and president, now deputy chairman of the Security Council.

He then explains that he considers me and Ale enemies, and that no one in Kazan wants to talk to us or answer our questions. We're better off visiting the museum. He reminds me he served in the FSB, and the mullah nods, clearly pleased. The message is clear: If we decide to stick around Kazan, we'll be in trouble. That said, in a demonstration of Russian Tatar hospitality, he offers us an unforgettable lunch: twelve courses, four waiters at our beck and call, and three hours of conversation that is as absurd as it is instructive. We start with meatballs in broth, then meander through courses of fish, meat, pike, chicken stuffed with eggs, sturgeon, boiled goose, horse sausage. They tell me the Tatar language has no word for "retreat," that the Tatars had been the best archers under Peter the Great, and that Mikhail Kutuzov, the general who defeated Napoleon, had been a Tatar. I point out that Kutuzov put down the Tatar resistance in Crimea in the late eighteenth century. "Yes, he lost an eye," Khairutdinov says, and the mullah nods. "We love to wage war. Am I right, Mansur?" "Yes," Mansur says. "We also fight against our demons."

I try to pursue the topic, but Khairutdinov changes the subject. "Sanctions have united us even more as a people," he says. As the skewered lamb arrives, Khairutdinov tells me that before the sanctions I would have been eating "shit lamb from New Zealand," but that this meat, tender and tasty, is from Tatarstan. Not only that, but up until yesterday, this very lamb was grazing just a few miles away. He raised it himself, he claims, and killed it with his little hands. His business is organic lamb and goose meat. He has stores all over Tatarstan, one in Kaliningrad and one in Sakhalin, on the Pacific. "There's no competition, it's amazing," he says. "Just think, we used to import geese from Romania and France. Now I export goose legs and cured meat to Turkey."

I ask why he never raised lamb or geese before the war, or why Russia, with all its intelligent and industrious entrepreneurs, produced so little and imported almost everything without generating significant income outside the oil and gas industry. The mullah looks me in the eyes for the first time and tells me this is precisely the Russian genius: "Buying without producing," he says. "Why should I make a bicycle if I can just buy one? I spend less money. Easy." Khairutdinov seems to think this answer flawless, though it contradicts his entire economic theory of organic geese.

When I tell them Kazankov, the boss at the collective farm, is also a fan of the sanctions, they don't seem surprised. I deduce that they've already been informed of our meeting. What's certain is that Khairutdinov and the mullah are none too happy about it. Khairutdinov rattles off Kazankov's long rap sheet. He calls him an anti-Tatar Communist who wants Russification. He says Tatarstan's success is annoying to the old Communist guard. "If people like him were in charge, they'd eliminate all minorities. But we believe in Putin. He protects us."

He tells us that many key positions, including the dean of the university, have been given to Tatars, who also hold top roles in refineries, tech, and the massive military industry, including in the new plants that produce strategic Tupolev bombers. "Putin says that we're the third capital of Russia," Khairutdinov declares, finally admitting the existence of a pact: The Kremlin allows the loyal, traditional Islam of the Volga to prosper, and in exchange, the mosques provide intelligence that keeps out Islamist cells and keep an eye on the troubled republics of Chechnya and Dagestan.

"That's enough now," Khairutdinov says suddenly. The others jump up, sliding their chairs back noisily. Alina seems uncomfortable, disappointed because she was looking forward to dessert and because we've established a rapport—she doesn't see us as dangerous Western enemies.

I ask her to relay our gratitude for the unforgettable lunch, and whether she thinks it helped placate Khairutdinov's hostility. Can we safely wander around Kazan? She shakes her head no, giving us a compassionate look. Khairutdinov understands, and nods to confirm that the sentence is final. He leaves without shaking our hands.

9

In Lenin and Oblomov's neighborhood

"Today we ask ourselves again: What do we do?"

THE MODEL STUDENT

Dimitri Rusin is an academic and tour guide who has agreed to show us around Ulyanovsk, the city where Vladimir "Volodya" Ilyich Ulyanov, more widely known as Vladimir Lenin, lived until 1887, when he moved to Kazan to pursue his studies. He's fifty years old, with a thick reddish beard and gray hair gathered in a ponytail, and he never appears in public without his straw hat. He speaks quietly, but is not afraid to say what he means, and never looks away when making his point, which right now involves an interesting anecdote about a young Lenin and his neighbor, Aleksandr Kerensky, who led the short-lived Russian Republic before it was overturned by Lenin's Bolsheviks.

As the story goes, Kerensky's father was a high school principal, who made a personal visit to Lenin's mother Maria Alexandrovna, here at Lenin Ulitsa number 70, then known as Moskovkaya Ulitsa, to give her a letter. It was a Sunday in late June 1887. "Based on her correspondence, there is a good chance that Fyodor Kerensky, the high school principal, arrived with his wife and six-year-old son Aleksandr, known as Sasha," says Rusin. In those days, Ulyanovsk was called Simbirsk, and it had the highest concentration of landed gentry, trade wealth, and large estates along the Volga—like Windsor on the Thames or Natchez on the Mississippi. But as history would have it, Simbirsk paid dearly for this record, suffering the worst Stalinist purges of the Volga and the demolition of hundreds of Russia's most exquisite villas and palaces.

The Ulyanovs and the Kerenskys lived about seven hundred feet from each other. There was a professional relationship between the elder Mr. Kerensky and Lenin's father, Ilya Nikolayevich Ulyanov, who had been in charge of education in the province of Simbirsk, where he'd opened 450 new schools. For his troubles, Ilya Ulyanov, son of a tailor and former serf, had been inducted into the Order of Saint Vladimir and elevated to the rank of nobility. When Ulyanov died of a brain hemorrhage, Mr. Kerensky's visit to his widow was an act of respect not just to his former boss but to an imperial official who had lent a great service to educational modernization in that corner of Russia.

The letter is still on the dining room table of Lenin's childhood home, which is now a museum. It extols Lenin's virtues as a high school student: "A model student, very talented, focused and intelligent . . . he has never given school officials cause for discontent through inappropriate words or actions. . . . He has always excelled in class and at the end of the course he earned a gold medal for significant advancement and model behavior. . . . Religion and discipline are the foundations of his education." It is a recommendation letter for entry to the law program in Kazan, and it specifies that Lenin shows "a sometimes excessive reserve and a standoffish attitude even toward peers the school holds in high regard."

It was a rather courageous visit, since everyone had distanced themselves from the Ulyanov family. Just over a month before his father's death, Lenin's older brother had been sentenced to death in Saint Petersburg for making the bombs used in the attempt on Czar Alexander III's life. Simbirsk, a monarchist stronghold, had turned its back on the Ulyanovs, even though they were loyal subjects of the emperor. "The principal wanted to show that the gymnasium didn't harbor hatred and was not interested in retaliation," Dimitri explains. "Leninism and Stalinism suppressed or eliminated anyone with ties to an enemy of the party. Entire families disappeared, along with friends. That boy and his mother," Dimitri says, pointing to a painting of them hanging in Lenin's bedroom, "would probably have been executed had it been the 1930s."

The principal's visit painted a picture of what this city—or these few blocks overlooking the Volga's spectacular shores—meant to the history of Russia.

THE FREEMASON

We're in a living room with an orange-stained wooden floor, a grand piano, a table, a chessboard, four Thonet chairs, and a large brass samovar. It's where tea was served that Sunday afternoon, when Vladimir, the model student, and Aleksandr, the principal's son, met for the first time. Aleksandr, in piqué clothes, probably played in Vladimir's little brothers' room, where wooden toys are still on display along with rag dolls and a rocking horse. He may even have gone into the sand pit in the garden to play *lapta*, a rural Russian version of cricket the Ulyanov family was fond of, or run into the orchard to catch butterflies. If the gooseberries were ripe, little Sasha might have nibbled at their bush, as Vlad is doing right now as I watch him from the second-floor window.

Forty years after that Sunday afternoon, Vladimir Lenin and Aleksandr Kerensky met again in Saint Petersburg. Both lawyers, both revolutionaries, both atheists, both determined to overthrow the autocratic regime, both leading exploited workers, both heads of government. But only one, the eldest, the first in his class, the Marxist with a brusque attitude, made himself indispensable. To the detriment of the other.

As the events of 1917 began to unfold, Kerensky was already on the scene. Soon thereafter, Lenin arrived from his exile in Switzerland. Trotsky and Nikolai Bukharin returned from their exile in America, and Lev Kamenev and Stalin were still political prisoners in Siberia. By early 1917, Kerensky was already a seasoned politician, a great lawyer who defended terrorists and Freemasons, and was even secretary general of the Grand Orient of Russia. Dimitri tells me that in Simbirsk, which in 1917 counted fewer than fifty thousand residents, there were five Masonic lodges. In the February Revolution and the months leading up to that turbulent October, Kerensky, a socialist, was the dominant figure on the scene: He was histrionic and theatrical and knew how to rile the people. He positioned himself as an indispensable leader, the only one who could keep the chaos at bay and mediate relations between the radical Left, Mensheviks, liberals, and monarchists. He envisioned a socialist revolution, but not a radical one. For example, he tried to forbid soldiers and workers from singing the "Marseillaise," the French national anthem. "His choices ended up triggering the Bolshevik Spring and the idol became the traitor, the coward," Dimitri says bitterly, as we sit on Lenin's childhood bed, his blue high school jacket hanging from a hook. The shelves contain his physics, chemistry, Latin, Greek, and French textbooks and a book called *Life of European Peoples*. Dimitri tells me that he has always loved Kerensky: He may be the only one in town who sides with the loser and is suitably punished for it by having to extol the myth of the winner to make a living. "Everything would have been different. But he made mistakes, he rode the revolution, and on the finish line, he handed the reins to Lenin."

THE AMERICAN CAR

Russia's fate was hanging in the balance. Kerensky was well groomed and narcissistic, and often dressed as a bourgeois revolutionary—today we might call his attire radical chic. He was small in stature but had a powerful voice, which he used to pontificate everywhere, as if he wanted to stem the tide of events with his presence. Kerensky joined the temporary government and mediated with the Soviets in Petrograd while Lenin returned from exile with an armored train carrying tens of thousands of marks sent from Germany, the empire's enemy. As minister of justice, Kerensky granted amnesty to political prisoners. In May 1917, he became minister of war as the conflict with Germany plunged Russia into deeper ruin. He encouraged members of the army to exercise their democratic representation by joining the Soviets, where the strength of the Bolsheviks was growing. Soldiers stopped listening to their czarist officers and started to follow the Bolshevik rabble-rousers, who counted on the repressed anger of the peasants. They were rotting in the trenches when they heard of the fall of the czar, news they greeted as a signal for everyone to go home. Yet the government still wouldn't negotiate peace.

According to my guide, Kerensky set off the rebellion and then dug his own grave by consolidating power for the Bolsheviks and Lenin. He refused to end the conflict with central European powers amid increased anger and desertion among troops. At the same time, he reinstated the death penalty for deserters, radicalizing them.

"If he did it on purpose, hoping to speed things up with the Constituent Assembly [convened after the February Revolution in 1917], he greatly miscalculated and showed a great deal of presumption. Lenin wasn't presumptuous—he was a cool and calculating fanatic," Dimitri says.

When Kerensky became head of government that July, he was no longer the people's savior. Trotsky and Lenin were now firing up the crowds. Soldiers and workers descended on the streets of Petrograd, red flags in hand. Kerensky repressed the revolt and ordered Lenin's arrest, but he went into hiding. When Kerensky came to believe that General Lavr Kornilov was preparing a military coup, he went back to Lenin, who gave him just enough rope with which to hang himself, Dimitri says.

That September, Kerensky's bourgeois government armed the Bolsheviks against the presumed coup plotters. Trotsky's Red Guards then used those same weapons to stage an assault on the Winter Palace. Lenin's party, which had won a slim minority in the revolutionary front, positioned itself as a defender of the rights of workers, peasants, and soldiers. Lenin became the savior of a nation in danger. Dimitri tells me that after that summer, Kerensky lost credibility among the revolutionaries, but his authority was still seen as the only way to anchor Russia to liberal Europe and follow the Constituent Assembly: "By then, Kerensky no longer cared about the revolution. He wanted to be the head of the first democratic government in Russian history. London, Paris, and Washington supported him in this."

When Kerensky's moment in the sun arrived—with the Constituent Assembly, parliamentary elections, a new Russian Republic—he didn't realize Lenin was also gearing up to lead the armed proletariat and seize power, regardless of the outcome of the elections, which turned out to be unfavorable to him: The Bolsheviks won only a quarter of the vote. Peasants had opted for Kerensky's revolutionary socialists. "Elections count for nothing," Lenin said. "No revolution has ever waited for a majority. History would not forgive the revolutionaries for any hesitation." The message was clear: Kerensky's government, led by the son of Lenin's old high school principal, was the only thing standing in Lenin's way. It had to be stopped.

Kerensky fled the Winter Palace a few minutes before the assault, amid cannon shots from the cruiser *Aurora*—he got away in a car provided by the American embassy. Lenin and the proletariat gained power in a country where Marx and Engels never could have imagined it happening, that is, in a semifeudal, peasant Russia that had never experienced an industrial bourgeoisie or political liberalism. Russia was going from one tyranny to another. Lenin thought the Petrograd example would soon be followed in London, Paris, Berlin, Rome, everywhere. In the meantime, 400,000 Bolsheviks held on to power just as 130,000 landowners had managed to do under the czar.

Kerensky fled to Paris and then to New York. Like Lenin, he never returned to his old stomping grounds on the banks of the Volga. His home is no longer standing, and even Dimitri doesn't know exactly where it was. Just that it was near the cemetery of the Intercession Monastery—a longtime burial ground for local nobles—which was excavated in the early 1930s to make room for a single tomb, that of his excellency the education inspector Ilya Nikolayevich Ulyanov, complete with a half bust on a large stone memorial and a young Vladimir Lenin leaning against it, looking meditative with an open book in hand, as if to say that sometimes, children are the ones who ensure their fathers' memories live forever.

"At a crucial crossroads," Dimitri says, "Russia took masochistic pleasure in going the wrong way. As if giving in to an innate attraction for the abyss."

SUBVERSIVE GOSPELS

Dimitri and I are sitting in the Ulyanov kitchen. The ocher walls and honey-colored oak cupboards are awash in light. Dimitri is at home here, so Mrs. Olga Saleva, the custodian, doesn't hang around to check on him (she gets mad, and rightly so, only when I ask if I can try on Lenin's wolfskin coat, which is hanging in the hall). And anyway, unless a group of Chinese tourists shows up, a deathly silence reigns in these low-ceilinged rooms where, until the fall of the USSR, people lined up for hours to get in.

We open the window and hear the unchained melody of a thrush in heat. Dimitri observes the swaying birches, gathering his thoughts. "In 1917, the Bolshevik way wasn't the only way," he says. "Kerensky shouldn't have ignored the democratic demands of the February Revolution, when the Bolsheviks were just a handful of people. He should have immediately convened the Constituent Assembly, launched an agrarian reform to lock in peasant support, and found a diplomatic solution to the war. Now this city might be named after Kerensky. The same goes for when Stalin died, in 1953. The Soviet Union could have chosen a clearer democratic path. And again in Yeltsin's day. So many lost opportunities in less than a century."

I express hope that it won't be like this forever. "If Russia can't come to terms with its Soviet past," Dimitri says, "I don't see any other way. The alternate reality perpetuated by the Soviet regime has created large gaps we haven't been able to fill. Putin is taking advantage of that. He's rewriting history, creating new myths to serve his own ends. All his speeches reference this alternative reconstruction. In schoolbooks, the revisionism is increasingly clear year after year. For example, imperialist literature on eastern Europe weighs heavily on relations with the Baltics, Poland, and Finland. If we don't get out from under that, we'll be crushed. It's time to ask ourselves, once again, What is to be done?"

What Is to Be Done? is a novel by Nikolay Chernyshevsky, which two generations of Russian revolutionaries have referred to as if it were their bible. A copy sits on Lenin's desk along with several volumes by Gogol, Turgenev's *Memoirs of a Hunter*, and a story about Spartacus. Chernyshevsky's book was banned at the time, and its presence on the desk of a seventeen-year-old Lenin might seem to contradict his image as a respectful high school student uninterested in anti-czarist subversion. But Dimitri knows how that book ended up in Lenin's house, a month before the visit from the Kerenskys. It came from the Peter and Paul Fortress in Saint Petersburg, in a package addressed to his mother containing the few possessions of her firstborn son, Aleksandr. He had been hanged with four other terrorists, despite taking full responsibility for the assassination attempt on Alexander III, whom he referred to as the "crowned beast" when the police picked him up, a cocked Browning in his pocket. He was a veritable Nikolai Stravrogin, the main character from Dostoyevsky's *Demons*.

Within days, Lenin had read the book, reread it, and through the figure of Rakhmetov, understood why his brother had died. This led him to take that first enormous step that crossed the line between the theoretical and the fight against the oppressor. He decided not to accept Russian history but to make it. Sixteen years after devouring that doctrine of subversion, he climbed to the top of the list of the Okhrana, the czarist secret police, and became the Lenin we know today. He wrote his own *What Is to Be Done?*, an ideological manual for the professional Marxist-Leninist revolutionary, a road map to power.

Dimitri shows more empathy for Lenin's brother, the defeated idealist assassin, than for the victorious socialist leader. He becomes emotional as he translates a letter Lenin's brother wrote to their mother on the eve of his execution. "Terror is the only force available to a minority pitting its spiritual strength and rights against the might of a dominant majority. Students are encouraged to develop their intellectual abilities, but then they are not allowed to use them in support of their country. There will always be Russians who are so devoted to their ideas and sensitive to the misery of their people that they're willing to give their lives to this cause."

THE SCRAP HEAP

Kerensky died in 1970, at eighty-nine years old, forty-six years after Lenin. There is no statue of him that I know of, while Lenin can be found on every continent, including Antarctica, despite the global de-Leninization that followed the fall of the USSR, when many Lenin statues were knocked down in former Soviet republics and in eastern Europe. In Russia alone, he still holds court in five thousand squares. "In truth, he hasn't really been buried yet," Dimitri says. "That mummy in the Red Square is still keeping an eye on us, and on Putin. Burying Lenin would be a revolutionary act, a liberation. No man can escape returning to the earth. But many believe that so long as Lenin remains where he is, Russia will never break free of its Communist past."

In 1970, two months after Kerensky's death and a hundred years after Lenin's birth, Ulyanovsk inaugurated a memorial to the Soviet leader. While Leningrad was considered the "cradle of the revolution," Ulyanovsk was to be the mecca of Communism. "They leveled the entire old town," Dimitri tells me as we walk down the avenue of the museums, where a tile fountain seems to have died of thirst many years ago.

Lenin's memorial grounds have been closed for years, receding back into the scrap heap. There are a few signs of restoration attempts, but the neglect is widespread and also affects Lenin's bronze bas-relief on the main building's facade, oxidized by the weather. The degradation did not spare the statues of the pioneers either, porous as tuff, the red of their handkerchiefs faded, the carnations dried out.

The memorial encompasses the Pioneer Park (named for the Young Pioneers, a Soviet version of the Boy Scouts), concert and conference spaces, a Marxist-Leninist school, and the two houses—taken apart and put back together—where the Ulyanovs lived on the banks of the Volga before moving to Lenin Ulitsa. The museum complex also houses a three-dimensional model and a photographic exhibition of historic Ulyanovsk, to show what it looked like before it was sacrificed on the altar of the Soviets. The facility is in modern Soviet style, covered in white marble, with a solemn and serious effect despite its massive scale. The space takes up a total of 430 acres—215,000 square feet of which is dedicated to the memorial itself—designed by architectural stars Boris Mezenchev, Janko Konstantinov, and Garold Isakovich, who were awarded the 1972 Lenin Prize in architecture. It's impressive—although regime architecture always strikes me as delusional in its brazen attempt to challenge the laws of history and hold on to power forever.

Dimitri could go on for hours, and often does, when Chinese tourists come to see Lenin Square and hear about the father of the revolution and all the works donated in his honor by socialist and capitalist countries alike. But tour groups are few and far between. All I see is a mother pushing a stroller over the jagged paving, tripping along as she goes.

IDEOLOGICAL DOPING

We're now at the riverbank, where we catch sight of one of the most spectacular views on the Volga: Four miles of water separate historic Ulyanovsk from the industrial suburbs on the eastern shore. Two bridges cross the river at this point: the Emperor Bridge, inaugurated in 1913—the last one built by the czars, which took only two years—

and the President Bridge, the first one built in post-Soviet Russia, which took twenty-three years and was finished in 2012.

The river is roiling, a strong wind blows, and people walk down the street holding down various clothing items with both hands. Dimitri's straw hat flies off twice. We head down to the dock to take a closer look at some bushes that have been pruned to spell out LENIN. A welcome sign for anyone arriving in Ulyanovsk by river. But it's practically unreadable and the *N* is completely gone. Gardeners have stopped trimming the hedges for lack of pay. "No funds are coming from Moscow," Dimitri says. "The memorial complex was closed about ten years ago for restorations but work never began. Putin has abandoned Ulyanovsk because it's the only region where the Communist Party is more popular than the ruling United Russia. But they're votes of despair, not ideology: Ulyanovsk has been the most deprived and violent place in Russia for thirty years. Putin wants to erase all remnants of Lenin's myth."

We continue our walk. Dimitri says the Kremlin's rubles would be very useful—if it reopened the memorial, maybe he could get a permanent position there—but Lenin is an "unmentionable" in Ulyanovsk, responsible for cursing the city by simple association. He was tolerated when he drew thousands of visitors, five thousand per day in the late '80s. "Now it's five thousand per year and they're almost always Chinese. You can't even find Lenin on fridge magnets anymore."

The wind sweeps away our words, so we shelter behind a broken portable toilet. The door slams with every gust. "With Stalin it's different. The propaganda machine has associated him with a glorious idea of the Soviet Union, unlinking him from Communism. Lenin is too cerebral—he doesn't fit into today's need for easy approximations. He's too European. Even though there's a statue of him in practically every square, he's a cumbersome stranger."

According to Dimitri, nostalgia for the USSR even appeals to people who didn't experience it. "Many young people adore Stalin—a frightening idealization. They link him to the idea of Empire, which is prevalent, deeply rooted, a sort of ideological doping. Stalin's the perfect drug,

simple to administer . . . greatness and imperialism. Our people are like that." Dimitri is upset, his lips are shaking. "I feel a catastrophe coming."

THE TWO CITIES

Ulyanovsk's new claim to fame, to overcome its Leninist lodestone, is the "mother of talent." In that, it's spoiled for choice. Streets all around the Russian Federation have been named after people born in Ulyanovsk: historian Nikolai Karamzin; poet Nikolay Yazykov, whom Pushkin called "a fountain of champagne"; poet and soldier Denis Davydov, who led a partisan war against Napoleon. It makes you wonder where Russia might have ended up without this little provincial city or, more specifically, these four blocks overlooking the Volga. Outside a restaurant in Lenin Square, there is a hideous stone sculpture of a daybed, bedside rug, and slippers to represent the slothful and sleepy Oblomov, protagonist of the eponymous book by Ivan Goncharov, another Ulyanovsk native. Turgenev considered him to be the best Russian writer of the nineteenth century even though—probably out of laziness—he only ever wrote three books. It took him three months to write *Oblomov*, his seminal work.

"This was where two opposite and irreconcilable Russian worlds met and became one," Dimitri says, gesturing at our surroundings. "There's Lenin, a permanent revolutionary who created a new humanity and a new society; and there's Oblomov, who lives in the past, disgusted by progress and by the new order it creates, who is horrified by action because nothing is worth doing and so he exists by inertia, without hopes or goals. Oblomov is the calm and conservative Russian, son of the expansive plains, with a great soul and no ambition for change; Lenin wants to save Russia from its torpor and unleash what it has been keeping bottled up inside. Here are two essential traits of the Russian spirit—gentleness and radicalness." Dimitri concludes, citing Turgenev, "So long as a single Russian lives, Oblomov will be remembered!"

Dimitri does not side with Lenin's but with Oblomov's point of view. He identifies with his great spiritual detachment from the world and its assets, and his awareness of his physical weakness and the ephemeral nature of human action. "It's different in the West," he says. "You have no choice but to act, defend your social position, your assets, and your comforts. We don't have this same sense of ownership, and we don't think that life should be driven by the enjoyment of material goods. It's funny how this city, as rich as it was, capitalist, in a way, was Goncharov's and Lenin's city. It was home to the reactionary and the revolutionary. Maybe they both hated it."

When Lenin wanted to highlight the bourgeois inclinations of the Mensheviks, an offshoot of his party, he called them Oblomovists, borrowing the imagery of the limp and defeatist character from his neighbor's novel. It soon became a cliché.

Goncharov was born fifty-eight years before Lenin, a stone's throw from his home. The son of traders and landowners, he would have been a prime target for the Bolsheviks. The sixteenth-century Goncharov palace—which rivaled the grand style of Italian architectural works in Saint Petersburg—takes up an entire city block and is almost as large as Lenin's memorial.

Much like his lethargic character, Goncharov spent his life in Saint Petersburg, but Oblomov's famous dream, the crux of the novel, is set in his family's estate on the Volga—a lost paradise called Oblomovko, where time slows down to a regular and repetitive beat, and its citizens refuse to seek out news from "out there." Boredom is a comforting balm, silence is an almost deathly slumber, the ideal is happiness without pretense and a life without surprises. "It's Russia's existential lethargy," Dimitri says. "After all, Oblomovko is the land of our dreams."

HOUSE OF DEATH

But Simbirsk wasn't a place out of a dream but a paradise on the Volga. And in the 1920s and '30s, Ulyanovsk was hell on earth.

To understand the roots of Ulyanovsk's campaign to undermine Lenin's legacy, we have to look at Pokrovskaya Ulitsa, a block from Lenin's house. It was one of Russia's most prestigious streets but became a road to perdition for suspected enemies of the people and Trotskyists, starting from a patrician home at number 73, known as the Sakhov House, that was nationalized in the revolution and then became NKVD headquarters. Dimitri tells me that in the late 1930s, when about five million Soviet citizens were swept up in the Great Terror, at least twenty-two thousand people were executed in its cellar—as noted by a memorial stone embedded in the gate—including the elderly abbess of the Intercession Convent, Ekaterina Dekalina, accused of starting a Fascist, antirevolutionary, Orthodox group. "They asked her what she thought of Soviet power, and she said she believed it to be the coming of the Antichrist. She was undressed and put up against the wall. She was recently canonized."

The infamous head of the NKVD at the time, Nikolai Yezhov—also known as the bloodthirsty dwarf—often used the building as his base of operations on the Volga. It was the region's slaughterhouse. Only one place saw more killings: another cellar, in the NKVD building in Kazan. They called it the Black Lake, and it became the university's version of Lubyanka, which was then the NKVD headquarters in Moscow and now houses the FSB. "Few Volga intellectuals made it out alive," Dimitri says. "Forty university professors were arrested and tortured in

Black Lake Park, thirty were executed on the spot or in work camps. In Simbirsk, none of the residents of these luxury houses survived."

Large amounts of capital started flowing into the city between the late nineteenth century and early twentieth, positioning Simbirsk as a center of the prerevolutionary Russian architectural movement. The blocks between Pokrovskaya Ulitsa and Lenina Ulitsa resemble the Jugendstil model neighborhood around Karlsplatz, in Vienna. They contain dozens of masterpieces designed by some of the greatest architects of the time. When Lenin died in 1924, the city changed its name to Ulyanovsk and two hundred stately homes and forty churches were demolished. It spared the country club where the assembly of nobles gathered, the mansion that housed the bank of the nobles—opened in 1911 and cleaned out by the Bolsheviks—and the Palladian-style agrarian university on the Volga, which became a nursing home for the *nomenklatura*. The Sakhov building, a French Renaissance–style home, was designed by Avgust Šade (another Ulyanovsk native). It is still widely seen as the house of death: It was the Ulyanovsk headquarters of the KGB and it now houses the FSB.

THE RED BELT

During our tour of Lenin's old neighborhood, we see many burnt-down houses, even beautiful stately ones. Dimitri explains that the owners hire criminals to burn them down to avoid the cost of restoring them to code. They'd rather build a new one just to stay in the only relatively safe neighborhood in the city.

Ulyanovsk has been under a curfew since the 1990s. In 2017, a group of mothers asked Putin to do something. "Our children are dying in the streets," they wrote. Ulyanovsk has the highest unemployment rate in European Russia, and it acts as a heroin-trafficking hub, according to the UN. Heroin travels to Astrakhan from Afghanistan and then up the Volga, where it is delivered to the Ulyanovsk mob. Gangs run the city, and even extort money from schools, where principals are forced to pay for protection. "The gangs shoot at the windows until they get their cut,"

Dimitri tells me. In 2007 there was a big fight in Lenin Square among two hundred armed minors, some with Kalashnikovs. It lasted all night and resulted in five dead and thirty wounded. According to Katya, Ulyanovsk became the epicenter of the drug trade around the year 2000, after leaders in the region—known as the "Red Belt" of the Volga for its Communist leanings—created a patch of resistance to oppose Moscow's reforms while continuing to spend on social assistance. It was a last stand against the reigning antisovietism. "Ulyanovsk was the last bastion of the Soviet Union in the new Russia, and industry withstood better here than in areas that had adopted the free-market experiment," Dimitri says. The city attracted thousands of immigrants from the East and the Caucasus. "They came to look for jobs among the Communists," Dimitri says. There was a huge demographic boom. Then it all came tumbling down as the free market swallowed up Ulyanovsk too. The factories closed and the city became one big ghetto governed by the mob. The only industry was the drug trade; officials and police became powerless or were paid off.

In response, Putin diverted two SOBR death squads from Chechnya. At the time, the mobster Sergey Kapralov, known as the Corporal, led an army of three thousand kids who controlled various slices of the city. Dimitri remembers a SOBR blitz near the Kamyshinsky market—everyone was made to lie face down on the ground except for the Corporal, who was sent to fight in the Caucasus for a few years. Upon his return to Ulyanovsk, he went back to managing prostitution and the heroin trade in all of southern Russia. He died of a heart attack in 2017. "They don't make bosses like that anymore," Dimitri says. "And there aren't as many drugs going around now. The city is now run by small cartels who live off extortion, flash-kidnappings, raids. The most powerful group is called the AUE [Prisoners' Criminal Unity]. Its members are between the ages of thirteen and nineteen. In 2020 the Supreme Court branded them a terrorist organization."

Ulyanovsk has become a way of life. It's the only place where the *gopnik* culture survives, where teenagers from disadvantaged suburbs adopt the codes and tattoos of convicts, like "doing the crab" (squatting, like prisoners do to avoid sitting on the cold ground), and shooting *blatnaya* videos, a music genre that romanticizes violence and racism.

The Beverly Hills of imperial Russia, Oblomov's Eden, the cradle of Leninism, is now a dying city. "Many see the front as their last chance," Dimitri says. He's already lost three friends in Donbas, while two of his wife's friends were widowed in the first month of the war. "There's nothing left here. They just come to film documentaries on baby gangs—we've become a freak show."

THE PRIVILEGED

It's late afternoon by the time we bid goodbye to Dimitri and cross the President's Bridge. For a long stretch of road, we head away from the Volga, and plunge into an amorphous, monotonous landscape. I wonder if wide-open spaces like these are what make Russians want to shake it all up, burn it all down, or drink. They certainly put the European gaze to the test—at any given moment, this landscape seems extraordinarily important or totally irrelevant. "Fill it with your imagination, or it stays silent," Vlad suggests.

We, too, remain silent on our way to Togliatti. We listen to bluesy rock, Jimmy Page, Eric Clapton, while our fatigue and tension grow compound, our thoughts pregnant with foreboding. The birch trees here are shorter, followed by fields of sunflowers as far as the eye can see. In the distance we see a row of migrating birds, a black line fluctuating in blue. I think of Dimitri's stories of those years of terror, when execution was a privilege, a way out of the horrific agony wreaked by torture to extract denunciations. The purges were so widespread that any Russian Communist with a small amount of power and any foreign Communist living in Moscow would have known about them. Why didn't they rebel? Or alert the world?

I reread a passage on evil by revolutionary anarchist Mikhail Bakunin. He believed that Russia's brand of evil is worse than its European counterpart, "not because the people of Russia are evil, on the contrary," he wrote:

> I think Russians have more good in them, more heart, more spirit than Westerners. But western Europe has a remedy to evil: public opinion and freedom. . . . This remedy does not exist in Russia. Western Europe sometimes seems meaner, but it's because evil is visible, and few things remain hidden. But in Russia, illnesses run deep and corrode the foundations of our social organism. Fear is the essential engine of Russia, and fear destroys all life, all intelligence. It's painful to live in Russia if you value truth . . . if you suffer for the oppression inflicted on your neighbor.

Then I think of Palmiro Togliatti, leader of the Italian Communist Party. In 1964, a week after his death in Yalta, Brezhnev named a new city after him, the one we're about to see. Togliatti had been one of Stalin's most trusted accomplices. Bakunin's formula didn't work on him: If a Westerner in Moscow didn't want to die, they had to forget the truth and toe the party line, and the simple fact that Togliatti survived, despite being a Comintern heavyweight—and became a Soviet citizen in 1930—while thousands of Western Communists living in Russia were imprisoned and executed, proves his full complicity in the purges. Like when he dissolved the Polish Communist Party in 1938, leading to the massacre of almost all Polish Communists in Russia. Like when he used the Lubyanka model in the Spanish Civil War, where he orchestrated the elimination of anarchist and anti-Stalinist opposition elements. People like Togliatti, who survived the purges, knew what was happening, but kept silent to save themselves. And they remained silent even after returning from Moscow. When Stalin died in 1953, Togliatti called him "a giant of thought, a giant of action." In 1956, he called Khrushchev destabilizing, and in 1957, he voted for the execution of former Hungarian Prime Minister Imre Nagy.

We arrive in Togliatti on the back of an infinite sunset—they're all like this until the Caspian Sea, as if the sun feared it may never again rise over Russia.

Italian car company Fiat built Togliatti in 1966 as a Soviet dream city, a car capital in the middle of the steppes. It took less than a year to expand it by fifty million square feet—a historic feat, a geo-economic operation that cost almost $1 billion and took place with the support of the White House and Ford at the height of the Cold War. Togliatti became a bridge between socialist and capitalist worlds, bringing American technology to the Soviet Union by way of Fiat.

We drive past the AvtoVaz facilities, which in 1970 churned out six hundred thousand Zhiguli cars per year: It was a version of the Fiat 124, beefed up to handle Soviet road and climatic conditions and named after the hills south of Togliatti, our next destination. A series of warehouses stretch for almost six miles, all numbered and with the same slogan written in red: "Together, for Russia, my country, my pride."

The writing appeared after the 2022 nationalization of Renault, which had previously held a majority share in AvtoVaz. At the time of the invasion of Ukraine, Renault was the biggest automaker on the Russian market, with forty-five thousand employees. Macron forced Renault to give it all up, thereby letting go of a big piece of its world production—almost seven hundred thousand cars were manufactured in Togliatti each year, the company's second-largest market, with five hundred thousand cars sold in Russia in 2021. Now this Renault plant belongs to the Russian government and is called Moskvich.

We hear sirens go off and jump in our seats—but it's just the start of the night shift. "Clearly they're doing just fine without the French," Katya says. The workers' parking lots in front of the buildings are full.

Nobody walks in Togliatti. It's like being in Los Angeles, with eight-lane highways flanked by side streets. But there are very few cars driving around. We often find ourselves alone at traffic lights. The winter must be terrifying.

From fifty-seven thousand residents in 1957, Togliatti grew to nearly seven hundred thousand as of 2024, yet it's not a real city, but a combination of three industrial districts (it is also home to chemical heavyweights that produce fertilizers and detergents), where smokestacks, apartment blocks, daycares, warehouses, and churches exist together along the Volga in a suffocating cloud of ammonia. The cement smeared across the city in the 1960s, which left no room for a single public garden, seems to have already eroded. Iron beams stick out of frayed apartment buildings, while steel rods peek out from under cracked sidewalks. Despite an invasion of hundreds of engineers, technicians, and workers from Turin in the '60s, there is nothing left of Italy in Togliatti aside from two restaurants with Italian names that serve vaguely European food. There are no statues to Palmiro Togliatti, nor do any of his quotes grace the brochures available at our modest hotel.

They say it's dangerous to walk around at night—there are baby gangs here, too. They say the port acts as a supermarket for drugs. We learn that Togliatti boasts a booming parallel automotive market. The local *lombardy*, a type of pawnshop (born in Lombardy, Italy, in the sixteenth century), specialize in pawning cars. Anyone in desperate need of a fistful of rubles can go to them and hand over their Lada. If they don't return the money with an interest of 10–20 percent within thirty days, goodbye Lada. Dozens of signs along the boulevards bear the writing LOMBARD. But where are all the pawned cars? At a bar, I learn that loan sharks park them outside factories, so they can blend in with the workers' cars. Russia's biggest secondhand car market is apparently right in front of the country's largest auto manufacturing plant.

We ask the barflies whether they feel the effects of the war. Togliatti is where we've noticed the highest concentration of recruitment posters. By now, we know this is a reliable indicator of poverty. "In the first months, they went to get the boys from the factory," they say. "They sent them off to training camps before they'd even had a chance to pack a pair of spare underwear. There are at least three funerals a day—it looks like they're building a new cemetery." I ask if mothers and wives are protesting, as they often do in eastern Russia. "A dead soldier is worth a bag of rubles here," says a man with several gold teeth. "That shuts up the women and families. It's different when the soldier has gone missing, which happens more and more. Then it's a big problem because you don't have a body to bury, and you don't get a penny."

They say the reward is about $80,000 per body, about ten times the average stipend of an AvtoVaz worker.

10

The island of pacifists

"Boys don't cry"

EXOTIC SMELLS

We start the morning off on the wrong foot after Vlad talks us into poking around the docks. In addition to serving the auto industry, the port appears to be a river-railway hub for the war economy, supplying the front through the Volga-Don canal—which begins south of Volgograd—and circumventing sanctions by exporting grain and importing civilian and military technology.

We pull behind a truck and stay close on its heels, pretending to be lost. But all the docks are inaccessible, and when we finally think we've found an opening, we realize the place is crawling with armed guards with dogs. We quickly pivot toward the Arch of Samara, a natural bend where the Volga loops eastward around the Zhiguli Mountains as if it were about to set out across the steppe, only to change its mind and swing back to its European riverbed.

The Zhiguli are technically mountains, but the highest peak stands at 1,200 feet. They guard the start of the bend like natural forts and are the last rise before the plains stretch out to the Urals—courtesy of the Paleozoic Era. They were the Arcadia of the empire, an idyllic destination for nineteenth-century bohemians. For Russian painters, such as Repin, they were a patriotic alternative to clichéd Western landscapes like the Italian Grand Tour, both the imitation of a model and a rejection of European standards in favor of Russian natural beauty.

Yet it takes us a long time to shake the smell of Togliatti's industrial periphery: As we continue our drive, we see crumbling warehouses among the brushwood, their tin roofs flapping in the wind. The river is a deep shade of rust. Willows grow in junkyards; orchids create pink carpets between old tires and train carcasses. "I'm in a world of shit, yes / But I am alive," Vlad bursts out, citing the final apocalyptic words of *Full Metal Jacket*.

We gradually climb into a forest of linden trees and oaks, until we reach thickets of pine trees and brambles. From up here, the Volga seems strangled by the Zhiguli Mountains. Cossack and Kalmyk bandits used to set up ambushes from this point, just as the Houthis today attack shipments on the Bab el-Mandeb Strait in the Red Sea.

In the eighteenth century, traders traveling between Europe and Asia feared the Zhiguli: Ships sailed through in convoys, escorted by gunboats financed by their governments. Sailing against the current was especially dangerous, because the going was slow and because they would be on their way back from the Indies at that point, laden with precious cargo. Captured pirates, as English merchant Jonas Hanway explained in 1743, were hanged with hooks stuck into their ribs. Anyone who helped them received the same treatment.

The landscape here is dotted with little summer homes, modest prefab dachas or slapdash cabins covered in asbestos roofing sheets and rough-hewn concrete blocks. Some are just huts surrounded by enchant-

ing gardens. We see some kayaks and a few bicycles, which we were beginning to suspect had been banned by the regime. Smoke from a few barbecues meanders through the birch trees; babushkas sell apples, onions, cherries and *varenye*, whole-fruit preserves, at roadside kiosks.

THE WITCH

At the Zhiguli Mountains we meet Levsha, which means "leftie," a thirty-two-year-old reggae singer and songwriter. He is wearing nothing but shorts, showing off his sculpted physique and dark skin, and eyeliner that makes him look like a guru of Eastern spiritualism. He is always smiling blissfully behind a black, well-kept Solzhenitsyn beard with no mustache.

Levsha is not on vacation. He lives here with his family—his wife Anna and their children—in a spacious, well-kept house they built bit by bit in a harmonious blend of wood and handmade bricks. The rounded edges of the interior remind me of anthroposophical Steiner designs. The whole family seems fresh off the boat from a commune in Goa; or from a peace-and-love documentary on 1980s Oregon. The children, blond and curly haired, are perfectly scaled miniatures of their parents: barefoot and dressed in natural cotton tunics.

Anna is so beautiful, it's almost uncomfortable. At once sensual and otherworldly, she talks like a priestess but moves like an odalisque. She says she is Russian, daughter of the Volga, which she speaks of as a divinity to be worshipped at the family altar. Any mystical spirit is welcome in her home, including that of the great oak tree in the garden, which she caresses gently, as if it were an elderly mother. Then she leans back against the trunk and fixes her emerald eyes on us. Her smile seems to gather energy directly from the tree's sap. "I'm a witch," she says, as if it were a job like any other. "And a shamanic healer." She looks younger than her thirty-four years. She's wearing traditional necklaces and an ocher dress painted with infusions of herbs from the Zhiguli Mountains. Her long, fine, wheat-blond hair sways in the wind with the tree's canopy. "Officially, I'm a nurse," she specifies. "And if I didn't have three children, they would have sent me to Donbas. But we're pacifists. We must be zombies to be killing our own brothers." Anna identifies as an antiestablishment pagan environmentalist. "But not in the sense you Westerners mean, of fighting the system because it's not modern enough. I fight the system of modernity, the idea of money and that time is useful only for amassing wealth. Of course, it's easier to live now compared to two generations ago, but people have forgotten why they live. Wellness should not be an end in itself but lived in love . . . which means sharing a plate of beans with you today, enjoying this nature together, thanking the Volga and all the gods."

Initially, Anna and Levsha seem like hippies through and through. They have recycled pacifist Western counterculture tropes from the 1970s and applied them to a Russian context. But they soon prove us wrong. Although they both express dislike for Putin's politics and police repression, they espouse his same cultural ideas, including the superiority of Russian spiritual values, the defense of the traditional family, and love of the ancestors and their sacred land. Their views are not unlike those of the Chechen brand-identity expert we met in Dubna.

Anna mentions Western ideas that are sullying traditional Russian culture. When I ask her if she's talking about LGBTQ+ culture, she says, "They're legitimate opinions, but in Russia we don't feel the need to spread this novelty." Levsha also holds a grudge against Western scientific materialism. "Instead of the mystery of the spirit, you expect the void of science to shine a light on the emptiness of your world. Millions of people live with no soul, in a brain fog." I point out that it's the same great blindness produced by Lenin's scientific application of Communism, but he doesn't agree. Anna, cradling her youngest child, says, "People like us, who hold the old Russia in their hearts, are the ones who safeguard the roots of Europe."

SPECIAL EFFECTS

After eating green beans and chickpeas with pine juice and *surica*, an invigorating infusion of thyme and mint, we join Levsha on a stroll. We take a path that climbs sharply up to a forest of pines and willow groves. At the top, it opens onto a clearing of thorny grass and giant thistles. A breeze sweeps through, bringing foreign scents that remind me of warm places—the Maghreb, or the tropics. When I tell Levsha this, he laughs. "Welcome to the Jamaica of the Volga, my friends!" he exclaims, spreading his arms wide like wind turbines.

The land is dry and sandy—it almost feels like walking on chalk. But Ale, who has a degree in geology, is more interested in the botanical variety of the underbrush than the surprising nature of the subsoil. He looks funny as he walks hunched over an avalanche chute observing what I think are ferns. "It's marijuana!" he yells, as if he's just spotted land from the stern of the *Pinta*. We soon realize the entire hill is covered in wild cannabis. So it is the Jamaica of the Volga. Levsha's hammock hangs by the cliff overlooking the Zhiguli Strait. He retreats there to smoke and compose Volga dub. "I, my friends, have been everywhere / I've met plants in faraway countries," he sings. "But I know what's best for me, the herb of Zhiguli / and I see the sun pissing itself laughing with us."

Volunteers come from all over Russia to harvest the marijuana. "Those parties used to last for weeks," Levsha says. "We played, we made love, and we prayed." The village was basically founded on the bounty generated by the microclimate and biodiversity of the Zhiguli Mountains. It's a sort of autonomous republic of the mind, watched but tolerated by the authorities. "But now they've banned gatherings. We could get jail time. Strange people have started to show up. Everything has changed and we're thinking of going to India or Serbia." Levsha offers us a hit from his pipe. Katya holds back, but it's only to highlight her disdain and increasing hostility for us.

Before the war, even Boris Grebenshchikov would come here. He's the Russian Bob Dylan, legendary front man of the Akvarium, the band that put Soviet rock on the global radar. Since then, Boris has become a guru: His translations of mystical Tibetan texts have made him an authority on acoustic reggae in the lower Volga, which doesn't draw inspiration from Jamaica or British ska, but from the extraordinary tradition of Kalmyk Buddhists. Levsha grew up under Boris's wing but they no longer speak because Boris is in exile in London: He openly opposed the invasion of Ukraine, was charged in absentia for discrediting the Russian army, and was deemed a foreign agent. Levsha could go to jail just for talking to Boris.

THE EXODUS

Levsha plans to make a reggae album about the tragic fate of the Buddhist Kalmyks of the lower Volga and the Don region. In the sixteenth century, he says, this population of Mongol extraction let go of its shamanic cults and converted to Tibetan Buddhism—responding to the call of their ancestral spiritual origins in Inner Mongolia. It created a sort of Buddhist exclave in the European southeast, precariously perched between Islamic Turks and Orthodox Russians. As Peter the Great had done to Tatars and Jews, he forced the Buddhist Kamlyks to convert or pay heavy taxes. They resisted, until 1771, under Catherine the Great, when the Torghut tribe, the largest and most devout of the Kalmyks, returned to their ancestral homeland in Chinese Turkestan—an exodus akin to ethnic cleansing. Some 150,000 of them left their pastures and lands on the Volga, where they'd lived a life of compassion and peace, loaded their yurts on camelbacks, and left with their cattle. They forded the Volga and followed the stars along the paths formed by Genghis Khan, now erased by the centuries. More than 100,000 died, slaughtered by cold and raids. Those who reached Manchuria became slaves to the Chinese emperor. Had they stayed behind, they would have become serfs for the German immigrants who replaced them.

Levsha and I agree that tolerance for minorities (so long as they posed no threat) gave Russia its epithet of "Empire of Diversity," and allowed it to rule the borderlands, since its army and bureaucracy were no match for the size of the empire. As a result of this diplomacy of temperate tolerance, at the start of the nineteenth century, all lands along the Volga were fully in the hands of the empire.

Yet Catherine the Great had been ruthless with the Cossacks: She took back all the ground they'd gained in the Pugachev revolts and deported entire communities to the northern Caucasus. Nonetheless, over the course of a generation, many Cossacks became loyal servants of the crown, a genuine bastion of czarism. Believing that Russia's backwardness was due to low population density, Catherine launched a repopulation campaign on the Volga. She deported millions of converted Christian Orthodox Kalmyks to the area around present-day Togliatti, by the Zhiguli Mountains (where they took up piracy), and gave lands and money to discharged soldiers and their families. Then, in 1762, she issued a decree to encourage foreigners (except for Jews) to settle there, in the hope of modernizing manufacturing and agriculture. Some thirty thousand Germans arrived from the Rhine and the Main and she gave them land on both sides of the river near Saratov, freedom of religion (they were mostly Lutherans, like her), tax exemptions, and no forced conscription. Those who were forced to settle on the eastern shore found themselves on the steppe, in the middle of nowhere, without even a hut. To survive their first winter, they dug holes in the ground and subsisted on roots. But within four years, they'd founded four hundred colonies and at the start of the nineteenth century, they already numbered fifty-five thousand. A century later, at the dawn of World War II, they counted four hundred thousand residents and were known as the German socialist autonomous republic of the Volga. "Before the Nazi invasion and Stalin's retaliation, it had been smooth sailing for them," Levsha tells me. They were especially prosperous on the European shore, the gentler and more fertile side, where Catherine had cleared out the Buddhist Kalmyks.

GLIMMERS OF HOPE

Levsha's reggae is the soundtrack of the pacifist pirates of the Volga. To reach their secret island hideout, we set out after sundown on a ramshackle raft made of pallets and surfboards. Vlad and Katya stay behind: The raft is too small. We wonder what they'll get up to alone, in the Jamaica of the Volga.

As we wait for the raft, in a floodplain between patches of vegetation, the water is black and murky and there is no other sound but the rustling of rushes. We may as well be heading out to sea—it's the same smell—which is all the more impressive when I remember this same river in its infancy, emerging meekly from the ground at the source. By now, we know the true force of that apparent fragility: We've seen it cut through enormous forests and overcome the ugliness and pain of modernity, like in apocalyptic Togliatti; we've already learned that in 1942 it traversed the hellscape of what was then Stalingrad, carrying islands of bodies. But so far, we've seen it flow only on its own time, through its own unfathomable world. Tonight, we feel it close and conspiratorial, as if it had been waiting for us all along.

We hear the gurgle of an engine and the raft appears out of the darkness. At the helm is Shukhrat, a Tatar in his forties wearing a wifebeater and a bandanna. He sports a short, well-kept goatee and his eyes gleam in the dark. He is a man of few words and measured smiles. We sail through the pitch black for about half an hour, under the bright lights and smoke trails of nearby industrial conglomerates. A noise alerts us to a large flock of low-flying geese heading north, then we hear the strangled sound of helicopters going south: no need for a GPS when you have the Volga, a natural navigator for humans and birds.

The island is called Shubert, because it's a fusion of the name Shukhrat with that of his friend Albert, who meets us on the dock with two cups of warm tea and two bouquets of wild orchids. He's also in his forties, outgoing, and so excited to see us he's almost emotional. Originally from western Siberia, he's blond with skin as white as snow. We follow a path through dunes and reed thickets until we arrive at the island's "square," where camping lanterns hanging from branches are emitting just enough light to give us an initial idea of the place. The bar on the corner exudes beach vibes and makes me want to grab a rum, but it serves only natural and alcohol-free drinks. Next to it flies a yellow, red, and green flag—the colors of this imaginary republic, like Costaguanain *Nostromo*—with a profile of Pushkin's face in the center. It's the corsair flag of Shubert Island.

Albert says there are only four rules in the community: no alcohol, no fights, no shit music, and no news about the war, on pain of being deported to "Russia." Kids are playing soccer, adults are lounging in hammocks and chatting, a young woman is reading a book to the light of a headlamp, a young couple is grilling eggplant.

Albert and Shukhrat have an epic friendship that was changed and deepened by the war. Shukhrat lost a son—he doesn't say how—and Albert sent his to Sweden. They first met in a time of extreme turmoil: both divorced, both upset by events in Ukraine, both defeated and unable to go on. Then one night they decided to stop drinking and to share their pain, their names, and their fate. "We could no longer accept reality," Albert tells me. "So we decided to build a new one." Shukhrat quit his job as an engineer, Albert left his as a security-systems technician. They pooled their savings and started to compose reggae. Right around then, a strip of sand magically emerged from the widest point of the river, where the water is still fairly clean. It was created as part of a project to build a bridge, the longest on the Volga. A work site had even been set up before the project fell through. "Environmentalists like to think it stopped because of their protests," Albert says. "Yeah, right—this is Russia! But we let them think that. The truth is that the war changed the government's priorities." The island is a half square mile of land unknown to maps but not to plants, which soon colonized it and transformed it into a riverine botanical garden. Albert and Shukhrat quietly began work, ferrying over essential infrastructure on a motorized raft. They held reggae raves. Soon they were joined by other fugitives, tents became houses, solar panels and small wind turbines replaced diesel generators, and someone set up a water-filtration system, a small plumbing network, and a makeshift library. They are now a community of about a hundred self-displaced people.

Some go back and forth to "Russia" and others have settled here with their families. I wouldn't say the adults look happy—the crude reality they left on the shore, a mere half-hour crossing away, remains an elephant around the bonfire—but they do seem serene. "We're taking some time off from the hard work of being Russian," says a young woman from Kazan as she folds her laundry. They hold poetry readings, yoga classes, meditation sessions. They sing reggae songs in Russian or the other languages of the Volga, such as Chuvash or Mari, using traditional stringed instruments like the balalaika and domra, or the accordion-like bayan. English seems to have been banned. Every Friday night, friends and musicians from Kazan, Samara, Togliatti, and Volgograd arrive by raft and put on a music festival.

The spirit of Shubert Island is based on the rediscovery of Russian mysticism, an idealized and utopian Eastern philosophy of nonviolence, freedom, and harmony among people, nature, and the cosmos. Islanders look east to retrace their steps, hoping to rediscover a spiritual space of redemption and hope. Europe and the West don't exist. Indeed, nobody asks us any questions, as if we came from a dull and predictable world that has nothing left to say for itself. "Nothing good comes from there anymore," Shukhrat says with a hint of bitterness. Albert picks up a guitar and starts jamming one of Levsha's reggae songs.

This is the summer of the prune and the pine
the summer of the *surica* and antimony
and under the blind rain we merge again.

Shukhrat joins in and they sing the chorus together.

All colors from yellow to green
all seas from fresh to saltwater
take me away and bring me here.

Albert is enthusiastic and open, and we talk for hours. He doesn't need to drink to become sentimental. He's enjoying his new life to the fullest. The rest of the islanders seem to ignore us, or perhaps they see our presence as invasive. Albert pitches our tent by himself to avoid friction.

Active dissenters are in prison or have left the country in droves. Those who don't accept reality ignore it and pretend to be apart from it, as during the siege of Sarajevo, where people would convince themselves that if they avoided looking at the snipers or mortars, they wouldn't be targeted. "We're not distancing ourselves from the world," Albert says. "But creating our own separate world. This is our country now, based on authentic Russian values. Everything is scary out there: It is no longer the Russia in which I grew up, the good Russia, the sweet, deluded, naive, and emotional Russia, where friendships like mine and Shukhrat's can thrive despite being difficult to explain. He's a strong, brave man, and kind, but his punches land heavy. We're two halves of a harmonious person that no longer lives in fear. All I can say is that Shukhrat and I escaped a Russia we no longer recognized. We found the real Russia within ourselves."

Albert identifies as a pacifist. "Where there is force, there is no freedom. Freedom exists only where there is integrity, where you don't have to be ashamed of your actions." He tells me about his childhood. "My mother raised me on her own from when I was five years old. She worked three jobs, and we ate *grechka* every day. I never demand anything because I think about what my mother went through. I was so proud of my country, of the Soviet Union. . . . Children love rhetoric, big ideas, and they don't know those are the things that corrupt the most." Albert says many of his friends who agree with him have decided to go abroad.

The lanterns have now gone out and Albert softly sings the last song, lightly strumming his guitar. Shukhrat sits apart from us, watching Albert with buttonhole eyes that sparkle in the dark.

You'll see a lighthouse on the way
blue sails will suddenly turn into wings
and the dock of hope awaits you
the dock of hope is the horizon
through the fog and the distance you'll see my light
can't you hear my voice gently calling?

The isolation of Shubert Island hasn't dampened all of Albert's suffering. After some hesitation, he tells me that before the war, he'd formed a special relationship with two Ukrainian YouTubers who spoke Russian. They shared a love of motorcycles and math games. He'd been planning on biking out to visit them in Donbas in February 2022. "They left me voice messages asking if I was their enemy now and why were we bombing them and killing them," Albert says in a cracked voice. "I still don't know how we ended up on the other side—it's terrible. They'll never forgive us . . ." Albert covers his eyes with his big bony hands. Shukhrat is looking away now, into the rushes, where the night is darkest. "What can I do? Only cry. But Mother used to say that boys don't cry."

BOTTOM OF THE BOTTLE

Katya drives us to our next stop, Samara, because she's not as hungover as Vlad, who is curled up, asleep in the back seat. He looks pale, with bright red lips. I look at him with a sense of defeat, but without resentment. It's time to plan our escape: We need to find a flight or a train before it's too late. Vlad has reached the end of his tether, which is the worst possible news for us, because we're totally dependent on him, and not just for logistics and translation: This trip never would have been possible without his willingness to work with two Western journalists traveling without a journalistic visa. Vlad trusts us and we trust him—sober Vlad, I mean. But he is unable to avoid the self-destructive drive to "tell his thoughts to fuck off," as he says, as soon as he hits a roadblock, in this case probably caused by his contentious relationship with Katya and a series of frustrating hookups he experienced before the start of our trip.

Just yesterday, at breakfast, he confessed his state of mind with his usual reckless candor. We know that Vlad is a *zapoy* type of guy, someone with a serious alcohol problem and a penchant for apocalyptic benders that can last days, even weeks, dulling one's consciousness as one plunges into the abyss in a desperate search for truth, sometimes taking leave of the world, often for good.

Someone we met along the way called it the "self-genocide of a people," saying Russia was baptized with holy water and "the devil's piss." The country started drinking practically since birth, in the fifteenth century, as part of a sort of vodka pact between the czar and the people: The state held a total monopoly over the production and sale of vodka, while the people were granted total freedom to drown in their despair. Vasily Grossman wrote that in 1917, intellectuals and revolutionaries would gather "around a cup of spiked tea. Lenin talked about the revolution over tea. But Stalin seems to prefer cognac." In the Soviet Union, where alcoholism quadrupled between the 1950s and '80s, 40 percent of state revenue came from the sale of vodka and other liquors. In the 1990s, 75 percent of murders were linked to alcohol consumption. In 2016, Putin lowered the prices, citing health concerns surrounding the production and consumption of *samogon*, a homemade vodka responsible for many deaths. In truth, it was a simple populist move to gain support. Alcohol is responsible for the deaths of more than 25 percent of Russian men before the age of fifty-five, compared to an average of 7 percent in the West. Alcohol is the top cause of divorce in a country with an already high rate—so much for traditional family values. Centuries pass, empires and regimes change, but for Russian men, the only tradition that seems inviolable is that of searching for oneself at the bottom of the bottle—and the *zapoy*, who drinks to the bitter end, is the most extreme representation of this often fatal spiral.

As Katya drives, she keeps the window down even when it rains, and smokes like crazy. Vlad mumbles that he just needs a few hours to get back in shape, which turns out to be true. When we get to Samara, he gets out of the van, yawns, stretches, and looks as good as new, for now. The receptionist at our hotel—in the vast and square outskirts of Samara—scrutinizes our European passports. She is small as a button, in her thirties, with piercings on her face, and wearing denim overalls. "The devil's mark!" she exclaims, pointing at the star on my passport cover.

"Excuse me?" I say.

"It's a pentagram, a Jewish symbol, like what the Bolsheviks used. Did you know that almost all the Bolsheviks were Jewish? Europe isn't Christian anymore—they control it."

"They, who?"

"The Jews, of course!" Then we spend about an hour listing all the stops we made and all the hotels we stayed at along the way. "These are the rules set by the police in Samara," the little antisemite explains.

BOURGEOIS PUPPIES

Samara is known as the Russian Chicago because of its great industrial drive and popularity with gangsters and jazz musicians. It also has scorching, humid heat in the summer and polar winters. Samara—a city of more than one million—also grew rapidly after the arrival of a new railway, the Trans-Siberian in this case, which was finished in 1850 (the Chicago Great Western Railway wasn't inaugurated until 1887) and which now bridges two worlds, two sides of the Volga, acting as a north-south connector between Moscow and central Asia and as a hub for grain exports.

I sit on the promenade under some linden trees, watching the wide beach turn pink under the languid sunset. It's an exclusive beach, an elegant waterfront club for the wealthy. On my many trips to the big rivers of the world, I have always found them packed with blue-collar swimmers or kids whose families couldn't afford to go elsewhere on vacation.

But Samara is different—the river is so vast here, people refer to it as the sea. The hedonistic parade of young, healthy bodies displaying an unshakable belief in life eternal and financial comfort looks more like Long Beach than Chicago. But maybe I'm being influenced by typical Western provincialism—when Samara already had an opera house, Los Angeles was still a fishing village. The real question is, How did I ignore the existence of this wondrous place on the easternmost point of the Volga, so close to the steppe? Has the West been blind to such beauty due to cultural prejudice against Russia? Or did Russia keep it hidden on purpose, concerned that its luxury, taste, and status might reveal a penchant for capitalist pleasures?

The war seems more distant from Samara Beach than it does from Warsaw or Tallinn, yet we're within drone's range. I have to watch out for the hordes of bicycles and electric scooters. I also notice many e-cigarettes. Well-dressed ladies stroll with their bourgeois puppies along a shaded promenade with flower gardens and contemporary sculptures. The promenade extends for a few miles between the beach and a terraced public garden. Nearby, the old town shows no signs of Soviet architecture—it is dominated by the turquoise and rose colors of end-of-empire patrician buildings. A series of restaurants, cafés, tennis clubs, and open-air dance clubs line the walkway overlooking the beach. A big wedding is being held in an iron-and-glass pavilion. Everything is white—the bride and groom, the guests, the waiters, the flowers, the tablecloths. The guards at the entrance, intimidating as they are, look like the stewards of paradise.

Ale is wandering on the beach as relaxed as if he were in Miami, photographing beach volleyball games, spectacular athletic feats, and joggers with golf visors. But aside from him, I'm probably the only foreigner. I'm an alien, an illegal, a voyeur in the very city that entices me the most on this trip. I want to experience it fully and speak to anyone—including those soldiers drinking beer on the terrace. But this is their world, and journalists with Western passports are advised to keep out. The less I exist, the better off I am. The lovely Samara is a big Putin stronghold. "It's the most aligned city in Russia," they told us on Shubert Island. "There's no room for stepping out of line. You can have a good time as long as you follow Putin's commandments." After the city opened up in the 1990s and homosexuality became legal (after being considered a mental illness in the Soviet era), it became a destination for the gay community, until about ten years ago. Then "suspicious" bars were closed, and now morality guardians patrol the rest. After a young man was beaten to death, his attacker received only a five-year sentence, the lowest ever handed down for murder. A nudist colony that had existed on an island near Samara since the days of the Soviet Union gradually became a shelter for trans people, until a 2021 raid left several people wounded. According to the people of Shubert Island, the ER denied them care. Avers LGBT, the only organization in town that gave the LGBTQ+ community any legal protections, is long gone. Now Samara is one of the most homophobic places in Russia.

THE TRAIN MAN

Trotsky couldn't stand Samara. The man I consider the greatest writer and socialist organizer of all time called it a "den of philistines, idolizers of money and looks." He wasn't referring to the hedonist Samara Beach. He was talking about the place he had bombed heavily when he commanded the Red Army during the civil war.

After the Bolshevik coup in October 1917, the city became the stronghold of the revolutionary socialists, who reconvened the Constituent Assembly to form a new (and legitimate) republican government. Not only was the city strategically important for railway connections, but Samara was the only place on the Volga where peasants were resisting the Bolsheviks. The Czechoslovak Legion—an army of about forty thousand anti-Austrian volunteers who'd been allied with the czarist army in World War I—agreed to help the socialist revolutionaries take Samara in May 1918, install a counterrevolutionary government, and found an army able to "liberate" the Volga from the Bolsheviks.

After taking Samara, Syzran, Simbirsk, and Kazan were next—the aim was to conquer Nizhny Novgorod and then Moscow. But that

September, Trotsky retreated from the eastern front and redirected his armored train at the Volga, the river that had always held the fate of Russia in its hand, and now that of the civil war—in which ten million had died and two million had been driven into exile in three years. "The bourgeois scoundrels of the Volga, the Urals, and Siberia will feel the pain, starting with Kazan," Trotsky declared. He took it all in just a few weeks, using the fleet he'd launched that spring. He mobilized the peasants by promising them a total and permanent confiscation of lands from the lords. He then set up a base in Samara to prepare the campaign against the Whites, who were advancing from the Don and northern Caucasus.

FICTION AND HAMMER

I climb up the garden steps to the main square. A monument to Valerian Kuybyshev—head of the revolutionary committee and people's commissar of the Red Army during the civil war—stands in its center. The city bore his name until 1992, when it readopted its former designation (a sort of spoils system governs Russian toponymy: When history changes, so do place names).

This was where a *Pravda* reporter, after seeing Trotsky speak, wrote that he was "dismantling the foundations of Samara with his voice, rousing the troops with the power of his words . . . saying 'Comrade soldiers of the Red Army!' and the roar was such that it sounded like a great storm." Trotsky was a great orator, endowed with almost mystical furor and an otherworldly strength: the qualities of a supreme leader. Lenin always showed Trotsky absolute loyalty and great admiration. While Lenin led the revolution, Trotsky had the terrifying task of defending it. But he disdained political confrontation. Despite embodying the revolutionary spirit better than anyone, Trotsky, famous for his armored train, missed his stop in the line of succession and handed his spot to Stalin. He had too much pride and contempt for the triviality of power. When a friend of his accepted a position in government, he said, "What a stupid and wretched ambition! He's giving up a place in history to settle for a ministry." British historian Robert Service, a fierce anti-Communist, in his biography of Trotsky dismantled the revolutionary image that has so fascinated the West, and painted him instead as a haughty man who overestimated himself and underestimated his opponents.

Trotsky had supported the Mensheviks in the early days of the revolution, so Stalin accused him of secretly siding with liberal democracies—even though Trotsky was more antibourgeois than Lenin and believed in the Marxist doctrine of the permanent revolution more than anyone. But he'd become dangerous: too brilliant, and after Lenin, Stalin believed, Communism needed to be managed, not intellectualized. Plus, that frenetic energy that had roused the masses and soldiers was no longer necessary: The Soviet Union couldn't afford to be led by a Red Bonaparte. So the *Pravda*, the same paper that had praised Trotsky during his campaign on the Volga, published a series of op-eds where Stalin declared "Trotskyism" to be the ultimate infamy, worse than czarism. In the 1930s the term became a tool of mass slaughter, an indictment that automatically carried a death sentence. Stalin even did away with General Kuybyshev, whose statue stands here in the square, because he was suspected of being loyal to Trotsky.

While descending the Volga, the only Trotsky image we found was a large amateur painting on display at a gas station in Rzhev. Ale even took a few photos of it, aware of how unusual it was. The attendant told us that he'd put it up in 2017, after Rossia 1, the main state TV channel—whose programming is directly approved by Putin—aired *Trotsky*, a series later purchased by Netflix. "He was erased from Russian history—even the end of Stalinism didn't lead to his rehabilitation," the attendant said. "I was hoping that with the hundredth anniversary of the revolution his time had come. But they just gave him another blow to the head, like when Stalin's assassin killed him in Mexico." In fiction, Trotsky appears as a revenge-obsessed, sex-crazed cyberpunk—inhuman, stingy, egocentric, ruthless. His Jewish origins are thrust into the spotlight—Trotsky was born Lev Bronstein into a wealthy Jewish family. Rather than rehabilitate him, Putin chose to celebrate the anniversary of the 1917 October Revolution through Trotsky, its most controversial figure, avoiding a confrontation with Lenin's memory, and ultimately discrediting the revolution itself. It was a warning to his subjects, a severing of Bolshevism from Stalin and the Soviet Union, myths the Kremlin seeks to promote.

The Trotskyist attendant had his own ideas about how Stalin's revenge plan against Trotsky had taken shape. It started during the civil war, when people were engaging in hand-to-hand combat, even within the Bolshevik elite.

Lenin sent Stalin to Tsaritsyn, today's Volgograd, which controlled communication channels among Ukraine, the Caucasus, and the steppes. His task was to oversee grain requisitions, but then Lenin ordered him to repress the enemies of the revolution. This was Stalin's first lesson in violence, when he ordered the ruthless execution of enemies, real or presumed. Genuine military tasks soon followed, since the White army had the city of Tsaritsyn in a chokehold.

During this time, Trotsky turned to the old czarist officers for help, many of whom obliged, perhaps to avoid going hungry. But Stalin refused to cede his decision-making powers to anyone, especially not to the czarists. He saw Trotsky's move as insubordination, which forced Trotsky to have Stalin recalled to Moscow. "In 1925, a year after Lenin's death, Tsaritsyn was renamed after Stalin, for his presumed military capabilities," the gas station attendant told us, proudly observing his painting of socialism's worst enemy. "What military abilities! Stalin didn't known squat about war. They changed Tsaritsyn's name only to ridicule Trotsky and his role as commander of the Red Army." The fact remains that it was in "his" city, in Stalingrad, that Stalin decided the fate of World War II and returned Russia to its imperial status.

LOVERS' LANE

Vlad promised: In Samara, the coolest city on the Volga, he'd buy us dinner. And he's true to his word. After leaving us alone all afternoon, Vlad and Katya (they stayed at the hotel to work off their hangovers) meet us downtown. It's not easy to find a restaurant—the best ones are full—but we eventually find an open-air spot hidden away in a dirty passageway between two streets. The atmosphere between us is almost peaceful: There is a certain harmony, and the tensions caused by alcohol and the feeling of an imminent blowout with Katya seem to have dissipated for now. The food is terrible and the wine is even worse, plus, it's warm. Vlad and Katya are the only ones drinking. After the first bottle of white, Vlad is exuberant, affectionate, says he's super happy to be with us, and we tell each other we hope to stay in touch after the trip. He wants us to know how important this experience has been for him, and how our human connection has made it unforgettable.

We start the evening off by taking stock of our time together, while perhaps also preparing for the approaching farewell. As soon as Vlad finishes his bottle, Katya orders another, looking like a bird of prey. Vlad doesn't stand a chance against her talons, or against the ones taking hold of him from within. By now, we're familiar with the pallor that descends on his face like a mask, causing his cheerfulness to fade and his jaws to clench as he burns through his cigarettes in four hits. I don't know how he gets onto the topic of death, but he starts telling us about someone he knows in Moscow who is practically giving him a preview of the afterlife. His eyes become wide and feverish. His logic is too complicated to follow while sober. Plus, Ale and I are distracted by the surreal conversation between Katya and a couple sitting next to us. He's a Spanish farmer, short and thin and about forty years old—he must be, come to think of it, the only foreigner we've come across this whole trip. She's from Samara, around thirty years old, slender, platinum-blond hair, and wearing a tight prune-colored dress. They met on Facebook, then he came to meet her before the war—they seem eager for us to know they had sex for the first time in a car on lovers' lane, which is apparently a lookout point on the Volga, where couples go to be alone. But the story takes a sad turn, because after spending time with the farmer in a small village in Extremadura, the woman couldn't take it anymore and returned to Samara. He's here now to talk her into changing her mind. He promises her that in five years—after his mother dies, as she's very ill, and after he's taken care of things at the farm—they will move to a bigger town, with three thousand people, where they have a movie theater and everything. The woman laughs and cries at the same time, aware of the absurdity of her situation and terrified at the thought of having to spend one more day with the farmer. She tells him she never really loved him and that this is their last dinner together, that he shouldn't entertain any illusions just because she got all dressed up and had a few cocktails. The farmer cites his trip in the middle of the war as proof of his love. He appeals to us, as if our judgment could save his relationship.

Meanwhile, we've lost count of the bottles. A street urchin who looks like James Dean approaches us, barefoot and carrying a bag over his shoulder. He's selling hand-decorated cushions. Vlad asks him a bunch of questions and we find out he lives in a hut on the "rich people's beach," and that the wounds to his face and arms are from a mugging last night, when his earnings were taken, along with his shoes. Vlad gives him a big hug, pours him some wine, and pats his head. He buys all his cushions. Vlad seems to have guessed what we're thinking, he sees that we care about him and that it hurts us to see him lost and alone. He rests his elbows on the table, closes his eyes, and holds his waxen face in his hands. "I want to tell you something, guys. We'll never be real friends, because I've never really had any."

ESCAPE PLANS

The following morning, we have a chance to get to know the little antisemite at the hotel reception desk. She's an elementary school teacher who makes ends meet with seasonal work. As she talks about her various jobs, her tales get taller, encompassing claims that climate change is a fictional crisis set up by DARPA, and that Putin was selected directly by God to save the world from the American Satan. We feign interest and shock. We want her to help us navigate Russian websites and find the best way to leave the country.

We've decided to go all the way to Astrakhan, whatever the cost. But we also know that once there, we'll hightail it. We're not about to drive back to Saint Petersburg with two burnouts and spend another week with them, risking a traffic accident, arrest, or bloody fights. "I'd rather enlist," Ale keeps saying. We've been feeling crushed by the weight of tensions with Katya. For days I've been sending daily messages to the Italian embassy in Moscow, checking in and providing our location and destination. I've been taking pictures of my notes and sending them to my wife, Gabriella.

First, we look for maritime connections on the Caspian, from Astrakhan to Baku in Azerbaijan, but the conspiracy theorist teacher-receptionist can't find anything—it looks like commercial routes have been closed. She suggests a train to Tbilisi, Georgia. As we're about to look for flights from Astrakhan, Vlad shows up. Alone. He looks gloomy, his cigarette trembling between his lips. He says, "The fucking police are involved this time." "Vlad, tell me you're shitting me." He isn't. After returning to his room last night, he took a shower, but when he came out, he found the room upside down. Katya had disappeared and her phone was off. He drove around looking for her. He did the rounds of the suburbs, with their copied-and-pasted rows of identical apartment blocks like crimes against urban planning. At five o'clock in the morning, he got a phone call. A Moscow police officer said he was a friend of Katya's, that she'd gotten lost, and that she'd called him. Vlad asked,"Why didn't she call me?"; "What do I know?" the police officer responded. "She said she didn't know where she was and asked me if I could have my colleagues in Samara pick her up. They're taking her back to the hotel now. Just wanted to let you know."

STALIN'S BATHROOM

When Katya finally shows up, she acts as if she has just returned from an extraordinary adventure. No one thinks it's funny. But now Vlad's the real problem. He stinks of alcohol—the adrenaline he burned overnight must have needed a boost. He is clearly at the mercy of his demons now, and we can no longer count on him. As Soviet poet Arseny Tarkovsky wrote, it is as if he were stalking us, "step by step, like a madman with a razor."

We also have our first fight. I need Vlad to find Stalin's bunker, but he is nowhere to be found. I'm in Kuybyshev Square, the city's administrative district, and the police are everywhere. Finally, I spot Vlad on the sidewalk across from me and yell at him for disappearing. He walks toward me, raises his voice, and threatens to punch me. I smell the stench of alcohol and smoke. I mentally review various scenarios, one more terrifying than the other, until I reach my hand out and Vlad pulls me into a tight embrace, as if begging for forgiveness. So much for our plans to meet Pyotr, who was supposed to guide me through Samara's underground, where a series of legendary tunnels connects the various World War II–era ministry buildings above.

I spoke to Pyotr briefly yesterday. He is known for descending into tunnels and ventilation ducts, a dangerous task, since much of the subterranean space around Kuybyshev Square is off-limits. "Object Number 2," he told me, was the largest shelter, built to withstand heavy bombing and chemical attacks. It was a part of Putin's 2022 civil defense plan. According to Pyotr, it had been renovated and was perfectly safe to enter. "That old world hidden in Samara's underbelly has suddenly drawn renewed interest," he said.

The Beria bunker is especially legendary. In the late 1930s, NKVD director Nikolai Yezhov lived in the building of the current courthouse, but spent most of his time belowground, where he'd built his own network of tunnels. Splatterpunk stories of torture chambers abound, where women were kept prisoner and abused until they died. There are even rumors of cremation ovens. Pyotr spends his time searching for them and says that the fun part is that "you never know if you're crossing a line, like whether you're entering a structure that is operating again, given the situation."

The Kalinin bunker, under the opera house, is a point of pride for him: Pyotr went in before the war and said it was perfectly in order, it just smelled of mold. Legend has it that Shostakovich finished his

Seventh Symphony in this bunker, after fleeing the siege of Leningrad, while the KGB once used it to hide Khrushchev from an angry mob.

But Stalin's bunker, known as "Object Number 1," might be the most famous. He built it in 1942 to resist Hitler, thereby making Samara the USSR's "spare capital" as the Germans prepared to launch their final assault on Moscow.

These days, it's a pilgrimage destination. A line of people, mostly in their twenties, announces the entrance to the bunker outside the post office building. I join a tour group and we descend to Stalin's apartment and an emergency operating room. Stalin's study has been decorated elegantly, with art deco sconces reminiscent of Moscow's metro system. The large desk is covered in red leather. Stalin's bathroom is small, but well equipped: shaving kit, white robe with a red hammer and sickle, copper bathtub. The bunker was never used, but the guide explains that it was renovated during the Cuban missile crisis and after the annexation of Crimea in 2014. Now, it could hold up to six hundred people for five days and it even gets cell-phone service.

Andrei, a twenty-four-year-old electrical engineer from Moscow, is here with three friends. I ask him why Stalin is the icon of Generation Z. "He was a winner," he tells me courteously as we study the original military map of the Soviet counteroffensive. "He's number one. We must fight evil like in the Great Patriotic War. Putin should follow his example, his pragmatism. Look at what he created in just a few weeks—it's crazy. It's the results that count. I think more people died in the '90s during the gang wars and from drinking. That was our first experience with democracy, the worst time in our history." I ask him if he is Communist. He brings his hand to his mouth to stifle a giggle. "I'm Russian. We don't do anything halfway. Being a real Russian today is a form of extremism."

11

The *batyushka* of the steppe

"Let's burn it all down"

THE LUCKY ONES

Balakovo, population two hundred thousand, revolves around two nuclear power plants and two of the biggest hydroelectric plants on the Volga, which supply half of Russia with electricity. Yet all its roads are dark. We arrive at nightfall, advancing cautiously, the smell of ammonia and tar in the air. In the light of the full moon, we see high-tension pylons rise in the distance like many Eiffel Towers. People gather around bonfires in their courtyards. We hear the echo of an accordion and a chorus, which somehow makes the scene eerier.

The only sign of life comes from the Lucky Pub, which is hosting a concert by Kiss, a popular local rock band. All the kids know their songs. The lead singer looks about seventeen, with waist-length blond hair, which she whips around as part of her performance. She is wearing a tartan skirt and black knee-high boots and sings very well.

We walk in to find a scene resembling the American Midwest, complete with fake-leather booths, a pool table, darts, french fries in baskets with checkered paper, chicken wings, and a neon sign reading "No war here," in English. All the patrons are white and blond, and I don't see a single tattoo. A group of dressed-up young women have gathered at two tables, probably for a bachelorette party.

There must be a careful watch over alcohol consumption, because Vlad and Katya are denied a second bottle of white wine. I join a group of young people smoking outside and I soon become the evening's breaking news, an exotic attraction. I am surrounded and pummeled with questions. Even the bass player from Kiss extends his break to ask me whether another world war really has broken out—his band mates eventually have to come and drag him back onstage. The English speakers of the group become translators—their most pressing question is what the West thinks of Russians. I don't perceive any hostility or propaganda. They seem genuinely worried and disoriented. I tell them I'm not here to judge, but to understand. A first-year medical student at Saratov expresses a sentimental vision—he is grateful for this difficult situation because of the unity it has created: His friendships have become stronger, people worry about one another. "If someone collapses, the rest of the group springs into action."

I ask what he means by collapsing, wondering if he means from drugs. He says his friends don't do any heavy drugs, but they drink a lot. "Someone I know from college died a few days ago. He was twenty-one." I ask what music they listen to and what they think of old rock bands like Akvarium, Mashina Vremeni, DDT—all on the Kremlin's blacklist. They laugh and say it's old-fogy stuff. And Shaman? Putin's favorite rapper? They laugh again, aware of his pro-invasion songs and his concerts in occupied Mariupol. How does *Ja Russki* go? Two girls who look like sisters intone the song, which always seems to be on the radio.

I breathe in this air
the sun looks down on me from the sky
I am what I am and no one can break me
because I'm Russian and I'll fight to the end
I'm Russian, my father's blood runs through me
I'm Russian and I'm lucky to be Russian so I can stick it to
the world.

They say the biggest problem is prices. One young woman, who studies biology in Samara, tells me her family can eat meat only twice a week, max. "We want to support local produce, but it's too expensive. A lot of us have to buy frozen meat from Georgia or Kazakhstan. And Dad is raising chickens now." There's a shortage of nails at worksites and little gas for European cars. The lights are often out in this city because electricity, which is produced locally, is twenty times more expensive here than in Moscow. They no longer buy Western makeup and perfumes, another student says, showing me her Chinese-made lipstick. "At the start of this mess, the Balakovo mall was deserted, shelves were empty. But now it's always packed on Saturdays. Zara and H&M have been replaced by similar brands from some Arab country," she says. Their iPhones are antebellum models. There are Apple products around, but only trinkets. One kid lost a cousin, who'd been a construction worker, at the front. "For now, if you're a student you're fine," he tells me.

They chase away an acquaintance who comes over and starts to yell something at us. "He thinks you're a spy," the medical student tells me, blushing. When I tell them I'm due to meet a priest tomorrow, they look flabbergasted. I ask if they know Father Mikhail Rodin. They do not. "Hands up who goes to church," I say. No one. "And your parents?" Reluctantly, two out of ten raise their hands.

A nice vibe has developed between us. I want to continue to probe their provincial lives, their disappointments, their dreams. Maybe ask if they wear those red Stalin T-shirts. But they put out their cigarettes and go back inside to watch the concert. When I make eye contact with them inside, on the dance floor or sitting on a fake-leather couch, I hint a smile and a greeting, but none of them reciprocates. Maybe I'm too old for a place like this, or too foreign.

THE APPLE OF DISCORD

Piotrovsky, the director of the Hermitage, suggested I meet a young *batyushka*, or priest, named Mikhail Rodin. "A very interesting man," he said. "He lives in Balakovo, a place forgotten by God." Father Rodin, who is forty-four years old and has four children, has never been to the Hermitage. He doesn't travel much—people go to him when they want his opinion on something. He's an ideological theologist of the so-called "true" Orthodox Church, aligned with the Old Believers. His home and basilica are on the industrial outskirts of the city, among the high-tension wires: The complex looks like a large chalet and smells of pine and candles. It's equipped with an oven for the communion wafer—"But my wife also uses it to make pizza," Rodin tells me—and a collection of rare icons, gifts from the faithful, kept hidden during the seventy years of Soviet rule. A 1627 mass book contains notes written in the margins in a blue ballpoint pen.

"We inaugurated it recently," says Rodin, who speaks excellent English. "It was raining hard that day, so there were only about fifty people." But the shortage of faithful doesn't seem to bother him. "Now it's time to fight like dogs for Russia's survival. Our faith and Russia's fate are inextricably linked," he says sweetly, while showing me the first pale tomatoes in his garden.

His church is financed by Robert Stubblebine, an American native living in Moscow. He is a VP and early shareholder of Yandex, the Russian Google, launched by his business partner and oligarch Arkady Volozh, who quit his job and moved to Tel Aviv after the invasion of Ukraine and consequent sanctions against him. Stubblebine, who is from Boston, gained Russian citizenship and became a devoted sponsor of the Church of the Old Believers.

He is not Father Rodin's only link to the United States. Father Rodin was raised in a family of hardcore Communist atheists and ignored the existence of God until he was fifteen years old. "I wasn't so interested in the meaning of life, but in the mystery of words and language," he tells me. "While searching for the roots of words, I found God, and when you find out that God exists, everything changes. But I didn't like the official Orthodox Church: I couldn't stand the hierarchies and all that arrogance. So I became Protestant. In those days, all sorts of American preachers were coming—you could take your pick. I found the Plymouth Brethren, the Christian movement of free churches. They seemed interesting, anarchist. Then I realized that this evangelization of Russia by Protestants and Catholics was an evil plan. And I went to the source of our great soul, that of the ancient Orthodox ritual, at the heart of the one true faith and the one true Russia."

We're sitting on a bench, in the shadow of the presbytery, illuminated by candles and by the large stained-glass window. Father Rodin has a gentle way about him, cool and collected. His long Moses beard is reddish, he has the ruddy complexion of a gourmand, and I sense a robust physique under the tunic. Every so often, he widens his clear, bulging eyes. I want to know more about these missionaries, or traveling salesmen in search of lost souls.

"It was a sort of free market for faith. Turkish and Arab missionaries also came, but they focused on historically Islamic communities." Those who attracted the most "clients" in these godless lands were the Americans. The Saratov region was especially fertile, given its past as the cradle of Russian devotion and industry. "The Seventh-day Adventists were a huge hit," Rodin recalls. "Their pastor would ask people to shout out their joy for Jesus, saying, 'Once again, let's sing: Jesus never fails!'" I tell Father Rodin that highways in the southern United States are plastered with dogmatic posters like that. I remember one from Georgia that read, "Jesus will give you eternal life. Interested?" I'd called the number on the poster, but no one answered.

Father Rodin is not in the mood for jokes. He says the experience was humiliating. "They treated us like savages." The missionary pastor had also suggested a special diet based on grains, fruit, and vegetables. Those who managed to quit smoking were called to the stage and given a little American flag. The most devoted received a Bible, which in those lean years could fetch a few precious kopecks on the black market. When Putin came, he had the FSB keep an eye on the Western preachers until they all left. But in Balakovo, the matter of religious preaching remains a delicate problem. "The FSB is making life impossible for Jehovah's Witnesses," Rodin says. "FSB agents have many families in their sights and have banned gatherings. It's a campaign of repression: They've tapped phones, conducted surveillance, done nighttime raids and searches, and seized Bibles and even children's history notes from school." He suggests criminal proceedings are based on fabricated evidence. Some followers have been detained for months. But it isn't clear whether he is denouncing the matter or simply acknowledging legitimate police action against religious impostors.

"We were persecuted for centuries, by the state and the church. We're used to hiding and keeping silent to survive," he says. I ask if he sees his new church as a sign that the Old Believers have gone mainstream, that they really have become Putin's anti-Western crusaders. Rodin admits this in a roundabout fashion, as he highlights the glorious days of religious persecution. "Freedom corrupts. When faith costs nothing, it's worth nothing; if it's dear, it's precious and true. The Russian soul was preserved by repression. The Old Believers bolstered their faith through suffering and social marginalization. When there's no freedom, you have to fight for God and truth, as in the Soviet Union."

But now the moment of redemption has come. Rodin is no dissident, but an interpreter of Putin's true Russia, one of the most apocalyptic voices on the stage. His change of heart began with the Kremlin's rallying cry in 2017, 350 years after the schism, when Putin went to the Old Believers' Church of Protection of the Mother of God in Moscow. He accepted the state's responsibility in their plight and recognized the religious legitimacy of the *raskolniki*, those dubbed schismatics. This was a big blow to Kirill's patriarchal church. Putin even authorized the issuance of passports to Old Believer exiles around the world so they could return to their motherland. More than four hundred new parishes opened in 2021. "There's no room for conflict in Russia's sacred mission," Rodin says. The *raskolniki* fully support the army but keep their distance from power. "You'll never see our patriarch, Kornili, bless tanks. But we do pray for our president and for those at the front. It's a tragic time. We must all be ready to die."

Putin's recognition is healing a wound that has been bleeding for centuries. It's a message of national-Orthodox identity and ideology, Rodin says. Endorsing an anti-Western spirit and loyalty to the traditions of the Old Believers means to endorse the reasons for the schism in the seventeenth century, born of a rebellion against liturgical reforms imposed by the Patriarch Nikon of Moscow, who wanted to return ritual practices to their original Greek roots. "That evil idea came from Ukraine that time, too," Rodin says. "Brought to Moscow by the theological academy of Kyiv, where they'd admitted Jesuit theologians and taught Latin and even Polish. Nikon was completely under the thrall of these demonic deviants. It was no accident," Rodin points out, still in his sweet and measured tone, "that the reform began in 1666—numbers that represent the Great Beast."

Nikon changed the mass books, the hallelujahs, the spelling of Jesus Christ's name. But the cornerstone of the *raskol* was defending the ancient Russian sign of the cross, done with two fingers—where the third member of the Holy Trinity is the forehead of the believer, the incarnation of the son of God. The new sign imposed by Nikon called for three fingers to represent what he called the "rationalist trinity." This may seem like splitting hairs, but the Nikonian Church was calling into question the very foundations of the nation, which held that Russian Orthodoxy was the only pure form of Christianity, and that Moscow had become the Third Rome after the fall of Constantinople. "Religion was and remains the only Russian ideology," Rodin concludes. Nikon ordered the destruction of medieval-style icons and promoted a new iconography inspired by European artistic trends. For believers of the "true faith," these were pagan and blasphemous deviations.

The resistance leader was archpriest Avvakum Petrov of Nizhny Novgorod, who had been an associate of Nikon. He believed the reform was anti-Russian and satanic, since the Greeks had compromised with

Catholics and Turks. He was sent to Siberia, then burned alive. Soon, a witch hunt was unleashed in all of Russia until the end of the eighteenth century: a large-scale persecution, with tortures and summary executions ordered by the patriarchs and carried out by the czars. Many *raskolniki* left Russia and founded communities in remote corners of the empire. Thousands of others chose mass suicide rather than surrender to the new order: In one monastery, 2,700 people set themselves on fire, a scene Mussorgsky recreated in one of his operas. Despite the persecutions, followers continued to grow in number, and the lower Volga never ceased to be a bastion of dissent against state authority and religious hierarchies. Even Cossacks ascribed to the antireformist movement, and the Old Believers had an active and decisive role in Razin's and Pugachev's peasant revolts.

Rodin explains that, aside from the various doctrines—including the most radical, which rejects power completely—"true faith" is based on egalitarian ideals. "Our priests, starting with Avvakum, lived among the people and refused all forms of privilege," he says. "Daily life and religion mixed together. Faith wasn't above everyday matters—the divine and the human were one and the same." Purges, marginalization, and religious repression turned the *raskolniki* into a separate Russian society, religiously traditionalist, but open to individual emancipation and technological progress. They married only within the religion, forming large families. The men never shaved their beards (paying a high tax when Peter the Great ordered all Russians to shave) and the women always wore a veil. Since they were locked out of the ranks of the nobility, they developed a talent for business and industry, especially in textiles.

In the second half of the nineteenth century, the Old Believers became the backbone of czarist Russia's economy. "To create wealth, capital must be distributed and become a common good," Rodin says. "Old Believers were great patrons of Russian avant-garde art. They also backed the revolution because it meant being on the side of justice, on the side of God." Batyushka Rodin agrees with Stalin, in that "Communism enacted a dream of justice that already existed in Russia before

Bolshevism, a dream that came true with the Battle of Stalingrad. Stalin built a strong and just country."

Rodin's expression suddenly changes, becomes more determined, as if he wants to highlight the gravity of his statements. He agrees to let us film him. I ask him, on video, what it means to be Russian. "We're influenced by the immense spaces around us, and the harsh climate," he says. "To survive we must live by certain principles. My uncle hunted hides in the Siberian taiga. The hunter closest to him was thirty miles away, the nearest town was ninety miles. He used to say that if you live in an isolated village in Siberia and a stranger arrives, you know he has struggled on the road for a long time and needs warmth, food, and comfort. This is why Russians are the friendliest and most welcoming people in the world. But if this stranger shows hostility, Russians turn into beasts."

I point out parallels in Russian relations with Ukraine, and he doesn't skirt the issue. "We were their friends and brothers for hundreds of years. Now we're enemies because we've seen their hostility. If your sister marries someone who makes her suffer, a Nazi who abuses her, what do you do? Stand back and watch? No. You free her, kill the Nazi that makes her suffer. Russian soldiers are ready to die. They never surrender, like in Stalingrad.

"In a land like this, you have to have a goal, a dream. Russians need to have something big to aim for. We dreamed of Communism, equality, and a life where no one is exploited by anyone. Each person the same as the next. If Russians believe in something, they believe it until the end. They believe in God. They're ready to die for their faith. They believe in Communism. They're willing to die for that. They believe in Russia and they're ready to sacrifice themselves for Russia."

"Even if it means using the atomic bomb, Batyushka?" I ask.

"Of course," he says promptly. "We're ready to sacrifice ourselves. Because if we don't win, we'll burn it all down. If we can't build a brighter future, then what's the point of living? Our president said what everyone is thinking. If we don't have the Russia we want, we're ready to martyr ourselves, sacrifice ourselves and the whole world if it's unjust and evil. There's no need for a world like that."

Rodin is still again, his bulging eyes admiring his imagined apocalypse, his arms spread out to indicate the inevitable demise of humanity. Ale is sitting next to me on the bench—we yearn to look at each other. "Boia de," he murmurs in the dialect of his native Livorno, in Tuscany. A candle is about to go out, its flame writhing until the last spasm. But Father Rodin isn't done. "Who used the atomic bomb? The West is willing to kill with nuclear weapons, but from a great distance, far from New York or Washington. We're willing to use the atomic bomb even if we all die."

Back on the street, it's raining, and the puddles emit oily reflections. I receive a voicemail from Albert, from Shubert Island. He has composed a new reggae song: "At sunset the Volga is bathed in pure light," he sings in English. "The same happens to my heart, when it's illuminated by love."

HIGH MASS

The following days are restless. Vlad and Katya take turns driving and do the same with their moods: There is a growing tension as we reach the finish line, of our trip and of the Volga. Ale and I decry the questions left unasked and the photos we didn't get to take, and the little time left to make up for those missed opportunities. Unaddressed emotions pile up as our patience runs thin. We tell Vlad of our plans to leave from Astrakhan. He's relieved. "I don't know how you managed to put up with this shitty situation for so long. It won't be easy getting back to Saint Petersburg given Katya's behavior. If you don't hear from me, it means I'm lying flat out in some morgue."

We can smell the air of the steppe from the car, a scent of bristly, dry grass. At night, a patchwork of galaxies appears in the sky, with opalescent nebulae in the east. "The steppe speaks to man about the freedom he has lost," Father Rodin had said back in Balakovo. I wonder what the steppe will tell us about Russia, and ourselves, once we reach the opposite shore.

We decide to stop in Saratov for two days to visit the home of Nikolay Chernyshevsky, author of *What Is to Be Done?*, and nineteenth-century composer Sergei Rachmaninoff's favorite conservatory. When we arrive, we learn that a High Mass is being celebrated at the seventeenth-century Cathedral of the Holy Trinity, one of the most ancient in Russia. Still reeling from Rodin's nuclear "sermon," we want to hear from the other side, followers of Kirill, patriarch of Moscow.

It's Sunday morning, the sixth after the Pentecost. The display of tiaras and golden headgear is impressive. Ignatius, the archbishop of Saratov and a big shot in the patriarchal hierarchy, is celebrating the mass flanked by no fewer than thirty deacons, subdeacons, rectors, hieromonks, clerics, and priests. The cathedral is packed, with 80 percent women, even young ones with long lacquered nails and wearing chaste, 1950s-style attire: knee-length skirts, geometric or floral shirts, muted scarves. I sit next to Anastasia, a woman we just saw adjusting her veil outside the cathedral.

The service goes on for a long time. The clerics hang back in the sanctuary, behind the iconostasis, waiting for the arrival of the angels, Anastasia explains. I wonder if the cherubs would be encouraged by the cavernous chant of a six-foot-tall priest, a bass tone that makes the columns shake and recalls the Mephistopheles of Feodor Chaliapin, the most powerful operatic voice of all time and the pride of Kazan. But Anastasia says it's supposed to warm the soul and inspire meditation.

The choreographed dressing of the archbishop, in front of the iconostasis, doesn't leave a single move to chance. In a triumph of gold, purple, and embroidery, the scene unfolds in a dramatic crescendo of choruses, incense, bows, and grandiose processions. Anastasia notices my mouth agape and whispers that this rite is a way to join in communion with the heavens. She looks up at the frescoes on the lower nave. "We believe that the service celebrated here on earth is only one part of the sacred and divine mystery that is constantly being celebrated in heaven." But according to Anastasia, who is studying the history of modern art, people risk "falling prey to worshipping the cult itself, which, in the end, is just superstition." This reminds me of Rodin's words on the ancient faith, when the human and the divine were one, "when there was absolute submission to providence and prayer occurred at all times, even while drunk, even while giving in to sexual pleasure." I await Ignatius's sermon, wondering whether he'll refer to current events or the advent of the Antichrist, a popular theme from Russian pulpits.

After the service, we walk to a café, where Anastasia slips off her veil and straitlaced gray sweater, takes down her hair, and lights a cigarette. She explains that Ignatius had spoken about Saint Philip, the bishop of Moscow under Ivan the Terrible, who was strangled for allegedly shedding innocent blood and practicing sodomy. The sermon had taken a controversial turn when Ignatius warned those who sought to canonize a killer, which Anastasia thinks is a reference to Kirill.

The second part of the sermon was dedicated to the memory of Saint Basil, bishop of Ryazan', southeast of Moscow. Basil, when he was bishop of Murom, would spend his nights praying in his cell. But someone started a rumor that instead of praying, he was living it up with a prostitute. Slander, of course, but people believed it, and some even said they saw a woman going in and out of his cell. He was put to death by lynching. Basil asked for one night to pray. In tears, he invoked the Lord, and at dawn, a miracle happened: He took the mantle of the Madonna off a sacred icon, threw it into the Oka River, and used it to sail upstream before the eyes of his slanderers. He landed in Ryazan, which became a great city, while Murom is now hardly on the map, as Ignatius told it. Anastasia recounts the story passionately, especially when she speaks of Basil grabbing the mantle. "Things like that can happen in Russia. Loads of miracles, I swear," she says.

SKULLS AND SHINBONES

Our crossing point is in Kamyshin, a city of one hundred thousand people, where it's easier to imagine that there is a war going on nearby. Mechanics, dockworkers, truckers, and hawkers selling cucumbers in the central market are all wearing some kind of military attire, from full camouflage to bits of uniforms in blue, gray, or army green. The only patches of color are the watermelon halves teetering on rickety carts at the intersections. The manager at our hotel tells us that four hundred citizens from this city have been killed or wounded. One family lost two sons and a third was left without legs.

We've left behind the flat expanses of grains and sunflowers and now, on the western shore, the landscape rises and dips intermittently until the Don and the Black Sea. Beyond the Volga, the wind flows freely, sliding across a yellow tablecloth of grass that looks like an ocean—as vague and wild a space as the Mancha must have been for Don Quixote, a place with enough solitude and freedom to make one's head spin.

We set off on the ferry in the early morning. The boat cuts diagonally for almost six miles as we look out on the northern side. Here it truly is the Great River. There is something ineluctable, ruthless, about it: no bridges, just water that splits the land. Now the river has more in common with the sky than with the worlds it separates.

I think of what we've learned along the way. Every truth was immediately contradicted with a new truth; every bright idea was soon extinguished by dark thoughts, obscured by the shroud of nihilism that suffocates the conscience, ours included. While yesterday—delighted by the incense in the Saratov Cathedral—we fantasized about a miraculous cultural and spiritual alliance between Europe and Russia, now, standing on the liquid edge of the Volga, the distance between the two worlds seems unbridgeable.

We set off under low, gloomy clouds and arrive in Nikolayevsk when the sun is already high and scorching in the clear blue sky. It is still early to visit Bater, the shaman we are due to meet, so we walk down a dirt road to a point where the current has eroded the shoreline, creating a sheer cliff of ocher clay. Vlad and Katya are asleep in the van, parked in a lot on the outskirts of the village of Bykovo. A monument bears the names of the 136 (out of 230 enlisted) villagers who died in the Battle of Stalingrad. Ale and I walk off in different directions to experience the steppe in this rough strip of coast. I cut across a flat patch of grass on brittle ground, raising dust and grasshoppers with each step. In the distance, I see a patch of shrubs and men on horseback herding cows. I'm intrigued by a slight dip in the land and climb down into it, only to find a pile of bovine bones, skulls, and horns. Hisses rise as a dozen snakes shoot across my line of sight and slither into the gaps between the bones. I quickly climb back up the escarpment. The grass is sharp as sheet metal and scratches like hell. I'm panting, trying to anchor my gaze and control my vertigo, or at least temper an abstract fear.

Ale and I meet up at the cliffs. We look at each other disoriented, speechless. He also saw snakes, after which he was overcome with chills, as if he'd come into contact with a malevolent presence. This is a powerful place, full of dark energy, and it seems to be heightening the tensions we already feel inside.

The river is eating away at the base of the sea stacks, while small landslides chip away at the cliff wall. The current slams against it, leaving a yellow plume in its wake. Our feet are an inch from the precipice, and we take a few steps back in fear that the wall might give in. I point out a flock of geese approaching from the south, flying some forty feet above the water in a tight V formation. It's as if their wing beats are paddling through the air, regular and efficient. They are too far away for Ale to photograph, but suddenly, the lead goose turns sharply to the right. The rest of the flock, disoriented, breaks apart and course-corrects in a haphazard order. In just a few seconds, they soar up to the level of the cliff and head straight for us, causing us to duck. They are large and numerous and it feels like they fly over us for a very long time. We feel a sort of collective breath, the displacement of air, the sound of the wings flapping. They are so close we could reach up and touch them. We can see their little round eyes watching us sidelong as they speed by, communicating a sense of amusement and mischief. It feels like they're winking at us. Then, as quickly as they came, they swerve back toward the middle of the Volga, resume their proper formation, and continue their migration. Why did they indulge in this little escapade, here of all places?

I want to ask Bater, the Kalmyk shaman, about the geese but he isn't the type that does rain dances, as I'd imagined. He is a healer, like Anna from the Zhiguli Mountains. We learn this as we wait in the prefab building he uses as a clinic. A hundred or so people, mostly young, are also waiting. Their faces bear witness to the history of the Caucasus and the entire Asian world to which Russia has hitched itself. A woman in her thirties tells us that "the master helps birth babies."

Before long, Bater comes out and ushers us into his office. He is almost fifty years old, small, youthful, with Mongolian features, terracotta skin, and long pianist fingers. He smells of natural soap and wears a red shirt from Loro Piana, a luxury designer brand. He immediately warns us that he doesn't have much time, noting that it takes many months to get an appointment with him.

The room is plastered with pictures of babies. He points at them as he rattles off their names, then says, "All my children!" He tells us he is the last hope for people who struggle to conceive. There are some four thousand of "his" children living in Russia and beyond. "The smell!" he exclaims, touching his nose: He uses smell to read patients' chemical composition and determine what's wrong. Then he works on nervous system disorders and vegetative functions, in three-minute sittings. He doesn't accept a single ruble, but sometimes payments in kind: a chicken, a lamb, winter boots. Those who wish to contribute can donate to a rehab center in Volgograd.

He says he's seen a sharp decline in fertility lately. "People are afraid of the war, which is a big factor. Young people are coming back from the front unstable, or they fear being called up. The war creates toxic adrenaline. But the real problem," he says, "is that we're not as human as we used to be. And if you're not human, you can't make children. We're poisoning our lives. Take nationalism. I haven't watched the news in twenty years, and I have no nation. I'm not afraid to say it: I have no nation! And I don't have a specific religion: At home I have a Buddhist altar and a corner for my icons. I respect all beliefs, even cults. There are pagan communities in this region and that's fine with me. I fight only the new religion of the internet. It gets into you like a snake and devours you. Never mind Nazism or Communism: The internet should be abolished if we want to be human and have children." I ask him how one becomes a shaman or a healer. He says his knowledge and power have been passed down to him through generations. He learned to use his sense of smell from his grandmother, who is ninety-five years old and still cures many people. I ask him if location is a factor, if this is a special place. "I call it the great womb!" he says. "Everything is boundless and confused in the steppe, but here on the Volga we have clarity, harmony, and peace because wars have consumed all the evil there was. We feel safe."

Then our time is up. "There are people out there who are suffering and who have come from very far away," he says. He stands, takes my hands and Ale's and looks us each in the eyes with affection, as if trying to capture a good memory. He hands me a sort of Muslim rosary with large red ceramic beads. "I thought of you this morning, grasping this amulet. Your trip will go well, don't worry. Everything will be fine." Anna had said the same before we crossed the Volga to Shubert.

THE PLAYGROUND

Volgograd, the former Stalingrad, is up next. The city that turned the tide of the twentieth century. Now that I am here, on the site of one of the most horrific crimes against humanity in history, a page written in the blood of more than a million young men, I think back to Piotrovsky's words. When we met at the Hermitage, he refused to call it Volgograd.

We learn of a group in town that is gathering signatures to restore the old name, which was stripped in Khrushchev's 1961 campaign against all things Stalin. Volgograd's regional Duma recently passed a law forbidding comparisons between the Third Reich and the USSR, on pain of fifteen days in prison. Putin renamed a nuclear-powered icebreaker *Stalingrad* and when he inaugurated a new bust of Stalin at the Battle of Stalingrad Museum-Panorama, he declared, "We're once again being threatened by German panzers . . . and once again, we've been called to push back Western aggression."

Volgograd is the most Soviet city we've seen on the trip so far. It was the ideological capital of the USSR and now Putin uses it to back his patriotic rhetoric of courage and sacrifice (the *passionarnost*) and the denazification of Ukraine—Stalingrad will not take one step back, according to Stalin's famous orders. It's also the most Soviet because after the battle, it was rebuilt from nothing: Forty-one thousand buildings had been reduced to rubble, and only seven thousand residents remained at the time of victory in February 1943, from a population of four hundred thousand before August 1942. Now Volgograd counts about one million people, and the city is developing around the western shore of the Volga, as it did then, just that its center of gravity has been moved to the heart of the Great Battle. It remains a giant of heavy industry, but it has also been reborn as a giant of memory.

The memorial is a city within a city, a huge sanctuary swarming with pilgrims. People are lining up outside. The building, a convex cylinder in reinforced concrete, looks like a nuclear power plant and stands next to the ruins of the Stalingrad mill, built in 1909 by the Germans of the Volga and then destroyed by their former compatriots.

Tatiana Rikazchikova gives me a tour of the building, explaining that there are ten times more visitors now than in 2021. "It has become the mecca of Russian patriotism: People come here to swear an oath, and to prove to themselves they are Russian even when times are hard." We circle around the four-hundred-foot-wide, fifty-foot-tall diorama of the last days of the battle. "It was simpler in Borodino or Waterloo because those lasted hours, not months," she says. The work is a masterpiece of late socialist realism, made by seven painters in 1982. It's a collage of heroic acts, like the moment General Vasily Chuikov's troops surrounded the German Sixth Army and then took Mamayev Kurgan, the hill where, until then, seventy thousand men had died each week: That single square mile marked the beginning of the German defeat, the start of Hitler's undoing, and a decisive turning point in the conflict. The scene also depicts the moment Mikhail Panikakha, who was already mortally wounded, turned himself into a human torch and blew up a panzer. And when Yulia Koroleva carried fifty wounded soldiers to safety. And the feats of sniper Vasily Zaitsev, who killed 225 Germans on his own, 11 of whom were also snipers. In the allegorical scenes, the sky above the line of German prisoners is black, perhaps to recall the representations of Catherine the Great's victories over the Turks, where cherubs play trumpets among the clouds.

Images of the heroes in Donbas run along the exterior walls of the museum. A banner of Stalin in a white uniform against a red background hangs next to a black-and-orange flag with the letter *Z*, the symbol of Putin's war. Children climb all over an old T-34 tank and the barrels of a Katyusha rocket launcher set up at the entrance as if they were part of a playground. Tatiana shows me photos of the eightieth-anniversary celebrations of the liberation of Stalingrad. Families of Volgograd soldiers who perished in Ukraine were given medals, including that of Corporal Anastasia Savitskaya, the first female soldier killed in Donbas. The event's slogan was "Their ancestors fought Fascism according to conscience and tradition. Honor to the heroes, death to Fascism."

"Our elders say that celebrations like these haven't taken place since the '50s," Tatiana says. She also tells me about a controversy that erupted in Tatarstan that illustrates a new awareness of minority rights in Russia. The statues on the memorial in Hero Square depict soldiers of the Red Army with white European features, while at least half of the young men who died on the hill were Tatars.

Volgograd is also very Soviet because only women drive the trams, which are red—manifestations of a proletarian pride that has disappeared elsewhere in modern Russia. Similarly, for the first time on the trip, we notice many policewomen in uniform and plain clothes diligently watching over the Mamayev Kurgan memorial.

It is almost evening when I climb the two hundred steps to the shrine at the top of the hill, blending in with a tour group. At sunset, the statue *The Motherland Calls* stands at the top of the hill against the iridescent sky, in all its 280 feet in height, sword included. Those who arrive here by boat pass under the Motherland wielding her sword, where it's customary to toss carnations into the Volga.

Khrushchev wanted the monument to be taller than the Statue of Liberty and face east, toward the steppe, which can be interpreted in two ways: either as a sign of détente with the West, or as a communion with Mother Volga, the new protector of the USSR. "We are Russians, we are children of the Volga," Soviet poet Yevgeny Yevtushenko wrote. The motherland would not turn its back on the sacred river, which Soviet writer Vasily Grossman likened to the River Jordan in his book *Stalingrad*. In the novel, he describes a scene where Marshal Timoshenko takes his troops to safety on the other side of the Don, before preparing for his mortal clash on the Volga. "Slowly, the soldiers removed their shoes, revealing blistered feet that had marched from the Donets to the Volga. The pain was such that even a gust of wind could cause great pain. The soldiers carefully laid out their mats as if they were bandages. The wealthiest washed with shards of soap, others scraped their bodies with nails and sand." Then Grossman asks, "As the soldiers reveled in washing their necks and heads, did they understand the symbolic meaning of those ablutions? For the fate of Russia, that mass baptism in the Volga before a desperate battle for freedom could have been even more consequential than the one in the Dnepr a thousand years before," referring to the Rus of Kyiv converting to Christianity—the same Dnepr now known as Dnipro, a battlefront in Putin's war in Ukraine.

I don't know how many steps I climb before I stop to watch two people going the other way. A soldier in his thirties, wearing a green T-shirt with several medals pinned to his chest, holds a little girl by the hand. As they pose together for a selfie, I offer to take their picture. I notice the Donetsk annexation flag on the man's beret, and that the girl's arm is missing just under her shoulder. I try to strike up a conversation: The man is civil and smiles, showing several gold teeth, but we have no means of communicating. I look around for Vlad, but there is no trace of him. My only option is to say goodbye. I think of the lost opportunity and the favorable situation, because there on the staircase, I saw no undercover agents.

THE SICK COUNTRY

Andrey Voronov-Orenburgsky is the author of eight books on the Battle of Stalingrad, one for each month of the conflict. I meet him in a large and luxurious apartment. He is a large, sixty-two-year-old man with a gruff appearance, but as we converse, he becomes increasingly amiable.

"The Nazis wanted to see the Volga?" he begins. "We sure showed them. By tying up their hands with barbed wire. They're all there, with my love." He points to the rows of books behind his dog, who is lying on the floor next to a bookcase. Voronov's historical novels detail the clash of the century almost hour by hour, house by house, body by body.

He refers to the Volga as the czarina, and it's his other love. "It separated two peoples, two regimes, two civilizations. The Germans considered it the eastern border of the Third Reich." I ask him whether he sees Vasily Grossman as competition and he dismisses me with a practiced answer: "He wrote memorable words on Jewish pain. Less memorable ones on Russian pain." I've never read anything by Voronov, but here, in his adoptive city, his books line the shelves of souvenir shops. Of the great Grossman, though, there is no trace even in the museum bookshop.

I ask him about Stalingrad's legacy, but he wants to dwell on the role the city and its river played in the battle. "In May 1942, the Germans occupied Kharkiv, eastern Ukraine, and then Crimea. Hitler postponed the attack on Moscow until after the winter and focused on the south, certain the Red Army was done for," he explains. "Breaking through the Volga at Stalingrad, in addition to humiliating Stalin himself, would give him control of one of the largest iron and steel hubs of the country, paving the way for an offensive on Astrakhan, the Caspian, and the oil fields of Baku, opening up the route to Asia. Having the Volga corridor in hand meant certain victory. Then Moscow would be just a detail."

Stalingrad managed to bring almost three hundred thousand civilians to safety across the river in just a few days. Those who stayed on this side became part of the *Rattenkrieg*, the rat war, as the Germans called it. The Red Army had no way out, no chance of retreating—the Volga was the famous point of no return. The crossing—exposed to German snipers and protected by Katyusha rockets from the eastern shore—was intended only for transporting the five hundred thousand wounded. Then, one day in February 1943, silence fell on both sides. The wind swept the air clean and the ruins of Stalingrad—the factories, buildings, forts—emerged from the fog as the Red Army claimed victory. Grossman wrote that the silence was the expression of the people's victory—not the marches, the orchestras, or the fireworks, but the quiet of a humid Russian night.

"The Germans had come to see the Volga. They got what they wanted," says Voronov. "We lined them up, some one hundred thousand prisoners, and took them to see the sacred river they had fought so hard to reach."

I ask what remains of that spirit. "Nothing," he says, seized by emotion. "This is a very sick country. It has destroyed everything those heroes created. Stalingrad strengthened the bonds between people. Russians were pacified. Victory brought a sense of compassion for all of humanity. We knew we'd stood up to evil, whom we'd fought, and why. Now Russians have become a powerless mass, unworthy of the USSR and the real Russia. And he . . . I don't know whom he's fighting or why. What I know is that we're fighting our brothers, our own Slavic brothers! He has plunged us into barbarity. They told us our borders were violated and that we're defending ourselves. But us who? Who are the ones defending themselves?"

I point out that he is terribly pessimistic. "How can we talk about the spirit of Stalingrad when we're shooting at our brothers? How can you talk about a 'wall of resistance' when Russia is consumed by chaos, by the *smuta*? Do you know what it means?" I say yes, it means turbulence, like in the seventeenth century. "What seventeenth century! We're in it now. But I know Russia can heal, it can be reborn like a phoenix, out of the ashes. And the heroes are awaiting their turn. And when the time comes, as Hemingway said, the bell will toll louder and louder, clearer and clearer, and the true heroes of Russia will appear. And it will be good for everyone, even the West, which denigrates us, which doesn't want us, which pushes us like rejects toward the East. I don't care what they say, time is always on the side of Russia, and our time will come. We'll stand up, make the walls shake, defend our dignity and the name of our ancestors, our *sobornost*, Orthodoxy, loyalty to the Russian army, the Russian idea; and we will bring goodness to the whole world. We'll bring the best of ourselves."

Voronov runs out of words, and air. He is breathless and exhausted by his heartfelt lament. He lights another cigarette to catch his breath. With a tender and teary look, he searches for his dog, who was lying there just a moment ago. "When she hears my voice change, she scampers off. My love is a scaredy-cat."

THE SIGN OF THE CROW

It is the day of our last crossing, though this time, we'll be traversing the steppe to reach the Caspian Sea. It is already scorching in the early morning, making it hard to imagine how these red-hot southern lands could turn into a polar climate in winter. It reached −40 degrees Fahrenheit in January 1943, and the Soviet infantry had to fashion gloves out of the skin of dead dogs.

Our next and final stop is Astrakhan, and a long journey awaits us. From there, we hope to take a boat to Baku, Azerbaijan, and maybe get a glimpse of the illegal trafficking between Russia and Iran along the Volga-Caspian corridor. But it is not clear whether passenger services are running. We are fascinated by the idea of spending time in Astrakhan, the "magical melting pot," as Voronov called it, but we feel like we've pushed our luck far enough. "Everything will be fine," the baby-making shaman said, as Ale continues to remind me. He often returns to those moments we spent on the cliffside and the migrating geese that winked at us. "What a frightening place. The energy was crushing my temples," he says. Now it's our turn to migrate.

There is no breakfast at the hotel, so we search for a café. We are on the outskirts of Volgograd—there hadn't been a single room available in town. In the van, we speak only when strictly necessary. Even the radio is off. To think that for a good part of the trip, we argued over which station to listen to. Those were nice moments, with Vlad and Katya singing along, she in her beautiful voice, and he with his passion for the blues.

We have a few hours left before our departure. I want to find the people organizing the referendum to restore the name of Stalingrad, or someone from the Communist youth Tatiana mentioned at the museum. This city needs further study, and I sense that I will leave with some regrets. For one, I can't stop thinking about the soldier and the little girl on the steps, those medals, that missing arm.

But Vlad seems off. Likely from another hangover. We drive around for half an hour looking for a place to eat. Finally, we head for the city center and drive down an elegant tree-lined street full of people strolling. We stop at the Massimo Café, which overlooks the park. We sit on the veranda, each of us stewing in our own thoughts. I watch the constant flow of people walking along the promenade: workers, tourists, a group of young priests. Then suddenly, hand in hand, there they are, the soldier and the little girl, in the same clothes they wore on the steps to the Mamayev Kurgan. They walk into the Massimo Café.

The little girl's name is Masha. She is almost five years old and has an oval face marked with scars and a half-closed eye. His name is Shukhrat, but he goes by Donetsky. He is a thirty-seven-year-old Tatar special forces officer—though he does not say which forces. He doesn't seem surprised to have run into us in a city of more than a million people. He, too, was sorry we hadn't been able to talk at the monument.

We head to the public gardens to film the interview under an oak tree. Katya takes Masha for a walk, and they set off hand in hand. Donetsky doesn't have much to say about his time at the front—nothing he wants to share with us, anyway. He is sitting on a bench in his tight green T-shirt, and it's clear that he built up his muscles in the field, not at the gym. He keeps his military beret pulled over his eyes and his arms crossed over his medal-studded chest. He's been fighting in Donbas since 2014 and is on Kyiv's wanted list. We ask him if he thinks himself a hero. "Yes," he says, flashing us his golden teeth. "President Vladimir Vladimirovich Putin has told me so!" He met Putin a few days ago, at a ceremony in Moscow during which the president personally pinned the medal of valor to his shirt—Donetsky points to the Saint George's cross on his chest. I ask him why he's in Volgograd. "I grew up in Kazakhstan," he says. "I'm here looking for volunteers. I have to recruit at least forty by the end of the week. Stalingrad is patriotism. People here believe in victory and know Russia cannot lose." A good place to go fishing, that is, like going to Lourdes to recruit priests.

His appearance is obviously a marketing ploy: He walks around with his medals pinned to his chest and a girl with no arm so that people will notice him and approach him. He climbs the Mamayev Kurgan hill three times a day, he says proudly. Masha is his daughter, but she doesn't live with him in Donbas. She and her mother moved to Rostov, on the Don, because Donbas was too dangerous—they were terrified. "We spend a few days together and then I go back to my duty." He says

he hopes that he and his men can take Odessa next. The only confession he lets slip, maybe because we're foreigners, is that he's in charge of several European and American volunteers of Russian ancestry.

Finally, he stands up to leave, saying he promised Masha a proper breakfast. Mozart's *Requiem* starts blasting from some nearby speakers. "This is Memory Park. Over there is the eternal flame to the unknown soldier," Donetsky tells us. "They play this music every day at eleven. Gives you the chills, doesn't it? This is Russia. A big heart." He pats his medals.

We stand there listening, and in that moment, an enormous crow swoops down and settles on the back of the bench, next to Donetsky, who reaches out to touch it. The crow inches away, seemingly unafraid, and turns to look at us. "When they do that, it means someone is thinking about you intensely," Donetsky says.

"In a good way or a bad way?" Vlad asks.

"I think good, but I could be wrong."

THE KALMYK MANCHA

After meeting the shaman, and before arriving in Volgograd, the four of us experienced a period of great peace, the last one we would share. We made a pit stop some forty miles before the city, at a trucker restaurant managed by an Azeri family that owns about a thousand sheep. We ate outside to admire the horizon. It was very hot, and the wind was lifting small dust funnels on the steppe. We also felt uplifted by the very good lamb *shashlik* and mutton-stuffed cabbage we were dining on.

I think back to those moments at a truck stop on the way to Astrakhan, after leaving Volgograd. Vlad and Katya were sleeping in the van. They were both worn out from driving the trucker's route—a black ribbon stretching into the desert, where there were no signs and where the only warning to travelers was provided by the rusty carcasses of vehicles that didn't make it. We have just survived a potentially fatal impact with a pothole.

Inside, Chechen, Circassian, Ingush, Kabardian, or Karachay truckers were staring at a silent TV screen displaying subtitles in Russian. Or maybe they belonged to one of the two hundred peoples of Dagestan, where they speak two hundred mutually incomprehensible languages.

Arab geographer al-Masudi called the Caucasus a mountain of languages, while Pliny reported that the Romans used 134 interpreters when dealing with local clans. We don't have this problem, since nobody wants to talk to us. And for the first time on the trip, we receive hostile smirks. When Ale begins to fumble around with his camera, three men stand up menacingly—those with the longest beards and the broadest shoulders.

Next we stop to visit a couple of cemeteries, one Islamic and one Christian—though it's hard to tell them apart, since there are no houses or villages around. Yet they each contain fresh graves, all of young people, and plastic flowers that haven't yet faded in the sun. But no trail of empty vodka bottles or toasts to the health of thirsty souls. Who will come to mourn the soldiers in the desert?

When we reach the Orthodox cemetery, Katya tells us what happened to Masha, the veteran's daughter. As they were walking in the park, she told Katya how she'd lost her arm. She was with her mom in Donbas, and they were running toward a shelter because the Ukrainians were pounding the city—Donetsk, maybe, Katya couldn't remember. But there had been a line out the door, and before Masha and her mother could enter, they'd been hit by a grenade. "My daddy is brave," she told Katya. "Did you see how many medals he has? I'm brave too, and this is my medal. I gave my arm for Russia." We are dumbstruck. I wonder how a five-year-old managed to articulate such an upsetting sentence; I can't help but think that she is being used to draw tears and enlistments from new volunteers. Katya, too, was moved, but the girl told her not to cry. "Everything will be okay, don't worry. I just wish I could see out of this eye again. Daddy says I'll get better—he never lies."

I look around. How many cemeteries have we visited over the past four thousand miles? How many times have we walked through this sense of emptiness, so akin to what death leaves behind? The only living residents are grasshoppers and the fist-sized spiders that crawl out of wrought iron crosses. What are spiders doing here in the scorched clay, which is cracked and just as dead as the fallen of this and other wars? Our shadows grow long across the graves as the sunset bleeds from the west. I imagine the silhouettes of Rocinante and Don Quixote's slim halberds beside us: We are the sad knights of this Kalmyk Mancha, where everything—bison, shepherds, camels, warriors, and tanks—has been flattened by infinite time. To the east, the waters of the Volga flow solitary, unaware of the sweet death that awaits it just a few miles away, in the delta's embrace. We see giants rise in the distance, or perhaps it's the dizzying effect of a landscape devoid of horizon. They are just a few windmills, but Don Quixote would have faced them anyway, full of principle, dignity, and honor as he was. He would have challenged the giants of our time, shown us what is worth fighting for, and torn down the veil of fallacies that everyone, in Russia and in the West, seems to believe are true. He wouldn't have thought twice about marching forth into the foolishness of this war. Perhaps only madness can stop us from mistaking appearance for reality.

In this emptiness I wonder where all the spirit guides have gone. Where are the voices of the desert, the predictions of doom as humanity worships at the altar of money and technology and the world amasses weapons, ready to pull the trigger?

ALTERNATIVE STURGEON

We continue our drive as sky and earth blend into one and the toasted colors of the prairie join those of the sunset, until the lights of Astrakhan finally appear before us. Then the landscape changes, and we see a city surrounded and besieged by the Volga, which branches off into the distributaries of the delta before diving into the Caspian Sea: one hundred miles of changeable, amphibious nature where zoology, geography, and history persist against all odds. Every wave of migration has attempted to build a civilization, only to be erased by the following wave, where a new elite could come in and wipe out a dominant neighborhood, a caravansary would be demolished to make room for a Grand Hotel, or an old bazaar would be undermined by rapacious trading companies.

Astrakhan stands at the border between the south and east of the Russian world. A commercial hub to welcome the gathering of peoples, religions, and goods that straddle continents. The winds of Persia, China, India, and Europe have all blown through Astrakhan, bringing nomads and merchants like flocks of birds.

"The nomads and the birds are all gone," says Olesya Sergeeva, a forty-two-year-old biologist who raises beluga sturgeon and produces caviar. She knows we aren't here to buy, but she still shows us around and gives us a taste of her version of reality, along with some caviar. "Astrakhan has lost its charm, and the delta pays the price of the devastation the Soviets wreaked on the river. They tampered with nature so much it may never recover. Like Gorky, I look at the Volga and see the inexplicable self-destructive force of the Russians." She tells us that over the past several decades, the water level in the Caspian Sea has dropped by twelve feet because of dams on the Volga, which also prevent sturgeon from swimming up the river to reproduce. The rest of the damage was caused by industrial and civil waste, fertilizers, pesticides, and overfishing: Wild sturgeon is practically extinct. "They're living fossils. They're two hundred million years old, but now they're going the way of the dinosaur. But not because of an asteroid." I tell her that in New Orleans, the Mississippi has at times been called the Great Sewer. A large catfish farm on the Mississippi Delta gave me the same impression of a neglect of the river, signaling that we no longer need it. But there was also a time when the Thames, in London, was known as the Great Stink. It seemed done for, but it recovered, and now even dolphins have been spotted swimming in it.

Sergeeva raises her sturgeons in large pools, where they produce prized caviar that is served at dinners in the Kremlin. It is grayer than the caviar that was available for a handful of rubles around the time of the fall of the USSR. She explains that this is the result of a process that she has invented: She extracts the sturgeon's eggs with a small incision, without killing it, an operation that can be done up to three times on the same fish. She manages 470 pools with a total of four hundred tons of sturgeon and assures us that the production level and sale of caviar remains the same as it was before the war. "No self-respecting party in Russia can forgo caviar," even, apparently, in the current situation. It costs $35 per hectogram (about 3.5 ounces) and her employees earn $600–$700 per month. She says that since Russia banned wild sturgeon harvesting in the Caspian, farms have proliferated, their numbers rising from three to sixty in five years.

Sergeeva is well known in Europe for her work in aquaculture. She could get a job anywhere, it seems to me, so why stay? "I was born here, I studied here, my husband is Russian, my son is Russian, I am Russian," she says. "I wouldn't say I'm a patriot, and I don't want to express my thoughts on Putin and the war. But I can assure you that my life has not changed." As other agribusiness entrepreneurs we've met along the way have done, Sergeeva praises the quality of products that are available now compared to before the sanctions. Although now, she has to procure feed from Iran instead of Europe. "We can get anything here. They're building new docks on the delta for container ships and oil tankers. Astrakhan is crucial for Russia. It always has been."

She tells us about her family. "I come from a Jewish family that arrived in Astrakhan in the nineteenth century, when they introduced barges and steamboats. You mentioned the Mississippi—at the time, the Volga was the Mississippi of Europe. It was a trade route between Saint Petersburg, even Manchester, and Persia and India. Astrakhan was a giant emporium on the mouth of the Caspian. The East India Company's local branch employed three hundred people."

By this point, Ale and I are mostly on our own. Sergeeva offers to take us to the Jewish, Armenian, and Iranian quarters: hard to spot the differences among them, since Cyrillic has Russified everything, minimizing any foreign distinctions. Large photos line the avenues of Glory Park of civilian volunteers supporting troops by camouflaging tanks and making pickles. Sergeeva points out the renovations along the canal that runs through the old town, the nineteenth-century wooden villas being converted to hotels or luxury apartments. "They seemed destined to collapse, but now that money is going around, Astrakhan has gone back to being European Russia's gateway to central Asia and India."

In the distance, we can see fighter jets zoom past at low altitude. They seem to be flying over the delta, though in this region of fluid realities, it's hard to tell what is land and what is water.

CASPIAN BREEZE

We are due to leave tomorrow on a flight to Baku. The only escape route is by air: The ports in Astrakhan and the Caspian waters have turned out to be genuine fronts in the war. There are checkpoints at all customs areas in the commercial port, while the passenger port has been closed since the fall of 2022. Even scheduled boats that used to stop at the commercial naval district, a few miles south of Astrakhan, are no longer in service and the area is off-limits to civilians. But we can still glimpse cranes loading and unloading a dozen cargo ships and three barges waiting at the widest point. We also learn of a project to expand the Don canal, which is sixty-three miles long. The Volga-Don canal was built under Stalin with the labor of seventy-five thousand prisoners and opened in 1952. It connects the Volga to Rostov-on-Don, from which one can reach Mariupol on the Sea of Azov, which is now controlled by the Russians. South of Volgograd, we'd tried taking a dirt road leading to the mouth of the canal, but we were intimidated by the presence of a helicopter hovering some three hundred feet above us. We stopped to gather pears and apricots instead.

Iran is building a railway to connect the Caspian Sea to the Persian Gulf, which will act as a pipeline to carry Russian oil to India. At the same time, Tehran has reportedly invested about $10 billion to develop the Caspian-Volga-Don corridor to bypass sanctions on the trade of agricultural goods, oil, wind turbines, spare parts, medicine, nuclear materials, and drones. It is impossible to verify, but Astrakhan is clearly central to the anti-Western economic bloc's efforts to turn to the East.

The riverfront is swarming with families and couples eating watermelon. The smell of grilled skewers fills the promenade, which is lined with prerevolution architecture. As we stroll, we spot a few long beards, uniformed soldiers, and a Cossack in full dress uniform with his girlfriend on his arm. Ale stops taking photos—his intended subjects cover their faces when they notice his lens.

What Russia is this? What era? We are at the tip of the Volga, at the edge of a boundless Russia. But we feel like we are about to enter into a new time—*na grani*—full of menace like the dark clouds on the horizon. Despite the wide promenade and gentle breeze from the Caspian, I start to feel claustrophobic.

Ale's last picture is a selfie of us on a restaurant boat. It reminds us of a sentence we read on a beam in a little bar in Venice, Louisiana, a shrimp-fishing village on the last clump of land on the Mississippi. "Wondering where you are, babe. When I think of you, I can't breathe, my brain explodes, my body shatters. You are my all." Seized by the emotion of the moment, we'd felt like those words had been worth the entire trip. And now? Now we are afraid of what could happen in the brief period before we board our plane to get out of here. We feel vulnerable. We are at the end of the road, where there are no more stops, landscapes, or stories to look forward to. The only remaining story is ours.

Closing Credits

We find Katya and Vlad at a bar near our hotel, empty bottles on the table. Vlad leads us upstairs to an outer walkway. He looks pale and tense, but we manage to talk through some logistics—we have to pay his fees, erase all signs of contact between us, and part on the best possible terms.

Then Katya materializes in front of us. She speaks to Vlad in Russian while pointing at us. Vlad looks at her, stunned and terrified. "She says she's going to report you. She's going to make some phone calls."

"Why should she?" I ask.

"What the hell do I know. Because she's crazy and she hates you."

The following morning, we knock on their door. We've decided to confront Katya, convince her that if they take us, she'll get in trouble too. We spent the night preparing a whole list of arguments. But we find Vlad alone, wandering through a graveyard of empty bottles.

We know we'll never see them again. But Katya's threat, now that we are facing our last mile of Russia alone, is ringing in our ears, amplifying the ticking of the bomb. Will we be ambushed in the closing credits?

The Astrakhan airport is guarded by armed soldiers with jeeps. The building isn't much larger than a bus station, and all eyes are on us. Ale pulls out the shaman's red amulet. "He said it would be all right," he whispers.

I've seen Ale in tense situations, and I know how unflappable he can be. During antiregime protests in Minsk, I saw him climb onto the roof of KGB headquarters to snap photos of students tossing flyers off the building. He barely escaped capture that night. I've seen him in Darfur, when our Land Rover broke down in the desert, in an area controlled by the Janjaweed, mounted militias that were massacring and torching entire villages. I see that same calm now, as we walk through the only passport-control gate and three officials arrive to stop him and take him to the FSB office. They also confiscate my passport, and we both end up in a small room with five agents, all very young. It's hard to say how much time we spend there, but I am keenly aware of every moment until we leave with our passports and take off for Baku.

They check our phones, but don't confiscate them; they ask questions about our trip, about this book, about why we chose to drive down the Volga. But they don't ask to see notes or photos. At one point, they zero in on Ale's residency in Miami, which appears on his Italian passport. But when he says he is from Tuscany, their attention shifts in a surreal way to the art scene in Florence, San Gimignano, Siena. One of the agents, who must be about twenty-five, apparently wants to showcase his overwhelming passion for the Italian Renaissance.

Russia is this, too: the electrified gaze of an agent with the infamous security services extolling the virtues of Brunelleschi.

We will never know why they stopped us, or why they let us go.

Acknowledgments

Even before the war, along with my colleagues at the *River Journal*, Nicola Scevola, Nanni Fontana, and Massimo Di Nonno, I had thought of reporting on Russia by way of the Volga—so my first thoughts go out to them, my partners in expeditions along the great rivers of the world. The idea came about as a narrative device to investigate a country that has become belligerent and off-limits to the Western press. I also want to reiterate the crucial role of my friend and photographer Alessandro Cosmelli in sharing the risks of this trip along with his open and profound interpretations of reality.

There is a long list of people who facilitated our jobs in Russia, agreeing to work with us before, during, and after our trip, but I'd rather protect their identities by not mentioning them by name. I don't know the names of the FSB agents who refrained from arresting us at the airport in Astrakhan: We will always be grateful to them.

I thank my publisher Giuseppe Russo because he continues to believe that reporting in the field is crucial to critical thinking. I also thank the whole crew at Gramma/Feltrinelli, especially editor Luca Soverini—working with him, in a molecular revision of this text, gave me an almost masochistic pleasure. I am also extremely grateful to two exceptional reader-consultants: my sister Tiziana—my own personal "literary high court"—and my dear friend Nicola. I also received invaluable help from Victoria Savvicheva and Giovanni Gobber, an expert in Slavic studies at the Catholic University of the Sacred Heart in Milan, who checked my Russian terms and references.

I stood firm in the face of the difficulties and discomfort wrought by this project thanks to my wife, Gabriella, who never stopped encouraging me and always prioritized my writing. I will never forget the generosity of Enza Pasquariello, who allowed me to take a long writer's retreat in her Milanese *izba*.

This trip and this book could not have been possible without the support of Tom Hundley and the Pulitzer Center in Washington, John MacArthur of *Harper's Magazine*, and Daniel Puntas Bernet of *Reportagen*. That a piece edited by Will Stephenson, related to this book, was featured on the cover of *Harper's Magazine* gave global prominence to this story and generated a flurry of lectures at US universities: My exchanges with students and professors highlighted the need to write this book in its entirety.

I especially want to thank Deborah Anne Cohen and former ambassador to Georgia Ian Kelly, of the Northwestern Buffett Institute for Global Affairs; my friend and colleague Joe Coleman at the University of Indiana; and Lynette Clemetson, director of the Wallace House Center for Journalists in Ann Arbor, Michigan. I also want to mention a few people who have contributed to this project in various ways: Gaia Light, Daniele Stefanini, Tiberio Mian, Ignazio de Roux-Mian, Maurice Walsh, Giovanni De Mauro, Pierluigi Vercesi, Linda Rexer, Francesco Battistini, Brad Wernle, Bob Rowley, Lilli Faccioli Pintozzi, Serge Michel, Paolo Mazzoli, Charles Eisendrath, Valerio Selle, Dora Di Scilla. And Tosca, our dog, who would love me even if I were illiterate.

Bibliography

NOTE: These sources are listed in the Italian editions consulted by the author. English-language editions, if available, are provided in parentheses for the convenience of our readers.

Blok, Aleksandr. *I dodici. Gli Sciti. La patria.* Translated by Eridano Bazzarelli. Fabbri Editori, 1998. (*Selected Poems.* Translated by Jon Stallworthy and Peter France. Carcanet, 2000.)

Chlebnikov, Velimir. *47 poesie facili e una difficile.* Translated by Paolo Nori. Quodlibet, 2009. (*Collected Works of Velimir Khlebnikov*, vol. 3: *Selected Poems.* Translated by Paul Schmidt, edited by Ronald Vroon. Harvard University Press, 1998.)

Giljarovskij, Vladimir. *Mosca e i moscoviti.* Felici, 2013. (Gilyarovsky, Vladimir. *Moscow and Muscovites.* Translated by Brendan Kiernan. Russian Information Services, 2013.)

Golovanov, Vasilij. *Verso le rovine di Čevengur.* Translated by Valentina Parisi. Adelphi, 2008.

Gor'kij, Maksim. *Infanzia.* Translated by Emanuela Guercetti. Giangiacomo Feltrinelli Editore, 2022. (Gorky, Maksim. *Childhood.* Translated with an introduction and notes by Graham Hettlinger. Ivan R. Dee, 2010.)

Grossman, Vasilij. *Vita e destino.* Translated by Claudia Zonghetti. Adelphi, 2008. (Grossman, Vasily. *Life and Fate.* Translated by Robert Chandler, introduction by Polly Jones. Everyman's Library, 2022.)

Majakovskij, Vladimir. "La nuvola in calzoni." Translated by Angelo Maria Ripellino. In *Opere scelte*, by Mario De Micheli. Giangiacomo Feltrinelli Editore, 1967. (Mayakovsky, Vladimir. "The Cloud in Pants." In *Selected Poems*, translated by James H. McGavran III. Northwestern University Press, 2013.)

Majakovskij, Vladimir. *Lenin*. Translated by Angelo Maria Ripellino. Einaudi, 1967. (Mayakovsky, Vladimir. *Vladimir Ilyich Lenin*. Translated by Dorian Rottenberg, introduction by Rosy Carrick. Smokestack Books, 2017.)

Pamuk, Orhan. *La stranezza che ho nella testa*. Translated by Barbara La Rosa Salim. Einaudi, 2015. (*A Strangeness in My Mind*. Translated by Ekin Oklap. Knopf, 2015.)

Puškin, Aleksandr. *La storia della rivolta di Pugačëv*. Translated by Ettore Lo Gatto. Quodlibet, 2023. (Pushkin, Alexander. *The Captain's Daughter*. Translated by Robert Chandler and Elizabeth Chandler. New York Review Books Classics, 2014.)

Rocca, Gianni. *Stalin. Quel "meraviglioso georgiano."* Mondadori, 1988.

Tarkovskij, Arsenij. *Poesie scelte*. Translated by Gario Zappi. Scheiwiller, 1989. (*I Burned at the Feast: Selected Poems of Arseny Tarkovsky*. Translated by Philip Metres and Dmitri Psurtsev. Cleveland State University Poetry Center, 2015.)

Tjutčev, Fëdor. *Poesie*. Translated by Tommaso Landolfi. Adelphi, 2011.

Illustrations

Frontispiece	Balakovo, Volgograd region. The Volga River east bank.
Page 6	Rzhev. Memorial to the Soviet Soldier.
Page 9	Volgoverkhovye. Church of the Savior Transfiguration at the source of the Volga River.
Page 25	Rzhev. Memorial to the Soviet Soldier. Young woman selling memorabilia.
Page 37	Rzhev. Visitors from Donbas singing Russian nationalist songs at the Memorial to the Soviet Soldier.
Page 47	Tver'. Military aircraft flying over the Proletarka complex, a public housing project.
Page 60	Tver'. Train tracks.
Page 62	Volgograd. Battle of Stalingrad Museum. Statue of Stalin.
Page 65	Yaroslavl. The Transfiguration Cathedral as seen from the ferry on the Volga River.
Page 81	Kazan. Mechanics taking a break.
Page 89	Dubna. Roadside house.
Page 103	Rybinsk. Valentina—widow of Pavel Tsibulsky, who died in Donbas as a volunteer—with her daughter Zarina.

Page 114 Yaroslavl. Teeneger wearing a Stalin T-shirt on the ferry to Kostroma.

Page 124 Yaroslavl. Young military school students working out.

Page 127 The Volga River west bank near Kostroma.

Page 146 Balakovo, Volgograd region. Steppe landscape.

Page 149 Mari El region. Kombinat Zvenigovsky's front gate, one of the last Soviet *kolkhozy* (collective agri-food company) of the Russian Federation.

Page 151 Mari El region. Most-valuable-workers pictures, Kombinat Zvenigovsky.

Page 161 Balakovo, Volgograd region.

Page 165 Verhanii Ochaki. Eugenio Yazheikin, Nadezhada Yazheikina, Svetlana Yazheikina, Nikolai Yazheikin, farmers.

Page 176 Verhanii Ochaki. Blind dog chained in front of a house.

Page 184 Kazan. Propaganda sign in the outskirts of the city.

Page 195 Ulyanovsk. Young couple at the bus stop.

Page 204 Samara. Young people playing beach volleyball at sunset.

Page 206 Samara. Young gymnasts practicing on the beach.

Page 228 Saratov. Mass in the Holy Trinity Cathedral.

Page 251 Volgograd. Kids playing on a World War II tank.

Index

Abkhazia, 143
Abramovich, Roman, 138
Afanasev, Aleksandr, 39
Afghanistan, 86, 126, 142, 198
agriculture, 90, 150–55; *See also* collectivization (collectivized agriculture)
Akhmatova, Anna, 42
Akvarium (rock band), 209, 229
Albanians, 143
Albert (friend of Shukhrat), 212–15, 237
alcohol and alcoholism, 10, 17, 22, 48, 51, 60, 67, 73, 76, 101, 216, 223, 225–27, 229
Ale (travel companion), *See* Cosmelli, Alessandro
Alekseev, Georgi, 61
Aleppo, Syria, 121
Alexander I, Czar, 31
Alexander II, Czar, 53, 90
Alexander III, Czar, 18, 179, 186, 191
Alexandra (wife of Nicholas II), 90
Alexandrov, Alexander, 94
Alexandrov, Russia, 134
Alexandrovna, Maria, 185
Alipius, Father, 20
All-Russian Extraordinary Commission, 41
Americans, 23, 73, 83–84; *See also* United States
Anastasia (art student in Saratov), 238–39
Andreeva, Maria, 55, 56
Andrew, Saint, 153
Andrey K. (Chechen), 68–72, 72, 79, 82, 87
Angola prison (Louisiana), 115
Anna (wife of Levsha), 206–8
antiglobalization, 92–93
antisemitism, 22, 217, 224
anti-Western nationalism, 51, 82–86, 126, 233, 234, 257
Antonov, Pavel, 138
Apple, 71, 230
Applebaum, Anne, 111
Arab countries, 155, 180
Arch of Samara, 204–5
Arctic, the, 34, 80, 135, 152, 156
Arctic Ocean, 111

Arendt, Hannah, 140–41
Ariston, 158
Arkhangelsk, Russia, 135
Armenia, 123
Artem, 177
Artur (singer), 128–30, 132, 144
Ashkenazim Jews, 120
Asia, 4, 18, 120, 122, 123, 136, 155–57, 179–81, 205, 247
"Asianism," 126
Assad, Bashir al-, 143
assassinations (assassination attempts), 17, 43, 53, 67, 74, 138–39, 179, 186, 191, 221
Astra Shipping, 138
Astrakhan, Russia, 1, 5, 120, 123, 132, 135, 167, 198, 224–25, 225, 237, 247, 249, 254–57, 257, 259
Atanasio, Bishop, 134
atheism, 11, 13, 15, 39, 50, 52, 162, 186, 231–32
"Atlantic" (term), 18
AUE (cartel), 199
Aurora (cruiser), 189
auto industry, 158, 202, 203
autocracy, 45, 70, 79, 93, 125, 137, 140–41
Avaev, Vladislav, 138
Avagumyan, Kamo, 158
Avar language, 35
Avers LGBT, 219
Avilon, 158
Avtodom, 158
AvtoVaz, 202
Avvakum Petrov, 40, 234–35
Azov, Sea of, 111, 257

Baba Yaga (folk figure), 40
Babel, Isaac, 42
Baghdad, 119
Baku, Azerbaijan, 247, 249, 257
Bakunin, Mikhail, 168, 200–201
Balakovo, Russia, 228–33, 237
balalaika, 213
Balkans (Balkan crisis), 83–85
Baltic region, 19–20, 28, 29, 34, 36, 84, 86, 133, 135, 191
Baltic Sea, 4, 111, 120
barley, 155
Bashkirs, 168
Bater (shaman), 240–42
Battle on the Ice, 123
Battleship Potemkin (film), 91
Batu Khan, 122
Baulin, Pavel, 63
Belarus, 28, 36, 82, 101
Belinsky, Vissarion, 32
Belomorkanal, 111
Beria, Lavrentiy, 226
Berlin, Battle of, 20
Berlin, Germany, 48, 189
bespredel, 139
billionaires, 137–39
birth rates, 181, 242–43
"biznes fever," 81
black market, 75, 233

Black Sea, 22, 32, 79, 111, 179, 240
Blair, Tony, 3
Blok, Aleksandr, 7
Boatmen of the Volga, The (painting by Repin), 104–6
bogatyri, 39
Bolsheviks and Bolshevism, 28, 52, 55, 58, 77, 90, 93, 98, 115, 124, 132, 150, 184, 187–90, 196, 198, 217, 219, 222; *See also* October Revolution
Boris Godunov (Pushkin), 140, 141
Bosnia, 85, 128–29
Botikov, Andrey, 138
bourgeoisie, 41, 53, 93, 173, 189, 196, 220, 221
boyars, 123, 124, 133–35, 137–39, 167, 168
Brezhnev, Leonid, 82, 94, 201
BRICS, 111, 156
British Empire, 2, 180
Brodsky, Joseph, 42
Brothers Karamazov (Dostoyevsky), 40
Buddhism, 209–11, 242
Bukharin, Nikolai, 187
Bulgakov, Mikhail, 42
Bulgaria and Bulgarians, 77, 120, 122
burlaki, 104–5
Burnt by the Sun (film), 91
Bush, George W., 86, 171
Bykovo, Russia, 240
Byzantium (Byzantine Empire), 16, 20, 93; *See also* Constantinople

Caesar, Julius, 167
Cambridge University, 54
Canaletto, 2
canals, 108–11, 204, 256, 257
capitalists and capitalism, 49, 55, 74, 110, 112–13, 126, 153, 163, 164, 170, 193, 196, 202
Caspian Sea, 1, 4, 5, 111, 120, 157, 167, 179, 225, 247, 249, 254–58
Catherine II (Catherine the Great), 3, 4, 40, 90, 110, 137, 164, 167–68, 180, 209–11, 245
Catholicism, *See* Roman Catholicism
Caucasus, 31, 35, 58, 71, 78, 86, 121, 129, 143, 163, 169, 178, 199, 210, 220, 222, 242, 253
caviar, 255–56
Central Intelligence Agency (CIA), 79, 139, 171
Chaliapin, Feodor, 238
Cheboksary, Russia, 111, 174–75, 178
Chechens (Chechnya), 11, 48, 67–68, 71, 80, 129, 130, 142–43, 158, 183, 199, 207, 252; *See also* Kadyrov, Ramzan
cheese, 155, 158, 160

Cheka, 41
Chekhov, Anton, 24, 32, 40, 106, 126
chelnoki, 75
Chelsea FC, 138
Chelyabinsk, Russia, 158
Cherkasov, Nikolay, 133
Chernyshevsky, Nikolay, 32, 191, 238
Cherry Orchard, The (Chekhov), 126
China and Chinese, 75, 119, 121, 126, 155, 157, 159, 190, 193, 194, 209, 210, 230, 255
Christianity (in general), 3, 10, 11, 14, 92, 92–93, 93, 110; *See also* Roman Catholicism; Russian Orthodox Church
Christopher, Warren, 85
Chuikov, Vasily, 244
Churchill, Winston, 28–29
Chuvash language and people, 4, 96, 153, 164, 174, 177
Circassians, 252
climate change, 224
Clinton, Bill, 82–85
Cold War, 18, 80, 83–86, 202
collectivism, 69, 110, 125
collectivization (collectivized agriculture), 97–98, 163, 165, 169, 172, 175–76
Comintern, 80, 201
Communist Party, 49, 75, 126, 149, 194, 201
Communists and Communism, 13, 19, 28, 31, 32, 41, 52, 55, 61, 68, 76, 77, 80, 93, 98, 99, 125, 150, 153, 159, 162, 163, 165, 170, 183, 192, 194, 199–201, 208, 221, 235–36, 236
Constantinople, 10, 14, 16, 32, 133, 234
consumerism, 81, 90
Copenhagen, Denmark, 171
copper, 136
Cosmelli, Alessandro (Ale), 2, 4–5, 23, 24, 59, 65, 79–80, 88, 101, 106, 115, 127, 130, 145, 152, 171, 181, 208, 218, 221, 223, 225, 237, 240–41, 249, 253, 256, 258–60
Cossacks, 3, 4, 28–29, 77, 93, 129, 132, 142, 165–68, 167, 168, 175, 205, 210, 235, 258
Covid-19 pandemic, 138
Crime and Punishment (Dostoyevsky), 18
Crimea, 14, 20, 21, 34, 37, 40, 78, 121, 142, 144, 154, 163, 182, 227, 247
Crusades, 16
Cuba, 86, 155
Cuban missile crisis, 227
Cuman nomads, 121
currency and currency exchange, 74, 75, 99
Cyril, 11

czar (term), 125
Czechoslovak Legion, 219
Czech Republic, 77, 84

dachas, 100–101
Dagestan, 129, 143, 183, 253
Dalmatia, 173
Dannon, 158
Darfur, 260
DARPA, 224
Davydov, Denis, 195
DDT (rock band), 229
death, beliefs about, 45–46, 223
Death in Venice (Mann), 24
Decembrist revolt (1825), 71, 140
Deir Ezzor, Syria, 141–42
Dejean, Maurice, 94
Dekalina, Ekaterina, 197
Dementyev, Andrey, 49
democracy(-ies), 21, 43, 71, 73, 75, 77, 78, 82, 85, 99, 126, 141, 142, 171, 188–91, 221, 227
Demons (Dostoyevsky), 18, 191
Deripaska, Oleg, 138
de-Stalinization, 94, 243
digital payments, 99
divorce, 71, 216
Dnepr (Dnipro) River, 122, 246
Doctor Zhivago (Pasternak), 42
domra, 213
Don River (Don region), 45, 111, 122, 124, 132, 166–67, 175, 209, 220, 240, 246, 251; *See also* Donbas; Volga-Don canal
Donbas, 27, 38, 48, 95, 102, 108, 115, 128, 143, 200, 207, 215, 245, 251, 253
Donets, 121, 246
Donetsk, 246
Donskoy, Dmitry, 30, 124
Donskoy Monastery (Moscow), 93
Dostoyevsky, Fyodor, 15, 18, 40, 50, 51, 92, 105–6, 125, 191
Dranova, Natalia, 25–27, 33
Dresden, Germany, 3
Drevlians, 11
Drina River, 128
drug trafficking, 48, 198–99, 203
Dubna, Russia, 5, 65–68, 72, 80, 87, 108, 207
Dugin, Aleksandr, 17, 45, 76–77, 126
Dugina, Darya, 17
Duma, 138, 149, 153
Duranty, Walter, 170

East Germany, 77
East India Company, 256
Egypt, 3
Eisenstein, Sergei, 91, 133, 134, 137
electricity, 97, 230; *See also* hydroelectric power
Engels, Friedrich, 189
England, *See* United Kingdom
Enlightenment, 54
Eskimo ice-cream sandwiches, 66–67

Estonia, 28, 103
Eurasia, 16–18, 54, 93, 180
Eurasian Academy of Cinematographic Arts, 91–92
Europe (Europeanism), 3, 4, 14, 16, 18, 40, 51, 53, 54, 78, 79, 83–84, 86, 92, 97, 109, 120–23, 125, 126, 135, 155, 157, 171–72, 180, 194, 200–201, 205, 234, 256; *See also* West, the
European Union (EU), 34, 91
Everyday Saints (Shevkunov), 19, 20
Ezzor (mercenary), 129–32, 140–45, 166, 174

Fairy Tales (Pushkin), 40
Fall of an Empire, The: Lessons from Byzantium (TV documentary), 16
famine, 169–70
Far East and Arctic Development Corporation, 138
February Revolution (1917), 187–90
Federal Service for Supervision of Communications, Information Technology, and Mass Media, 43
Fermi, Enrico, 68
fertility rates, 242–43
fertilizers, 68, 154, 202, 255
Fiat, 201–2
Figes, Orlando, 141
film, 91–92, 133, 134, 137
Finland and Finns, 28, 29, 60, 158, 191
Firebird (folk figure), 40
Five-Year Plan, 110, 111
Fomenkov, Artem, 164–69, 172–74
Ford Motor Company, 112
Fortum, 158
47 Easy Poems and One Hard One (Khlebnikov), 147
France and the French, 4, 28–30, 94, 112, 143, 155, 170, 182, 187
Francis, Pope, 21–22
Frankel, Jan, 35
freedom, 19–20, 43, 71, 82, 136, 152, 201, 210, 214, 233
Freemasonry, 187
FSB (Russian federal security service), 5, 15, 21, 44, 67, 108, 129, 152, 173, 182, 197, 233
Full Metal Jacket (film), 205

Gagarin, Yuri, 52
Gamzatov, Rasul, 35
gangs, 58, 74, 198–200, 203, 227
Ganicheva, Marina, 36–39, 39, 41, 44, 44–45, 45–46
Garbo, Greta, 156
Gazprom, 158
Gazprombank, 138
GDP, 73

geese, 182–83
"Generation P," 79
Genghis Khan, 54, 120, 122, 126, 210
Georgia, 14, 78, 102, 142, 143, 230
Germany and Germans, 4, 28–29, 53, 55, 73, 77, 83, 112, 122, 123, 125, 154, 158, 188; *See also* Nazis (Nazi Germany); Volga Germans
Gibbon, Edward, 121
Gilyarovsky, Vladimir, 147
glasnost, 20, 80
Gogol, Nikolai, 15, 191
gold, 136
Golden Horde, 120–21
Goncharov, Ivan, 2, 106, 195–97
gopnik culture, 199
Gorbachev, Mikhail, 71, 83, 85, 134, 138, 160
Gorky, Maksim, 2, 32, 41, 44, 52, 55, 56, 96, 97, 105, 111, 173, 174, 179, 255
Gorky, Russia, *See* Nizhny Novgorod, Russia
Govor, Alexander, 158
"Grasshopper, The" (Chekhov), 106
Great Depression, 73
Great Patriotic War, *See* World War II
Great Terror, 197–98
Grebenshchikov, Boris, 209
Grishin, Sergey "Scarface," 138
Grossman, Vasily, 42, 100–101, 246–48
Grozny, Russia, 67, 143
Grozny model, 121
G7, 157
Guevara, Che, 166
gulags, 12, 17, 20, 41, 42, 71, 74, 78, 111, 136
Gumilev, Lev, 17, 93, 126
Gypsies (Romani), 101–2

Haaretz, 17
hammam, 11
Hanseatic League, 133
Hanway, Jonas, 205
Harry, Prince, 138
Haval (automobile), 159
Havana, Cuba, 22
Heart of a Dog (Bulgakov), 42
Helsinki, Finland, 4
Hemingway, Ernest, 43, 45, 248–49
Hermitage, 3, 173, 231
heroin, 198, 199
History of Pugachev, The (Pushkin), 168
Hitler, Adolf, 20, 26, 28–29, 31–33, 76, 86, 122, 170, 227, 244, 247
holodomor, 169–70
homosexuality, 219; *See also* LGBTQ+ community and culture

Houthis, 205
Hugo, Victor, 43
Hungary, 77, 84, 122, 201
huzun, 97
hydroelectric power, 88, 108, 228
Hyundai, 158

Ibn Battuta, 123
ibn Fadlan, Ahmad, 119–20
Idiot, The (Dostoyevsky), 40
Ignatius (archbishop of Saratov), 239
IKEA, 81
Ilyin, Ivan, 92–93
India, 4, 112, 121, 138, 157, 255–57
industrialization, 110–13, 156, 162–63
inflation, 73, 157
Ingush people (Ingushetia), 143, 252
Inner Mongolia, 209
intellectuals, 33, 41, 42, 44, 45, 81, 170, 197–98, 216
"International, The," 94
internet, 43, 79, 99, 242–43
Ioann, Father, *See* Perevezenkhov, Ioann
Ipatiev Monastery, 131
iPhones, 230
Iran, 4, 111, 157, 179, 249, 256, 257
Iraq, 86
iron (iron production), 54, 112, 136, 247
Isakovich, Garold, 193
ISIS, 143
Iskra (newspaper), 55
Islam (Islamism), 2, 3, 10, 71, 120, 122, 132, 142, 178–81, 183, 209, 232, 253
Israel, 154, 159
Istanbul, Turkey, 97; *See also* Constantinople
Italy, 16, 41, 68, 154, 155, 158, 170, 201–3, 225, 260
Ivan III (Ivan the Great), 124–25
Ivan IV (Ivan the Terrible), 70, 91, 113, 132–37, 139–40, 239
Ivan the Terrible: The Boyars' Plot (Ivan the Terrible, Part II) (film), 133, 134, 137
Ivanovich, Ivan, 137
izby, 26, 100–101, 176

Jalaletdinov, Mansur Hazrat, 181, 182
Janjaweed militias, 260
Japan, 98, 111, 112
Japan, Sea of, 121
Jerusalem, 10, 11
Jesuits, 234
Jews (Judaism), 10, 120, 209, 210, 217, 221; *See also* antisemitism
John, Elton, 66–67

John the Apostle, 109
Jones, Gareth, 170
journalists, 22, 24, 38, 43, 50, 115, 152, 215–16, 218

Kabardians, 252
Kadyrov, Ramzan, 67, 158
Kalinin, Mikhail Ivanovich, 49–50, 163
Kaliningrad, Russia, 36, 182
Kalka River, 121–22
Kalmyks, 4, 166, 168, 205, 209, 209–11, 210, 241–42
Kalyazin, Russia, 95, 108
Kamenev, Lev, 187
Kamyshin, Russia, 239–40
Kanokov, Arsen, 158
Kapralov, Sergey, 199
Karachay people, 252
Karadžić, Radovan, 85
Karamazov, Mitya, 51
Karamzin, Nikolai, 195
Karelia, 29, 78
Katya (travel companion), 5, 22–24, 38, 65–68, 70, 72, 75–76, 79, 87–88, 95–96, 101, 107–8, 116, 128–30, 132, 144, 145, 172–78, 199, 202, 209, 211, 215–17, 222–23, 225, 229, 237, 240, 250, 252, 253, 259
Katyn Massacre, 11, 50
Kazakhstan, 84, 230, 251
Kazan (galley), 180
Kazan, Russia, 5, 71, 119, 132, 135, 150, 153, 161, 168, 169, 178–85, 197, 213, 220, 238
Kazankov, Ivan, 149, 152–64, 179, 183
Kazankov, Sergey, 149–50
Kerensky, Aleksandr, 184–85
Kerensky, Fyodor, 185
KGB, 5, 15, 19, 21, 75, 80, 81, 94, 158, 227, 260
Khairutdinov, Farid, 178, 179, 181–83
khans, 122–23; *See also specific khans, e.g.:* Genghis Khan
Kharkiv, Ukraine, 247
Khazars, 119–20
Khlebnikov, Velimir, 2, 147
Khrushchev, Nikita, 12, 20, 201, 227, 243, 246
Khrushchevkas, 25, 173
Kino (rock group), 57
Kirill I, Patriarch, 1, 12, 15, 21–22, 233, 238, 239
Kiss (Russian rock band), 228–29
kolchozy, 97, 150, 153, 163, 166, 177
kommunalka, 56
Kondopoga, Russia, 78
Konstantinov, Janko, 193
Korean War, 36
Kornilov, Lavr, 71, 188
Korobstov, Andrei, 34
Koroleva, Yulia, 244–45
Koshchei (folk figure), 40

Kosovo, 86, 143
Kosovo, Battle of (1389), 16
Kostroma, Russia, 116, 125, 127–33, 144, 166, 174
Kovalchuk, Yuri, 138
Kovalev, Andrei, 89–92, 94–95
Kovalevskaya, Sofya, 54
Kozyrev, Andrei, 82–86
Kremlin (Moscow), 137
kremlins, 132
Krupskaya, Nadezhda, 41
krysa ("protection"), 74
kulaks, 3, 104, 112, 113, 162–64, 179
Kulikovo, Battle of, 124, 126
Kul-Sharif Mosque (Kazan), 180
Kumarin, Vladimir, 58
Kursk submarine disaster, 118
Kutuzov, Mikhail, 30, 32, 182
Kuybyshev (city), *See* Samara, Russia
Kuybyshev, Valerian, 220, 221
Kyiv, Ukraine, 11, 109, 169–70, 234; *See also* Rus of Kyiv
Kyrgyzstan, 86, 159

lamb, 182, 252
lapta, 186
Lavrov, Sergey, 67
League of Nations, 170
Lel, Katya, 130
Lena River, 2
Lenin, Vladimir, 2, 10, 19, 30–32, 41, 42, 58, 60–61, 65, 69, 86, 90, 91, 98, 104, 106, 149, 151, 162, 179, 184–200, 208, 216, 220–22
Leningrad (siege of Leningrad), 30–32, 36, 98, 192, 227
Levant, the, 120, 121
Levsha (reggae singer/songwriter), 206–11, 213–14
LGBTQ+ community and culture, 21, 70, 207–8, 219
Libya, 142
Life of the Archpriest Avvakum, The, 40
Limonov, Eduard, 45, 77
literature, 39–45, 106, 195–97
Lithuania and Lithuanians, 28, 123, 126, 135; *See also* Poland-Lithuania
livestock, 155, 158–61, 175, 182
Lloret de Mar, Spain, 138
lombardy, 203
Los Angeles, Calif., 218
Lubyanka, 15, 21, 42, 197
Luhansk People's Republic, 38, 108–10
Lukoil, 138
Lutherans, 210

Macron, Emmanuel, 202
Madonna, 103
Mafia, 74

Maganov, Ravil, 138
maize, 155
Makfa Group, 158
Mal, Prince, 10–11
Malaysia, 157
Mamai Khan, 124, 126
Mamayev Kurgan, 34, 244–45, 250, 251
Manchester, England, 256
Manchuria, 210
Mandelstam, Osip, 42
Manhattan Project, 65, 68
Mari El Republic, 96, 150, 163
Mari people, 4, 164
marijuana, 208
Mariupol, 121, 229, 257
Markelov, Leonid, 160–61
Markle, Meghan, 138
Marx, Karl, 19, 189
Marxism, 41, 44, 221
Mashina Vremini (rock band), 229
Masudi, al-, 253
Matlock, Jack, 83
Mayakovsky, Vladimir, 34, 42
McDonald's, 23, 158
Medvedev, Dimitry, 181
Mein Kampf (Hitler), 28
Memoirs of a Hunter (Turgenev), 191
Memorial Society, 81
Mendeleev, Dmitry, 66
Mensheviks, 221
Mercedes-Benz, 158
Merkel, Angela, 3
Metchnikoff, Élie, 53
Methodius, 11
Metro-Goldwyn-Mayer, 91
Mexico, 155, 221
Mezenchev, Boris, 193
Michael I, Czar (Michael Romanov), 131
Michigan, Lake, 1
middle class, 33, 80
Mikhail S. (philologist), 48–58
"Mikhailov" (KGB agent), 21
Mikhalkov, Mikhail, 94
Mikhalkov, Nikita, 91–92
Mikhalkov, Sergey Vladimirovich, 94–95
Milošević, Slobodan, 70, 85
Minin, Kuzma, 131, 174
Minnikhanov, Rustam, 178–79, 181
Minsk, Belarus, 260
Mississippi River, 255, 256, 258
MKB Raduga, 87
Moldo-Russian War, 142
Moldova, 142
Molossians, 129
Molotov, Vyacheslav, 28
monasteries, 39, 132–33
Mongols, 30, 54, 93, 112, 120–26, 126, 135, 166, 209
Morozov, Savva Vasilyevich, 53, 55–56
Morozov family, 47, 55

Morozova, Varvara, 55
Moscow, Battle of, 12, 20, 30–34, 227, 247
Moscow, Russia, 1, 4, 14, 15, 17, 20, 21, 44, 75, 93, 111, 114, 120, 122, 134, 135, 138, 139, 168, 170, 197, 201, 219, 222, 225, 227, 230, 233, 234; *See also* Muscovy
Moscow and the Muscovites (Giljarovsky), 147
Moscow Art Theater, 42, 55
Moskvich (automobile), 202
Motherland Calls, The (statue), 245–46
multiculturalism, 3, 78
Munich agreement (1938), 84
Münnich, Christoph von, 18
Murmansk, Russia, 34
Muscovy, 123–25, 131–33, 135
Muslims, 71–72, 128, 136, 180–81; *See also* Islam (Islamism); Tatars
Mussolini, Benito, 1
Mussorgsky, Modest, 40
Myanmar, 121
Mykonos, 117
mysticism, Russian, 213

Nagy, Imre, 201
Napoleon, 29–31, 122, 168, 175, 182, 195
narod (*narod* movement), 78, 141
national debt, 80
nationalism, 39, 78, 124, 125, 126, 169, 234, 242; *See also* anti-Western nationalism; Slavophiles (Slavic nationalism)
Native Americans, 77
natural gas, 68, 80, 136, 138, 156, 182
natural resources, 136; *See also specific resources*
Navalny, Alexei, 35, 78–79
Nazis (Nazi Germany), 12, 14, 20, 26–36, 92, 100, 170, 211, 236, 243–45, 247–48; *See also* World War II (Great Patriotic War)
Netflix, 221
Netherlands, 155, 160
Neva River, 104, 123, 180
Nevsky, Alexander, 30, 123, 125
new economic policy, 162
New York Times, 170
New Zealand, 182
Nicholas I, Czar, 140
Nicholas II, Czar, 22, 90, 153
Nicholson, Jack, 92
Nikolayevsk, Russia, 240
Nikon, Patriarch, 167, 234
1990s, economic chaos of, 72, 73, 75, 85
Nizhny Novgorod, Russia (formerly Gorky), 5, 12, 13, 105, 111, 112, 127, 131, 132, 164–68, 172, 219, 234

NKVD, 197, 226
nomenklatura, 75, 154, 198
North Atlantic Treaty Organization (NATO), 34, 38, 70, 73, 76, 82–86, 86, 126, 136, 142, 143, 171, 172
North Korea, 155
North Sea, 1
Northern Crusaders, 123
Northern Fleet, 73
Norway, 73
Novatek, 138
Novaya Gazeta, 22
Novgorod, Russia, 120, 123, 135; *See also* Nizhny Novgorod, Russia
nuclear power (nuclear weapons), 37, 65, 66, 72, 80, 81, 87, 153, 228, 236–38, 243, 257
nudist colonies, 219

Oblomov (Goncharov), 106, 195–97, 200
October (Bolshevik) Revolution, 31, 41, 49, 54, 55, 70, 110–11, 161–63, 168, 192, 197, 219–22, 235
oil (oil industry), 4, 68, 73, 75, 80, 136, 138, 141, 153, 154, 156, 157, 247, 257
Oka River, 239
Okhrana, 192
Old Believers, 167, 168, 181, 231, 233–34, 234, 234–35
Oleg (ex-con), 58
Olga, Princess (Saint Olga), 10–11
Olginski Monastery (Tver'), 11–14
oligarchs, 75, 134, 137–39, 157–58, 231
Olkhovsky, Andrei, 158
Operation Barbarossa, 29–31
Operation Deliberate Force, 85–86
Operation Mars, 26, 27
oprichnina (oprichniki), 134–36
Orbán, Viktor, 179
Orlov, Elizbar, 14
Orwell, George, 170
Ostashkov, Russia, 50
Ottoman Empire, 97, 132; *See also* Turkey; Turks

pacifists (pacifism), 207, 211, 214
Pag, Isle of, 173
Pamuk, Orhan, 96–97
Panikakha, Mikhail, 244
Paris, France, 171, 189
"Paris" (building in Proletarka), 57, 58, 60, 61
passionarnost, 17–18, 32, 93, 244
Pasternak, Boris, 42, 44
Pavel (fallen soldier in Ukraine war), 95, 101–4, 106, 107, 113
Pavlov, Innokenti, 15
Pavlov, Ivan, 53
Pechorin, Ivan, 138

Perevezenkhov, Ioann, 95, 108–10, 112
periodic table, 66
Persia and Persians, 16, 119, 121, 167, 255, 256
Persian Gulf, 257
Peter the Great, 72, 113, 132, 139, 140, 167, 182, 209, 235
Petrograd, 49, 188, 189
piatiletka, 110, 111
Pilnyak, Boris, 110–11, 111
Piotrovsky, Mikhail, 2–4, 173, 231, 243
Platonov, Andrei, 52
Plekhanov, Georgi, 32
Pliny the Elder, 253
Plymouth Brethren, 232
Poland and Poles, 28, 30, 30, 34, 50, 84, 114, 122, 123, 126, 130–32, 135, 140, 174, 191, 201
Poland-Lithuania (Polish-Lithuanian Empire), 40, 112, 135
politburo, 30, 31
Politkovskaya, Anna, 43
Pontecorvo, Bruno, 68
populism (populist movement), 106, 167, 216
potholes, 175
poverty, 42, 73, 80, 203
Powell Doctrine, 121
Prague Spring, 84
Pravda, 220, 221
Presidential Council for Culture and Art, 44
Prigozhin, Yevgeny, 4, 70, 129, 130, 132, 140, 166
princes, Russian, 121–24
Pristina, Kosovo, 143
privatization, 73, 75, 157
Proletarka (housing complex near Tver'), 47–49, 52–53, 55–61
Protensya, Sergey, 138
Prussia, 29
Pskov-Caves Monastery, 19–20
Pugachev, Yemelyan, 166–68, 210
purges, 20, 28, 29, 54, 111, 135, 185, 200, 201, 235
Pushkin, Aleksandr, 15, 32, 40, 136, 140, 141, 168, 195, 212
Putin, Vladimir
  and agriculture, 153, 155
  alcohol prices under, 216
  "Atlantic" concept of, 18–19
  authoritarianism of, 10, 77–78, 80, 81, 140, 171
  and Chechnya, 11, 67, 129, 142–43
  civil defense under, 226
  and Crimea annexation, 40
  and de-Stalinization, 20, 243–44
  and Aleksandr Dugin, 17, 76, 126
  early pro-Western politics of, 86
  and economic sanctions, 111
  in European press, 171–72

and FSB, 5, 20, 59, 233
"Grozny model" of, 121
and Ivan Ilyin, 92–93
Ivan the Terrible statue commissioned by, 139–40
and Kosovo, 143
and Lenin myth, 192, 194
and Lokomotiv Yaroslavl crash, 117–18
and Nikita Mikhalkov, 91, 92
and Muslims, 71, 178, 181
and Alexei Navalny, 78–79
as neo-imperialist, 17, 34, 98, 125
and oil, 157
and oligarchs, 134, 137–39, 157, 158
and *passionarnost,* 18, 32, 244
and Mikhail Piotrovsky, 3
popular support for, 37, 82, 98, 99, 153, 162, 183, 207, 218–19, 224, 251
and Yevgeny Prigozhin, 4, 70
and Russian national anthem, 94
and Russian Orthodox Church, 1, 15, 18–19, 21, 22, 99, 233–34
and Russia's Soviet past, 191
and Rzhev monument, 34, 36
in Saint Petersburg, 3, 85
and Siberia, 136
and *smuta,* 70, 71, 132
and Syria, 143
and Tatars, 178, 181, 183
and *Trotsky* television series, 221–22
and Ulyanovsk, 194, 198, 199
and Ukraine war, 50, 77, 82, 102, 121, 144, 171, 227, 245, 256
and writers, 39, 41, 43–45
"Putin's henchmen," 81
Pyotr (guide in Samara), 226–27

Rachmaninoff, Sergei, 238
Radio 7 (radio station), 23
Radio Retro, 23
raskolniki, 167, 233–34, 234, 234–35
Rasputin, Valentin, 45, 111
Razin, Stenka, 166–67
Red Army, 27, 29, 32–33, 35, 77, 115, 126, 164, 219, 220, 222, 245, 247, 248
"Red Belt," 199
Red Cross, 11
Red Guards, 189
Red Sea, 205
Red Square (Moscow), 10, 135–37
Red Star Belgrade (soccer team), 128
Renaissance, 16, 54, 260
Renault, 202
Repin, Ilya, 104–6, 205
Revolution of 1905, 55
Rikazchikova, Tatiana, 244, 245, 250

Rimsky-Korsakov, Nikolai, 40
roads, Russian, 175
Robin Hood, 166
rock bands, 57, 70, 209, 228–29
Rodin, Mikhail, 230–37, 237–39
Roman Catholicism, 14, 21–22, 39, 54, 92, 123, 125, 126, 135, 232, 235
Romani people, 101–2
Romania, 77, 182
Romanov dynasty, 53, 54, 90, 123, 126, 131
Romans (Roman Empire), 2, 10, 167
Rome, Italy, 189
Roosevelt, Franklin Delano, 170
Rosneft, 158
Rosselkhozbank, 155
Rossia 1 (TV channel), 221
Rossiya (bank), 138
Rostov-on-Don, Russia, 14, 251, 257
Rotenberg, Arkady, 138
Rotenberg, Boris, 138
Rozenbaum, Alexander, 72
rural areas, 90, 97–100, 163, 172
Rurik dynasty, 10
Rus of Kyiv, 10–11, 119–22, 122, 246
Rusin, Dimitri, 184–200
Russian Academy of Sciences, 68
"Russian Bear," 40–41, 50
Russian Cinematographers' Union, 91
Russian civil war, 31, 71, 169, 219–22
Russian national anthem, 94–95
Russian Orthodox Church, 1, 10, 11, 14–16, 18–22, 26, 30, 39, 43, 54, 77, 85, 86, 91, 109–10, 123, 128, 132, 133, 153, 167, 180–81, 197, 209, 210, 231–34; *See also* Old Believers
Russian Popular Legends (Afanasev), 39
Russification, 38, 183, 256
Russkiy mir, 18, 39, 125
Russophobia, 171
Russo-Polish War, 28
Ryazan', Russia, 239
Rybinsk, Russia, 5, 89–91, 94, 95, 101–5, 107, 111
rye, 90
Rzhev, Russia (Battle of Rzhev), 25–28, 27, 32–36, 56, 115, 221
"Rzhev Meat Grinder," 25, 27, 34–36, 45

Šade, Avgust, 198
Saint Basil's Cathedral (Moscow), 10, 135, 136
Saint Petersburg, Russia (formerly Leningrad, Petrograd), 3, 5, 22–24, 34, 49, 54, 58, 71, 75, 76, 85, 87–89, 96, 104, 108, 138, 171, 177, 180, 186, 188, 189, 191, 196, 225, 237, 256

Sakhalin Island, 182
Sakharov, Andrei, 81
Saleva, Olga, 190
Saltykov-Shchedrin, Mikhail, 51
Samara, Russia (formerly Kuybyshev), 5, 31, 204–5, 213, 215, 217–20, 222–27, 230
samogon, 216
samozvanec, 140
sanctions, 4, 34, 45, 68, 71, 91, 111, 116, 149, 154–59, 162, 179, 182, 183, 204, 231, 256, 257
Sarai, 123, 124
Sarajevo, 129, 214
Saratov, Russia, 5, 111, 168, 210, 229, 232, 238, 240
Sarkozy, Nicolas, 143
Saudi Arabia, 180
Savitskaya, Anastasia, 245
Sberbank, 156–57
Schenck, Joseph, 91
Schenck, Nicholas, 91
Scythians, 4, 120
"Scythians, The" (Blok), 7
Sechin, Igor, 158
secondhand car market, 203
Sekret (rock band), 70
September 11, 2001 terrorist attacks, 86
Serbs (Serbia), 16, 70, 77, 85, 85–86, 109, 128, 143
serfs (serfdom), 53, 104–6, 168, 185, 210
Sergeeva, Olesya, 255–57, 256–57
Service, Robert, 137, 221
Sevastopol, Russia, 34, 144
Seventh-day Adventists, 232
Sheksna River, 104
Shevkunov, Tikhon, 14–22
"shock therapy," 73
Shostakovich, Dimitri, 167, 226–27
Shubert Island, 211–15, 218–19, 237, 243
Shukhrat (Tatar acquaintance), 211–15, 250–51
Shukshin, Vasily, 168
Siberia, 2, 17, 24, 31, 32, 42, 49, 55, 75, 78, 104, 111, 112, 136–37, 156, 187, 212, 220, 235, 236
Siberia, Siberia (Rasputin), 111
Silk Road, 123
Simbirsk, Russia, *See* Ulyanovsk, Russia
Simferopol, Russia, 144
Slavophiles (Slavic nationalism), 16–18, 32, 54, 77, 125; *See also* anti-Western nationalism
smuta, 70, 71, 79, 93, 105, 113, 131, 248
sobornost, 38, 249
SOBR, 129, 131, 141, 199
socialist realism, 61, 172
Solidarność, 126
Sophia, Abbess, 11, 15

Sorokin, Vladimir, 141
South Ossetia, 143
Southeast Asia, 155
Soviet-German nonaggression pact (1939), 28
sovkhozy, 150, 153, 154, 159, 160, 163
Spanish Civil War, 201
Spartacus, 166, 191
Sputnik (vaccine), 138
SS, 76
Stakhanovite awards, 150–51
Stalin, Joseph
  authoritarianism of, 10, 177
  bunker of, 225–27
  death of, 57, 190, 201
  deportations of, 3
  and de-Stalinization, 94, 243
  during Great Patriotic War, 28–32, 211, 243–45
  and industrialization/collectivization, 88, 108, 112, 113, 156, 169–70, 257
  and Ivan the Terrible, 91, 137, 140
  and Mikhail Kalinin, 49–50
  and Katyn Massacre, 11
  as leader, 72, 98, 134
  on Moscow, 111
  resurgent popularity of, 19, 20, 37, 77, 103, 104, 118, 149, 151, 153, 194–95, 226–27, 235–36
  in Siberia, 187
  and Soviet national anthem, 94
  and Leon Trotsky, 220–22
  and writers, 41–44
"Stalin stoves," 60
Stalingrad (Battle of Stalingrad), 26–28, 32–34, 36, 37, 71–72, 111, 211, 222, 236, 240, 243–51
Stalingrad (Grossman), 246
Stalingrad (icebreaker), 243
Stalinism, 51, 152, 161–62, 186, 221
"Stalin's revenge," 22
Starbucks, 158
steel production, 54, 75, 112, 247
steppe, 4, 52, 119, 120, 125, 126, 172, 180, 218, 222, 237–38, 240–41, 243
stock market crash (1929), 170
Stolypin, Pyotr, 43
Stravinsky, Igor, 40
streltsy, 132
Stubblebine, Robert, 231
sturgeon, 255–56
subsidies, 155, 157
Suez Canal, 156
sunflowers (sunflower seeds), 116, 119, 155, 200
Susanin, Ivan, 131–32, 143
Suvorov, Aleksandr, 30, 32
Swedes and Sweden, 4, 30, 92, 112, 123, 212
Switzerland, 33, 55, 92, 93, 187
Syria, 14, 129, 141–43

Tajikistan, 142
Talbott, Strobe, 83
Tallinn, Estonia, 218
Tambovskaya Bratva (gang), 58
Tamerlane, 32
Tarkovsky, Arseny, 225–26
Tatars (Tatarstan), 3, 4, 40, 71, 110, 120, 136, 150, 163, 168, 175, 178–83, 209, 211, 245, 250–51; *See also* Mongols
Tatiana (grocery store owner), 117–19
Tbilisi, Georgia, 143, 225
Tel Aviv, Israel, 231
Telegram, 23
television, 16, 43, 45, 80, 99–100, 221
Tendryakov, Vladimir, 52
Teutonic Knights, 123, 133
Thames River, 2, 255
"Third Rome," 125, 133, 234
Thunberg, Greta, 156
Tiber River, 1
Tiberinus, 1–2
Tichomirov V. (philosopher), 116, 125–26, 133–36, 139
Tigers (Serbian paramilitary unit), 128
Tikhon, Father, *See* Shevkunov, Tikhon
Timchenko, Gennady, 138
Time magazine, 20
Timoshenko, Semyon, 246
Tinkov, Oleg, 158
Tito, Joseph, 49–50
Togliatti, Palmiro, 201, 203
Togliatti, Russia, 60, 111, 159, 200–203, 205, 210, 211, 213
Tokhtamysh Khan, 126
Tolstoy, Aleksey, 111
Tolstoy, Leo, 15, 32, 40, 179
Torghut tribe, 209–10
toska, 56
trade, 4, 119–21, 123, 157, 205, 256, 257; *See also* sanctions
trans people, 219
Transnistria War, 142
Trans-Siberian Railway, 54, 217
Trotsky (television series), 221
Trotsky, Leon, 19, 29, 115, 187–89, 219–20, 220–22
Trotskyists (Trotskyism), 49, 197
truckers, 252–53
Tsaritsyn, Russia, *See* Volgograd
Tsoi, Viktor, 57
Tula, Russia, 179
Tunoshonka River, 117
Turgenev, Ivan, 125, 191, 195, 196
Turkestan, 209
Turkey, 75, 155, 157, 159, 182
Turkoman language, 119
Turks, 16, 30, 32, 122, 168, 209, 235, 245; *See also* Ottoman Empire
Tver' (galley), 180
Tver', Russia, 5, 11, 27–28, 33, 47–51, 53, 58, 61, 120
Tvertsa River, 49

Twain, Mark, 105
Tyumen, Russia, 31
Tyutchev, Fyodor, 69

Uglich, Russia, 111
Uglich River, 95, 108
Ukraine (Ukraine war), 10, 14–15, 15, 17, 19, 22–23, 28, 31, 33, 34, 36, 37, 39, 43, 48, 50, 67, 72, 78, 79, 82, 84, 86, 91, 95, 99, 102, 109, 113, 115, 118, 121, 129, 131–32, 138, 141, 142, 144, 149, 155, 158, 160, 162–63, 169–73, 179, 207, 209, 212, 218, 222, 229, 231, 236, 242, 245, 246, 251, 251–52, 256
Ulitskaya, Ludmila, 43–44
Ulyanov, Ilya Nikolyevich, 185, 190
Ulyanovsk, Russia (formerly Simbirsk), 2, 5, 86, 106, 184–86, 192–99
Uncle Vanya (Chekhov), 40
unemployment, 75, 80, 157, 198
UNESCO, 114
Union of Russian Writers, 36, 41, 44, 44–45
Union of Soviet Writers, 41, 42
United Arab Emirates, 180
United Kingdom, 28–30, 32, 53, 55, 112, 123, 138, 162, 170, 175, 209
United Nations (UN), 86, 143
United Russia party, 79, 194
United States, 3, 23, 29, 30, 50, 52, 53, 73, 76, 82–86, 91, 98, 102, 121, 136, 141–42, 155, 170, 171, 175, 189, 224, 231–33
Universal Exhibit (Vienna, 1873), 106
Ural Mountains, 31, 112, 150, 156, 176, 205, 220
Ural River, 4
Ushakov, Fyodor, 36–38
Uzbekistan, 12, 86

Valdai Hills, 1, 10, 50
Valentina (Pavel's widow), 101–4, 107
Varshavsky, Alexander, 158
Vasileva, Ivanovna Lidya, 150–51
Vasilievich, Nikolai, 151
Venezuela, 155
Venice (city-state), 16
Venice, Italy, 90, 258
Vercingetorix, 167
Verdun, Battle of, 169
Versailles, Treaty of, 28
Vienna, Austria, 48, 106, 198
Vietnam, 86, 121
Vietnam War, 36, 142
Vikings, 10
villages, 97, 98, 100

Virgin of Vladimir, 31
Viśegrad, Bosnia, 128
Vlad (travel companion), 5, 10, 22–24, 38, 65–67, 72, 74, 87–88, 95–97, 100, 101, 106–8, 116, 117, 128, 130, 172–78, 186, 200, 204, 205, 211, 215–17, 222–26, 229, 237, 240, 246, 250, 252, 259
vladika, 133
Vladimir, Prince, 10
Vladimir, Russia, 123
Vladivostok, Russia, 23, 26, 138
vodka, 27, 67, 129, 177, 216
Volga (automobile), 75
Volga (galley), 180
Volga Flows to the Caspian Sea, The (Pilnyak), 110–11
Volga Germans, 110, 164, 210–11
Volga River
  agriculture along, 155
  in art and literature, 106
  Baltic aura of, 66
  Buddhists of, 209–11
  Bulgarians and, 120, 122
  burlaki of, 104–5
  canals and dams, 110–11, 204, 255, 257
  and collectivization, 163–66, 168
  easternmost point of, 218
  during Great Patriotic War, 3–4, 26, 27, 31, 33, 247–48
  hydroelectric plans on, 228
  Ivan the Terrible and, 132–33
  monasteries and convents along, 12, 48
  Mongols and, 120–26
  monuments along, 34, 49, 68
  Motherland Calls statue on, 245–46
  and popular revolts, 166–68
  during the purges, 185, 197–98
  "Red Belt" of, 199
  restoration of city centers along, 90–91
  Romani people of, 101
  in Russian civil war, 115, 219–21
  source of, 1, 9, 11–14, 24, 50, 211
  Stalin and, 3, 11, 88
  Tatars and, 180–81
  as *the* river of Russia, 2, 4, 72
  trade and boat traffic along, 4, 116–17, 119–20, 123, 157, 179, 198, 256
  Vikings and, 10
Volga-Don canal, 204, 257
Volgograd, Russia (formerly Tsaritsyn and Stalingrad), 3, 5, 34, 70–71, 111, 204, 213, 222, 242–46, 250–52; *See also* Stalingrad (Battle of Stalingrad)

Volkswagen, 158
Volozh, Arkady, 231
Voltaire, 4, 181
Voronkov, Konstantin, 78
Voronov, Yuri, 138
Voronov-Orenburgsky, Andrey, 247–49
vranyo, 50

Wagner Group, 4, 129, 130, 141, 144, 166
Wałesa, Lech, 84
War and Peace (Tolstoy), 40
War & Sanctions blacklist, 154
Warsaw, Poland, 84, 132, 171, 218
Warsaw Pact, 86
waste (waste management), 98–99, 255
Weimar Republic, 73
West, the, 18, 20, 21, 70, 71, 74–75, 79–82, 90, 91, 93, 99, 109, 117, 118, 196, 207–8, 229, 237; *See also* anti-Western nationalism
Westerners (Western sympathizers), 24, 72–73, 118, 125, 201
What Is to Be Done? (Chernyshevsky), 191, 238
What Is to Be Done? (Lenin), 192
"What Will Russia's Dismemberment Do to the World" (Ilyin), 93
wheat, 90, 120, 155, 162, 169
White Guard, The (Bulgakov), 42
White Sea, 32, 111
Whites (Russian civil war), 31, 220, 222
Winter Palace, 55, 189; *See also* Hermitage
Witte, Sergei, 54
women's emancipation, 53, 54
World War I, 11, 73, 169, 188
World War II (Great Patriotic War), 3–4, 12, 13, 19, 20, 25–28, 60, 82, 104, 170, 211, 226–27, 244–45, 249; *See also* Stalingrad (Battle of Stalingrad)

Yabloko party, 78
Yakunin, Gleb, 21
Yalta agreement (1943), 84
Yandex, 231
Yaroslavl (galley), 180
Yaroslavl, Russia, 5, 91, 114–18, 122, 166
Yasnaya Polyana, 179
Yazykov, Nikolay, 195
Yekaterinburg, Russia, 90
Yeltsin, Boris, 45, 59, 73, 77, 80, 82, 84–86, 94, 142, 160, 191
Yevtushenko, Yevgeny, 246
Yezhov, Nikolai, 197, 226
YouTube, 215
Yugoslavia, 49, 85, 173

"Z," 37, 166, 227, 245
Zaitsev, Vasily, 245
Zakharova, Maria, 67
zakvaska, 90
zapoy, 216
Zarina (Pavel's daughter), 101–3, 107
Zelensky, Volodymyr, 121, 171
Zhiguli (automobile), 202
Zhiguli Mountains, 205–10, 242
Zhukov, Georgy, 26
zilkop, 39
Zinoviev, Nikolai, 151
Zvenigovsky District, 149–50
Zyuganov, Gennady, 149